WAR OF THE WORLDS: FROM WELLS TO SPIELBERG

JOHN L. FLYNN

Galactic Books

Owings Mills, Maryland

Galactic Books
Post Office Box 1442
Owings Mills, Maryland 21117-9998

War of the Worlds:
From Wells to Spielberg
By John L. Flynn

PRINTING HISTORY
First Edition / June 2005

First published in the United States

Acknowledgements: Most of the photographs used in this book were issued by the original production companies at the time of the release for publicity purposes, and we make no claim as to ownership or copyright. We are simply reproducing them for the purpose that they were originally intended. Some of the photos are copyright of Paramount Pictures; some are courtesy of Timothy Hines at Pendragon Pictures; some are copyrighted by Warner Brothers. We also wish to thank Ed Gross for his assistance and reporting on this project.

Editor: Wendy Bush
Design & Layout: John L. Flynn

Library of Congress Cataloging in Publication Data
Flynn, John L. War of the Worlds:
From Wells to Spielberg
1. War of the Worlds--History and criticism. I. Science fiction films--
History and criticism. II. H.G. Wells--Plots, themes, etc. III. Title.

ISBN: 0-9769400-0-0

PRINTED IN THE UNITED STATES OF AMERICA

10   9   8   7   6   5

TABLE OF CONTENTS

Dedication:

For Wendy, with love

INTRODUCTION

As we look back over the vista of modern science fiction, we are struck by the fact that the outstanding stories in the field - the ones that endure - are those that almost invariably have as their wonder ingredient true or prophetic science. It is these stories that arouse our imagination and make a lasting impression on us which succeeding years do not seem to obliterate. H. G. Wells had considerable output of true science fiction, with the accent on science. Wells's best and more enduring story was The War of the Worlds.
—*Hugo Gernsback, May 1959*

For more than a hundred years, since the release of H. G. Wells's most famous and influential novel, readers, radio listeners, and moviegoers have been tantalized by the prospect of an invasion from Mars. When *The War of the Worlds* was first published in 1898, his Victorian audience responded very enthusiastically to the depth and resonance of his latest "scientific romance." The feeling of an impending apocalypse, which was present in all of Wells's earlier works, reflected the anxieties of his readers as they faced the turn of a new century and the very real prospect that their world was coming to an end. The novel also revealed the fears that most of his countrymen felt as the sun began to set on the British Empire and other world powers came to rattle their sabers in defiance at the island nation. His book was also one of the first that depicted mankind on the run, fleeing from a merciless enemy that had no regard for human life. Wells made specific references to actual places, like Woking, Middlesex, and London, devasted by the alien invaders. While such scenes of mass destruction and death are all too familiar to us in light of what happened on September 11, 2001, they were startlingly fresh and nightmarishly overpowering to those living in 1898. Thankfully, Wells's invasion was the stuff of fiction, not prophecy, and the Martians never arrived with their death rays, tripod machines, and poison gas. But that has not stopped his tale of an interplanetary conflict with Mars from resonating with subsequent generations of people.

In the late 1930's, thanks to a very clever radio adaptation, more than a million people in the United States believed the Martians had established a "beachhead" at Grover's Mill, New Jersey, and were attacking major cities up and down the East Coast. Orson Welles's "War of the Worlds" broadcast on October 30, 1938, forty years after the publication of the original novel, disrupted households, interrupted religious services, created traffic jams, clogged communications systems, and generally created a panic that disabled America one Halloween eve. In the 1950's, during the science fiction boom, George Pal unleashed his own Martian invasion, and thrilled and frightened millions of moviegoers with "The War of the Worlds." His 1953 film became the biggest and most successful motion picture in Paramount's history, and paved the way for dozens of alien invasion films that flourished in the fifties. Thirty-five years later, the Pal film inspired a short-lived television series and a whole host of imitators, including "Mars Attacks!" and "Independence Day," that frightened yet another generation.

Now today, more than a century after the Martians launched their first wave, we stand poised for not one but two new "War of the Worlds"—the big budget extravaganza from Steven Spielberg and the smaller, more faithful adaptation by Timothy Hines. And while not much is certain in our world, it is almost guaranteed that, before the box office returns are even counted, Wells's invasion from Mars will frighten and tantalize and thrill another generation of fans.

This book is a tribute to H. G. Wells, one of the few giants of literature, his most famous and influential novel, *The War of the Worlds*, and those adaptations that have been inspired by it. Often, as a science fiction author, I am asked to name the best novel or film in the genre. A fan will approach me after I've spoken on a panel at the World Science Fiction Convention, or a caller will telephone the radio show that I've just done, or the host of a television show will ask me after I've just appeared as a guest—they all want to know what I think. And I try to give them a thoughtful answer, by saying that there are many wonderful works of science fiction. From *Dune* by Frank Herbert and *Stranger in a Strange Land* by Robert Heinlein to "2001: A Space Odyssey" and "Planet of the Apes." I know what I like, and often my response cannot be expressed in a simple declarative statement or two in much the same way that another person might fumble to express his enjoyment of a Philly cheesesteak or a glass of Merlot or a baseball game at Wrigley Field. But the fact of the matter is that there is only one book that stands out, head and shoulders above all of the rest, and that is *The War of the Worlds*. And I think we all would agree the same is true for its cinematic adaptations as well. Honestly, I can think of no other author or no other story that defines of the genre of science fiction better than H. G. Wells and *The War of the Worlds*.

—John L. Flynn, Ph.D.
April 1, 2005

Chapter One: H. G. Wells

For the writer of fantastic stories to help the reader to play the game properly, he must help him in every possible unobtrusive way to domesticate the impossible hypothesis. He must trick him into an unwary concession to some plausible assumption and get on with his story while the illusion still holds. And that is where there was a certain slight novelty in my stories when they first appeared. Hitherto, except in exploration fantasies, the fantastic element was brought in by magic. Frankenstein, even, used some jiggery-pokery magic to animate his artificial monster. It occurred to me that instead of the usual interview with the devil or a magician, an ingenious use of scientific patter might with advantage be substituted. That was no great discovery. I simply brought the fetish stuff up to date, and made it as near actual theory as possible.

–H. G. Wells, June 1934

Herbert George Wells was born on September 21, 1866, the third son of a British shopkeeper in the London suburb of Bromley. "Bertie," as he was affectionately called by his parents, apprenticed as a draper, then later, a chemist, before leaving in 1883 to become a teacher's assistant at Midhurst Grammar School. He obtained a scholarship to London's Normal School of Science, and studied biology under T. H. Huxley, an activist and proponent of Darwin's Theory of Evolution. Darwin's "bull dog," as Huxley was known in scientific circles, made a huge impression on Wells, and may have been the inspiration for Dr. Moreau and his other literary scientists. However, his interest in education faltered, and in 1887, he left without a degree. Wells returned to teaching, taught in private schools for the next four years, delaying the exams for his Bachelor of Science degree until 1890.

In 1891, he settled in London, married his cousin Isabel and continued his career as a teacher at a correspondence school. In 1893, while teaching and working at the University Correspondence College, Wells wrote two textbooks, and dabbled in scientific journalism. After several years, he left Isabel for one of his brightest students, Amy Catherine Robbins, whom he married in 1895.

He began his literary career in earnest in 1895 with the publication of his first novel, *The Time Machine* (originally published as "The Chronic Argonauts" in Science Schools Journal, 1888; expanded and revised in 1895), a "scientific romance" that speculated about the evolutionary future of mankind. The human species becomes divided into the gentle Eloi and the bestial Morlocks, both of which ultimately become extinct as life as we know it gives way to a new, totally alien life-form. What made the novel so impressive was that H.G. Wells had created the first device for traveling in time; with the time machine, man was suddenly able to control his journeys backward and forward. By taking his anonymous time traveler on a trip into the distant future, then returning him safely to the present, Wells established the pattern for most modern time-

travel stories. Though it would take another thirty years, or so, for the notion to finally take root, Wells's invention not only gave time travelers mobility but also changed the way in which many other writers would approach the subject of time travel.

His second novel, *A Wonderful Visit* (1895), featured an angel fallen from Heaven who cast a critical eye on Wells's own bourgeois Victorian society. This was his first attempt at social criticism, and established the pattern that would run through much of his work. Like Jonathan Swift before him, H.G. Wells felt an obligation to hold a mirror up to his world, and show people the true folly of their lives when left in the hands of unjust politicians and leaders.

The Island of Dr. Moreau (1896) was the most radical and imaginative of his early writing; by implying that Darwin's evolutionary

Herbert George Wells

theory was a way to eradicate the injustices and hypocrisies of his contemporary society with a kind of genetic engineering, Wells touched off a firestorm of controversy. When the novel was first published in the spring of 1896, critics were outraged by the story of a scientist populating a remote island with beasts surgically re-shaped as men. *The London Times* led the cries of outrage by referring to his third novel as a "loathsome and repulsive" book. Other newspapers called Wells "a professor of the gruesome" and "a past master in the art of producing creepy sensations." *The Saturday Review*, which had frequently published articles and stories by the young author, hired Sir Peter Chalmers Mitchell, the famous zoologist, to write the literary review of this new novel. In the April 11, 1896 issue, Mitchell passed judgment on Wells with the damning

opinion that he was a scientific heretic.

H.G. Wells was angered by this review, but ironically Mitchell's criticism only helped to fuel interest for the book among the curious public. After the leading humor magazine, *Punch*, published a parody titled "The Island of Professor Menu" by James F. Sullivan, one of the most widely read humorists of his day, booksellers could not keep *The Island of Dr. Moreau* on the shelves of their London bookstores.

On November 7, 1896, Wells published a letter to the editor of *The Saturday Review* defending his book, and pointing out to Mitchell and all of his other critics that recent scientific experiments with animals had substantiated the thesis of his novel. He wrote: "I knew of no published results of the kind I needed [when I first penned *The Island of Dr. Moreau*]. But

Wells at 60

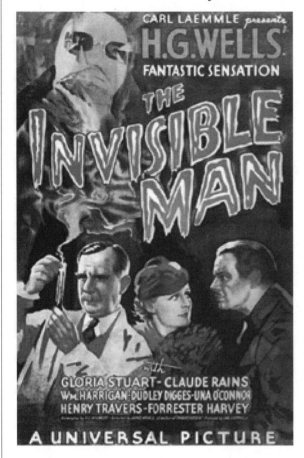

the *British Medical Journal* for 31 October 1896 contains the report of a successful graft by Mr. May Robson, not merely connective but of nervous tissues between rabbit and man. I trust, therefore, that Natural Science will now modify its statements concerning my book, and that [Mitchell] will now wax apologetic." Wells never did get his apology, but it was in the publicity surrounding *The Island of Dr. Moreau* that H.G. Wells became famous.

His follow-up novel was *The Invisible Man* (1897). Like Dr. Moreau, his protagonist Jack Griffin is a scientist with lofty ideals. He discovers an invisibility serum, and tests it on himself. Driven mad by the side effects of the drug he imbibes, Griffin becomes the scourge of the countryside. His benevolent dreams for mankind turn evil, and he, too, must be punished for meddling in the natural order of the universe. Jack Griffin represents both a savior and a demon as the forces of good and evil struggle for control of his very soul.

As with his previous novel, Wells was exploring the relationship between science and superstition. Both Moreau and Griffin were created in the image and mold of Frankenstein, but neither feels the need to show any remorse for what they have done. They are both fed up with the hypocrisy of their conservative scientific colleagues who find their ideas outrageous, yet at the same time profess to embrace rational thought. Moreau and Griffin's resistance to their outmoded ways of thinking makes the two Wellsian doctors seem almost heroic. In rejecting the old systemic and creationist views of the species, they clearly align themselves with Darwin, Huxley and others who see man as the product of millions of years of evolution. Wells did not view science and scientific inquiry as inherently evil. To him, science was not a religion with lots of arcane rituals and superstitious beliefs, but rather a powerful tool that can help man reshape his world. Dr. Moreau and Jack Griffin are the first true scientists of the twentieth century. Not burdened by guilt or the feelings of shame of his Judeo-Christian ancestors, they pursue a line of scientific inquiry to its inevitable and ultimately tragic conclusion. While theories may be proven faulty and conjectures found to be incorrect, Science itself is never wrong. Wells felt there was no need to recant his solemn interest in science even if it made his mainstream critics uneasy.

H.G. Wells left London for the peace and solitude of the English countryside, and moved into a home in the small village of Woking. There, he wrote diligently at his dining room table, penning some of his most famous tales. His best-known short stories included

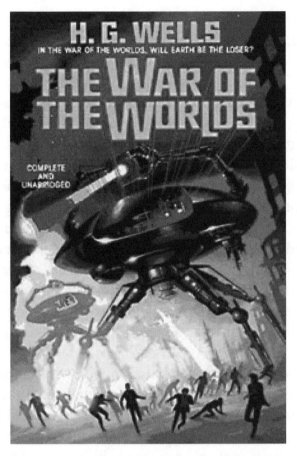

"A Story of the Stone Age" (1897), in which Wells traveled back in time to the moment in which Man evolved from his bestial ancestors; "The Star" (1897), a cosmic disaster story involving a star that goes supernova and the civilization it destroys; "A Story of Days to Come" (1897), a tale in which technology still relies on poverty to maintain class divisions; "The Man Who Could Work Miracles" (1898), and many others. Most of the stories combined Wells's interest in science and technology with his growing social conscience.

Like many other Englishmen of his day, Wells also discovered the joy and excitement of bicycling. He began cycling around Woking and the English countryside, and kept a journal of the sights and sounds of his adventures. Much of that found its way into a cycling romance called *The Wheels of Chance* (1898).

While he was putting the finishing touches on his latest book, his brother Frank recommended that he write a tale about an invasion from another world. Intrigued by the idea, Wells considered the locations of his cycling book, and started to outline a plot that would take full advantage of his locales. H.G. Wells recorded in his diary how he "wheeled about the district marking down suitable places and people for destruction." At the same time, he read an article in *The London Times* about English explorers to Tasmania who had acted so very callously towards the indigenous population that they had virtually wiped them out with the germs and technology they had brought with them. Wells was outraged, and struggled with his own conscience as a fellow Englishman. He decided his latest work would be a very personal one, in that it would take place in surroundings that he knew, but he also made a point of connecting the story to evolution, technology, and science. What if a superior race of beings from another world, as evolutionarily superior as humans are to apes, used their superior technology to conquer Earth? Would human beings survive such a conflict?

In a letter to Elizabeth Healey, a female friend in London, he wrote: "I'm doing the dearest little serial for Pearson's new magazine, in which I completely wreck and sack Woking-killing my neighbors in painful and eccentric way-then proceed via Kingston and Richmond to London, which I sack, electing South Kensington for feats of peculiar atrocity." Wells relished in shocking his friends with details of his latest work, and with *The War of the Worlds*, the author was very literally destroying the world that they knew and loved. He was also playing on the fears the public had as the end of the century was drawing to a close. The prevalent mood known as fine de siecle, or "end of the age," made his contemporaries nervous. Many people thought the world would end at the stroke of midnight on December 31, 1900, and some were actually preparing for the catastrophic event that signify the end. What better way to destroy the world than with an invasion from outer space!

When *The War of the Worlds* first appeared in 1898, the novel was a huge success, and was very well received by Wells's critics. For instance, in the February 10th issue of *Nature*, Sir Richard Gregory wrote: "*The War of the Worlds* is even better than either of these contributions [*The Time Machine* and *The Island of Dr. Moreau*] to scientific romance, and there are parts of its which are more stimulating to thought than anything that the author has yet written."

For the first time in literature, H.G. Wells introduced the reading public to an alien being intent on world domination. While somewhat of a cliché today, the notion that monstrous invaders from another world would travel vast cosmic distances to conquer Earth was a completely new one in his day. And the fact that Wells made his ruthless invaders Martians was even more clever. At the time, people around the world were obsessed with the daily discoveries being made of the Red Planet by scientists like Percival Lowell, Giovanni Schiaparelli, and others. Stories about canals and the possibility of an ancient alien civilization on Mars fueled book sales for *The War of the Worlds*. And with rampant feelings about an impending apocalypse, which he had purposely exploited in his novel, Wells enjoyed his greatest triumph.

No other work of fiction H. G. Wells wrote after *The War of the Worlds* quite matched its imaginative scope, even though he continued to produce fine work. *When the Sleeper Wakes* [1899] was Wells's most blatantly socialist work to date, imagining a future in which the socialist revolution has taken place. Governed by an elite body of ruling intelligentsia, the masses of humanity have finally achieved social equality and justice, and live in perfect harmony. When an ordinary man (the "sleeper") from his time wakes from an extended period of suspended animation, he finds that the world has achieved a kind of utopia, complete with fabulous flying machines and miraculous advances in science and medicine. The story mirrored his own take on socialism, not the socialist doctrines that were being espoused by Marx or other radical leftists, and made Wells seem like a champion of the lower classes.

H.G. Wells continued writing many other "scientific romances," including *The First Men in the Moon* (1901), *The Food of the Gods* and *How It Came to Earth* (1904), *A Modern Utopia* (1905), *In the Days of the Comet* (1906), and *Men like Gods* (1923), but as the twentieth century dawned, Wells seemed to be lose all interest in writing tales of science fiction, and gradually turned his prolific pen to mainstream works, histories, and social commentary.

Like *The Wheels of Chance*, his realistic novels drew heavily from his own experiences. *Love and Mr. Lewisham* (1900), *Kipps* (1905), *Tono-Bungay* (1909), and *The History of Mr. Polly* (1910) were all set in the present day, and dealt with contemporary social issues that people in the middle class experienced. *The New Machiavelli* (1911) was a political satire, and *Bildungsroman, The World of William Clissold* (1926) was his pretentious attempt to write a three-volume literary novel. Other mainstream works included *The Undying Fire* (1919), *Mr. Blettsworthy on Rampole Island* (1928), and *The Autocracy of Mr. Parham* (1930). Wells also wrote several non-fiction books about history; his most famous was *The Outline of History* (1920), but other books, like *God the Invisible King* (1917) and *The Science of Life* (with Julian Huxley, 1930), were equally popular.

A revolutionary proponent of "free love" and women's rights, Wells also penned *Ann Veronica* (1909), an important and revealing novel about the place of women in society. As a member of the Fabian Society, Wells believed that social reform could be achieved by a new political approach of gradual and patient argument, and used his clout as a best-selling author to promote many Socialist issues as a means to change society. Those books included *The Salvaging of Civilisation* (1921), *The Open Conspiracy: Blue Prints for a World Revolution* (1928), and *The New World Order* (1939). Many of his critics dismissed Wells

H.G. Wells Bibliography

Novels:
* The Lord of the Dynamos (1894)
* The Time Machine (1895)
* The Wonderful Visit (1895)
* The Island of Doctor Moreau (1896)
* The Wheels of Chance (1896)
* The Invisible Man (1897)
* The War of the Worlds (1898)
* Love and Mr Lewisham (1899)
* The Sleeper Awakes (1899)
* Anticipations (1901)
* The First Men in the Moon (1901)
* The Sea Lady (1902)
* The Food of the Gods (1904)
* Kipps (1905)
* A Modern Utopia (1905)
* In the Days of the Comet (1906)
* This Misery of Boots (1907)
* The War in the Air (1908)
* Ann Veronica (1909)
* Tono-Bungay (1909)
* The History of Mr Polly (1910)
* The New Machiavelli (1911)
* Marriage (1912)
* The Passionate Friends (1913)
* The Wife of Sir Isaac Harman (1914)
* The World Set Free (1914)
* Bealby: A Holiday (1915)
* Boon, The Mind Of The Race... (1915)
* The Research Magnificent (1915)
* Mr Britling Sees It Through (1916)
* The Soul of a Bishop (1917)
* Joan And Peter (1919)
* The Undying Fire (1919)
* The Secret Places of the Heart (1922)
* Washington and the Hope of Peace (1922)
* Men Like Gods (1923)
* The Dream (1924)
* Christina Alberta's Father (1925)
* The World of William Clissold (1926)
* Meanwhile (1927)
*Mr Blettsworthy on Rampole Island (1928)
*The King Who Was A King (1929)
* The Treasure In The Forest (1929)
* The Autocracy of Mr Parham (1930)
* The Bulpington of Blup (1932)
* The Shape of Things to Come (1933)

as a Marxist, but he was very quick to point out that his desire for social change was based on true Socialism. In *The World Set Free: A Story of Mankind* (1914), H.G. Wells explained many of his controversial beliefs in a prophetic novel set against the backdrop of a world war between Imperial Germany and Britain's "Central European Allies." Both sides invent an "atomic bomb," which is the first time the term was used, and inflict atomic warfare on the other. The world is utterly destroyed in the conflict. From out of the ashes of the old world, a new order rises that establishes a generous and just world state.

Of course, when the First World War began (as a conflict between Germany and the Allied Nations) shortly after his novel was published, Wells feared that the world might indeed face total annihilation. He changed his pacifist beliefs, and supported Britain's entry into the Great War, writing a pamphlet entitled "The War That Will End War." Its title became proverbial almost instantly, and we still remember it today as the hopes of his generation for the First World War. After the war was over, H.G. Wells was the first to call for a League of Nations, so that nations could work out their differences peaceably without war. But he was also bitterly disappointed with the actual League that developed, and wrote critically for reform. Regrettably, his indictment of atomic warfare in *The World Set Free: A Story of Mankind* (1914) did not prevent the world powers (especially the United States) from racing to develop and ultimately use atomic bombs in the decades that followed.

Wells's enormous gift for prophecy was also apparent in many of his other writings as well. In "The Land Ironclads" (1903), he anticipated the use of tanks in war, and in *The War in the Air, and Particularly How Mr. Bert Smallways Fared while It Lasted* (1908), he suggested how aerial bombardment might wreak so much havoc on civilians on the ground. *New Worlds for Old* (1908), *What is Coming* (1916), *War and the Future* (1917), *The Work, Wealth and Happiness of Mankind* (1931), and *The Fate of Homo Sapiens* (1939) all provided speculative glimpses into the world of the future by laying out a historical road-map for change. *The Shape of Things to Come* (1933), which was developed into the 1936 science fiction film "Things to Come" (based upon a script by Wells), represented the climax of his literary career.

He returned to London during the 1930's, and began writing his autobiography. He was profoundly disturbed by the rise of Fascism in Germany and Italy, and wrote pamphlets denouncing Hitler and his accomplices. In *The Holy Terror* (1939), Wells examined the psychological development of a modern dictator based on the careers of Stalin, Mussolini, and Hitler. During World War Two, he lived in a London flat off Regent's Park, and walked his own fire watch during the Luftwaffe's Blitz of the city. His last book, *Mind At The End Of Its Tether* (1945), expressed pessimism about mankind's future prospects, concluding that Man was doomed because he could not and would not adapt himself to his technological circumstances. He died quietly at home on August 13, 1946.

Evidence of his influence in Hollywood can be found, even to this day, in recent films such as "The Island of Dr. Moreau" (1999), the DreamWorks version of "The Time Machine" (2001), and "The War of the Worlds" (2005), as well as the unspoken but obvious (and rather clumsy) copies of his original ideas and themes in films like "Independence Day" (1996), "Mars Attacks!" (1996), and "Hollow Man" (2000). Other films based on H. G. Wells's work include "The Island of Terror" (1917), "Things to Come" (1936), "The Invisible Man" (1933), "The Island of Lost Souls" (1933), "The Man Who Could Work

* *The Croquet Player (1936)*
* *The Man Who Could Work Miracles (1936)*
* *Apropos Of Dolores (1937)*
* *Brynhild (1937)*
* *The Camford Visitation (1937)*
* *Star Begotten (1937)*
* *The Brothers (1938)*
* *The Holy Terror (1939)*
* *All Aboard for Ararat (1940)*
* *Babes In The Darkling Wood (1940)*
* *You Can't Be Too Careful (1941)*
Non-Fiction:
* *Text-Book of Biology (1892-93)*
* *Honours Phsiography (1893)*
* *Mankind in the Making (1903)*
* *New Worlds For Old (1908)*
* *The War That Will End War (1914)*
* *God the Invisible King (1917)*
* *The Outline of History (1920)*
* *The Salvaging of Civilization (1921)*
* *A Short History of the World (1922)*
* *The Way the World Is Going: Guesses and Forecasts of the World Ahead (1928)*
* *The Open Conspiracy: Blue Prints For a World Revolution (1928)*
* *The Science of Life [with Julian Huxley and G.P. Wells] (1930)*
* *The Work, Wealth and Happiness of Mankind [2 volumes] (1931)*
* *Experiment in Autobiography: Discoveries and Conclusions of a Very Ordinary Brain [Since 1866] [2 volumes] (1934)*
* *The Anatomy of Frustration (1936)*
* *World Brain (1938)*
* *The Fate of Homo Sapiens (1939)*
* *The New World Order (1939)*
* *Phoenix (1942)*
* *The Conquest of Time (1942)*
* *The Happy Turning: A Dream of Life [chapbook] (1945)*
* *Journalism and Prophecy 1893 - 1946 edited by W, Warren Wagar (1964)*
* *H.G. Wells in Love: Postscript to an Experiment in Autobiography (1984)*
Short Story Collections:
* *The Stolen Bacillus (1895)*
* *The Country of the Blind (1911)*
* *The Empire Of The Ants (1925)*

Miracles" (1936), "The Invisible Man Returns" (1940), "Kipps" (1941), "Invisible Agent" (1942), "The Invisible Man's Revenge" (1944), "The Passionate Friends" (1949), "The History of Polly" (1949), "The War of the Worlds" (1953), "The Door in the Wall" (1955), "Terror Is a Man" (1959), "The Time Machine" (1960), "First Men in the Moon" (1964), "Village of the Giants" (1965), "Half a Sixpence" (1967), "The Twilight People" (1973), "The Invisible Man" (1975), "Gemini Man" (1976), "The Food of the Gods" (1976), "The Island of Dr. Moreau" (1977), "Empire of the Ants" (1977), "The Time Machine" (1978), "The Shape of Things to Come" (1979), "The Invisible Man" (1984), "War of the Worlds" (1988), "The Time Machine" (1992), and others. H. G. Wells and his second wife Amy Catherine Robbins also became characters in "Time After Time" (1979).

H. G. Wells in 1936 on the set of William Cameron Menzies's production of "Things to Come." Wells himself wrote the screenplay, based upon his nonfiction work The Shape of Things to Come (1933).

CHAPTER TWO: THE NOVEL

No one would have believed in the last years of the nineteenth century that this world was being watched keenly and closely by intelligences greater than man's and yet as mortal as his own; that as men busied themselves about their various concerns they were scrutinized and studied, perhaps almost as narrowly as man with a microscope might scrutinize the transient creatures that swarm and multiply in a drop of water. With infinite complacency men went to and fro over this globe about their little affairs, serene in their assurance of their empire over matter... No one gave a thought to the older worlds of space as sources of human danger, or thought of them only to dismiss the idea of life upon them as impossible or improbable... Yet across the gulf of space, minds that are to our minds as ours are to those of the beast that perish, intellects vast and cool and unsympathetic, regarded this earth with envious eyes, and slowly and surely drew their plans against us...

—Chapter One, The War of the Worlds

The most famous and widely read of all his "scientific romances," *The War of the Worlds* (1898) assured the reputation of H. G. Wells as a master storyteller and visionary for his day and for all time to come. When the novel was first serialized in *Pearson's Magazine* in 1897, then later published in book form in January of 1898, the critics responded in both Britain and the United States with laudatory reviews that hailed it as a work of true genius. The unnamed reviewer for *The Academy* wrote in his January 29, 1898, review: "Mr. Wells has done good work before, but nothing quite so fine as this. He has two distinct gifts - of scientific imagination and of mundane observation - and he has succeeded in bringing them together and harmoniously into play." The American reviewer echoed those same sentiments, writing in the May 1898 issue of *The Bookman*: "Among the younger writers of his day, Mr. Wells is the most distinctly original, and the least indebted to predecessors. *The War of the Worlds* is a very strong and a very powerful book."

The struggle between humans and their otherworldly counterparts is so archetypal that it can be traced back to some of the earliest works of modern science fiction. In fact, six years before H. G. Wells penned his classic novel, Robert Potter unleashed the first story of alien invasion with *The Germ Growers* (1892). The London-published Australian novel introduced space dwellers that took on the appearance of humans in order to cultivate a virulent bacteriologic strain in different parts of the Earth as part of a plan to conquer the planet. With a storyline that more resembles Jack Finney's *The Body Snatchers* (1955) than *The War of the Worlds*, Potter's novel was probably not widely read, and is therefore largely forgotten today. Most people credit Wells with the first confrontation between humans and aliens.

Ever since his superior Martians first invaded the English countryside in *The War of the Worlds*, the idea of two highly successful species competing for resources and survival has fascinated science fiction writers. Karel Capek, who introduced the word "robot" to literature, envisioned an alien invasion story as a "takeover" tale with *The War of the Newts* (1936), while John W. Campbell Jr. introduced the first shape-shifting alien in "Who Goes There?" (filmed as "The Thing," 1951 and 1982). Frederic Brown's classic story "Arena" (1944) finds the fate of a human-alien conflict being decided by single combatants on an equally-alien world. The aliens in Arthur Clarke's *Childhood's End* (1953) and Clifford Simak's "Kindergarten" (1953) remain totally indifferent to man's existence as though humans are mere ants beneath their feet. Similarly, the man-eating plants in John Wyndham's *Day of the Triffids* (1951), the monster wasps of Keith Roberts' *The Furies* (1966), or the aquatic demons of Brian Aldiss' "The Saliva Tree" (1966) view humans as

Original illustrations from the 1898 publication.

simply a means to propagate their own species. These stories, and countless others like them, have all told the same, familiar tale. Humans have been threatened by alien creatures in pulp fiction as often as helpless heroines have been threatened by mustached villains in melodrama. Sometimes the stories are allegories of racism and xenophobia, reflections of cold war paranoia or metaphors for incurable diseases; but more often than not, they are simple adventure tales which force humans to confront their worst nightmares and fears.

Today, *The War of the Worlds* is seen as the forerunner of several branches of science fiction literature, including themes related to aliens, alien invasion, first contact, interplanetary war, and the end of the world. One could argue that H. G. Wells created single-handedly everything that has been written about in the field of science fiction, and the impact of his work has been as great, if not greater, than any other author who has ever written in the field. His powerful prose tells the story of Martians, fleeing from their own world because of depleted resources, invading the Earth, landing near London, and destroying or conquering all before them. Any effort by the humans to halt the Martian advance is crushed by the unstoppable alien invaders. The fate of civilization and even that of the human race remains in doubt until the very end of the book when a common germ eliminates the Martian menace.

Wells not only invented the myth of an invasion from space but also wrote a disturbingly realistic portrait of his own world which included very real characters and setting. His boastful artilleryman, superstitious curate, and energetic medical student are believable if not wholly sympathetic figures that were based upon people he knew in Woking and Surrey. And Wells bicycled the route the Martians take on landing so as to add the greatest degree of verisimilitude. He also tapped into the fears his reading public had as the end of the century was drawing to a close. The prevalent mood known as fine de siecle, or "end of the age," made many people think the world was going to end at the stroke of midnight on December 31, 1900; some were actually preparing for the catastrophic event that signify the end. What better way to destroy the world than with an invasion from outer space!

Ironically, Wells's masterpiece was born in the simplest and most prosaic way. While he was taking a break from editing the final draft of *The Wheels of Chance* (1898), his brother Frank suggested the idea for his next book. Years later, H. G. Wells recalled the incident in his autobiography, which was first published as an article in *The Strand* (February 1920): "We were walking together through some particularly peaceful Surrey scenery.

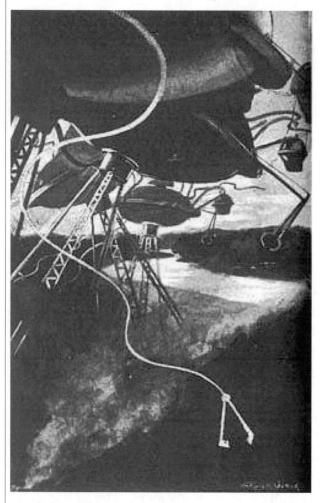

'Suppose some beings from another planet were to drop out of the sky suddenly,' said he [Frank], 'and begin laying about them here!' Perhaps we had been talking of the discovery of Tasmania by the Europeans - a very frightful disaster for the native Tasmanians! I forget. But that was the point of departure."

Intrigued by the idea, Wells began to consider the details of his plot. He had read the account of the English explorers to Tasmania in *The London Times*, and while he was outraged by what had happened to the native Tasmanians, the scientist in him had seen that as nothing less than a confirmation of Darwin's evolutionary theories about the survival of the fittest. In a struggle for existence, only the fittest survived, and the rest perished. His aliens, therefore, became a Darwinian competitor that sought to displace mankind for Earth's valuable resources. Though somewhat of a cliché today, the notion that monstrous invaders from another world would travel vast cosmic distances to conquer Earth was a completely new one in his day. And the fact that Wells made his ruthless invaders Martians was also inspired by the day's events.

At the time, people around the world were obsessed with the daily discoveries being made of the Red Planet. From 1894 to 1897, the slightly elliptical orbit of Mars brought its position in space particularly close to the Earth, and that rare cosmic event led to a great deal of observation and scientific discussion. Italian astronomer Giovanni Schiaparelli reported seeing "canali" on Mars in 1894. When the Italian word, which means "channels," was mistranslated as "canals," speculation about life on the Red Planet reached a fever pitch. In Flagstaff, Arizona, from May 24, 1894, to April 3, 1895, Percival Lowell observed Mars with one of the most powerful telescopes in the world, and made 917 drawings and sketches of the planet. Most of his sketches included an elaborate canal system that ran presumably from the northern polar regions to the arid plains near the equator. These canals fertilized the land, and were the only habitable tracts of the Martian surface as the remainder was desert. Another observer, M. Javelle of Nice, France, claimed to have seen a strange light on Mars, which stimulated speculation that there were not only canals but also cities with lights and industry.

The view that beings immensely superior to man lived on Mars was first put forth by another distinguished observer of Mars. M.E.M. Antoniadi suggested in a July 1897 epigraph that "perhaps the least improbable - not to say the most plausible - clue to the mystery still attaches to the overbold and almost absurd assumption that what we are witnessing on Mars is the work of rational beings immeasurably superior to man, and capable of dealing with thousands and thousands of square miles of gray and yellow material with more ease than we can cultivate or destroy vegetation in a garden one acre in extent." Antoniadi's speculations about the intellectual status of the Martians supported much of what the novel espoused.

Wells wrote *The War of the Worlds* in response to several other historical events as well. He remembered reading about the island of Java and the account of the explosion there in 1883 of Mount Krakatoa, in which 50,000 people were killed and the Earth's climate was drastically changed for a whole year. Wells imagined what the destructive power must have been, and gave his Martians equally formidable weapons to destroy the cities and towns they encountered. He also made one of his characters (partially based on the astronomer Javelle) Lavelle of Java. Wells was also very concerned about the unification and military buildup of Germany, and feared that a war in Europe was immanent. His speculation was prescient. War did break out in Europe nearly twenty years later, and the instruments of war (poison gas, aerial bombardment, and land ironclads) were all predicted in his novel.

And finally, H. G. Wells had just finished reading both Alfred Bate Richards's *The Invasion of England* (1870) and Sir George Chesney's *The Battle of Dorking* (1871), in which England is invaded by a militaristic Germany. Both novels warned against Britain's military complacency, and told the story from a semi-documentary fashion. Wells borrowed their technique to tie his interplanetary war tale to specific places in England that were familiar to his readers. (Orson Welles who created the famed 1938 radio broadcast would rely on the same technique.) In fact, H. G. Wells never relaxes his hold on the commonplace, everyday life of his characters, and that makes the horrible, almost lurid events of the story seem very real.

The novel is divided into two distinct sections or books. In *Book One*, "The Coming of the Martians," H. G. Wells introduces us to an unnamed narrator, an author of scientific texts and a student of moral philosophy, who is living at Maybury Hill in the English countryside near Woking. Like the unnamed narrator in *The Time Machine* (1895), this narrator is a thinly-disguised version of Wells himself. Of course, in order to present the narrative from the first person point-of-view, Wells had to resort to some clever tricks. For one thing, the narrator is a learned scholar, a scientist and a friend of a local astronomer named Ogilvy: this gives him access to the world of astronomy when most of the news about the first projectile from Mars is not commonly talked about. Another method used is that the narrator is speaking from six years after the action has taken place, so that information that would not have been available during the Martian invasion is now know. And finally, he becomes an eye-witness of the events that follow, including the construction of the Martian war machines, their advance on London, the defeat of the military, the flight of the populace, and ultimately the death of the invaders when they succumb to the Earth germs, or he converses with people in the story who have seen what has happened.

In the beginning of the book, the narrator explains that the Martians "regarded this earth with envious eyes..." and concluded that the aliens invaded Earth because they had completely depleted their own resources. He draws several parallels between the Martians'

treatment of humans and Britain's treatment of its colonial subjects, in particular the disaster in Tasmania. He refers to a "great light" seen on the planet Mars in 1894 - the same great light that was observed by Javelle - says that was six years before the time when he is writing. At first, Earth's astronomers were perplexed about what to make of the light; some speculated that it might be the sign of an intelligent alien civilization, while other dismissed it as a fire caused by a falling meteorite. Only later did they realize that it was the vanguard of invading forces, being shot toward Earth as if out of a gun. (The use of gigantic guns rather than rockets or shuttles to launch space vehicles may have been borrowed from Jules Verne's 1865 novel, *From the Earth to the Moon*.) Furthermore, the narrator mentions how the appearance of gas explosions is observed on Mars at regular 24-hour intervals.

Later, the narrator describes a "falling star" shooting through the atmosphere high over Winchester heading eastward. The meteorite, which is in fact the first Martian projectile, impacts the common between Horsell, Ottershaw, and Woking. In the early morning hours, his friend Ogilvy finds the "thing" half buried in the sand pits, and when the top starts to unscrew, he determines that it is actually a hollowed-out cylinder with occupants inside. He draws a connection to the gas explosions on Mars, and determines the cylinder is actually an interplanetary craft. Ogilvy tells Henderson, the local reporter who in turn telegraphs the news of the discovery to *The Daily Chronicle*. News spreads rapidly throughout the county, and residents from the three villages flock to the landing site of the first projectile on Horsell Common.

The narrator soon joins the crowd of people surrounding the huge hole where the cylinder lay, and listens to them speculate about the Martians. They all imagine that a peaceful dialogue is possible, and they become very excited when suddenly the Martians begin to emerge from the cylinder. He describes the scene: "A big grayish, rounded bulk, the size, perhaps, of a bear, was rising slowly and painfully out of the cylinder. As it bulged up and caught the light, it glistened like wet leather. Two large dark-colored eyes were regarding me steadfastly. It was rounded, and had, one might say, a face. There was a mouth under the eyes, the lipless brim of what quivered and panted and dropped saliva. The body heaved and pulsed convulsively. A lank, tentacular appendage gripped the edge of the cylinder, another swayed in the air . . . There was something fungoid in the oily brown skin, something in the clumsy deliverance of the tedious movements unspeakably terrible. Even at this first encounter, the first glimpse, I was overcome with disgust and dread. Suddenly the monster vanished." (*Chapter Four*) But, as the mass of people press around the pit to see what has happened to the Martian, a metallic tentacle slithers out of the cylinder's opening, and vaporizes the majority of the people with an unknown Heat-Ray.

Traumatized by what he has seen, the narrator flees home, and tells his wife what he has seen. Until this time, he had thought that Martians could not survive on earth because of the differences in gravity. He speculates about the course of evolution on Mars, and determines that the Martians have so focused their lives on intellectual pursuits that they have all gone to brain. They cannot move as swiftly or as easily on Earth because the gravitational

force is so much greater than what they have grown accustomed on Mars. He tries to persuade his wife that they will be safe, but then a second cylinder impacts on the English countryside.

Suddenly, as the narrator sits with his wife on the terrace of their home, he hears gunshots and loud thunder. The British army has gone out to meet the Martians, but their antiquated weapons are no match for the Martian Heat-Ray. The alien invaders ignite everything in their range, and easily destroy the army troops. The narrator and his wife, whose house would also soon be in the range of the Heat-Ray, flee to his cousin's home in Leatherhead. Leaving his wife in safe hands, the narrator heads back to Woking where he plans to help his neighbors and friends escape.

He then witnesses the landing of the third cylinder, and observes for the first time the Martian tripods: "Seen near the thing was incredibly strange, for it was no mere insensate machine driving on its way. Machine it was, with a ringing metallic pace, and long flexible glittering tentacles (one of which gripped a young pine tree) swinging and rattling about its strange body. It picks its road as it went striding along, and the brazen hood that surmounted it moved to and fro with the inevitable suggestion of a head looking about it. Behind the main body was a huge thing of white metal like a gigantic fisherman's basket, and puffs of green smoke squirted out from the joints of the limbs as the monster swept by me. And in an instant it was gone." He knows that the mechanical appliances will make the Martians undefeatable.

Back at the narrator's home at Maybury Hill, he meets the Artilleryman. He learns the man is from a regiment of the army that has been destroyed by the Martians' Heat-Ray, and he is shocked and barely able to speak. They decide to hide together in the house during the night, and hope the Martians pass them by. There is not another living soul in Woking. In the morning, they decide against the plan to return to Leatherhead because this would lead them directly to the third cylinder and its massing army. Instead they head for Weybridge via Byfleet. The two men travel together until they come upon a lieutenant of a cavalry unit in Byfleet, who tells the Artilleryman where he can find a superior officer to whom he can report. The army is in such disarray that he has trouble finding out who is in charge. By midday, they reach the junction of the Thames and Wey rivers, and are nearly discovered by four Martian tripods striding towards the river. Fortunately, the army destroys one tripod while the others continue to move downriver towards London.

When the Martians attack and destroy Weybridge and Shepperton, the narrator is separated from his companion. He dives under the water to save himself from the Heat-Ray, then later escapes by boat in the direction of London where he meets the Curate, who is sort of an assistant clergyman.

In *Chapter Fourteen*, the narrative switches to events in London, and is told second-hand through the experiences of the narrator's younger brother, who is a medical student working for an imminent examination. Even though the first cylinder had landed on Thursday and fighting broke out on Friday, most Londoners do not recognize the threat of the Martians and continue with their daily Saturday routines. They feel they are safe as London is so far removed from Horsell Common. Only when the newspapers begin printing the truth about the Martians' tripod machines and the heat-way do people ac-knowledge the enormity of the menace, and leave the city in a panic.

On Sunday, not long after the fourth cylinder impacts near London, the Martians deploy their sec-ondary weapon; poison gas is sprayed over all the fields and villages, and kills most of the humans and livestock in its path. The next day the narrator's brother escapes from Lon-don, rescuing Miss Elphinstone and her sister-in-law as the Martians lay waste to the city. Together, they attempt to cross the Great North Road, but are held up by swarming, panic-stricken crowds. Eventually, they reach the coastline and board a paddlesteamer bound for Ostend, Belgium. From the deck of the ship, they witness the destruction of two other Martian tripods by the warship *Thunder Child*, which rams the invader's machines like a torpedo.

In *Book Two*, "The Earth Under the Martians," H. G. Wells re-introduces us to the unnamed narrator as he sets out for Leatherhead to save his wife. Accompanied by the Curate, they try to avoid the areas of the English countryside poisoned by the Black Smoke or the forests that are burning because of the Heat-Ray. They take refuge in an empty house in Halliford, and are trapped when the fifth cylinder lands. Imprisoned in the ruined house, the narrator describes the Martians machines and creatures that operate them: "They were, I now saw, the most unearthy creatures it is possible to conceive. They were huge round bodies - or, rather, head - about four feet in diameter, each body having it front of it a face. This face had no nostrils - indeed, the Martians do not seem to have had any sense of smell, but it had a pair of very large dark-colored eyes, and just beneath this a kind of fleshy beak. In the back of this head or body - I scarcey know how to speak of it - was the single tight tympanic surface, since know to be anatomically an ear, though it must have been almost useless in our dense air." (*Chapter 2*) For the first glance, the narrator believes they look rather like animals than like humans, and are surprised by their lack of a physical body. To him, they seem like brains with tentacles, and little more than that.

Hours later, while still hiding in the ruins of the house, the narrator witnesses how the alien invaders treat captured humans. The Martians "took the fresh, living blood of other creatures, and injected it into their own veins." Like vampires, they drink blood for their nutrition. The narrator is sickened by what he sees, and resolves to escape. But the Curate cannot stomach the truth about the Martians, and loses his reason. Subsequently, he rages against a Martian tripod machine, and is killed by its tentacles. The narrator hides in the coal cellar of the house.

After twelve days without food and water, he risks using the water pump, and discovers much to his delight that the Martians have left the pit in front of the house. He tries to attract the attention of a stray dog, but it flees in terror. Later, he escapes from the house, and wanders through the woods, feeling the total stillness. At first, the narrator thinks that he may be the last man left alive on Earth, but then he meets the Artilleryman on Putney Hill. The Artilleryman has come to accept the collapse of civilization, almost welcome it, and has made exaggerated plans for living in the sewers like rats in order to assure mankind's survival. He no longer regards most of his fellow human beings. He views the cowards who surrendered to the Martians as less than human, and plans to exact his revenge against them as well as the invaders. In time, he hopes to take control of a Martian war machine, and turn the Heat-Ray on them. The narrator concludes the Artilleryman has gone insane.

Setting off alone to find other survivors (and possibly his wife and cousin), he reaches London, and hears an unearthly howling coming from a Martian tripod. The Martians are dying. On Primrose Hill, he finds the Martian base has become a mass grave of alien bodies. Human germs have annihilated them. Looking over the edge of the pit, the narrator writes: "The Martians [were] dead! Slain by the putrefactive and disease bacteria against which their systems were unprepared; slain as the red weed was being slain; slain, after all man's devices had failed, by the humblest things that God, in his wisdom, has put upon this earth." (*Chapter Nine*)

With these simple-minded sentiments, Wells brought his novel to a satisfactory conclusion. In the *Epilogue* to *The War of the Worlds*, we learn that his narrator returns home safely, three days later, to discover that his wife and cousin did not perish in Leatherhead as he had feared, and are waiting there for him. Both of them have survived the total devastation and horror of the Martian invasion, and want nothing more than to rebuild their shattered world. By contrast, the narrator takes pause to walk among the ruins of the Martian war machines, and reflect on mankind's legacy. Like Wells, he muses philosophically about the virtue of natural selection. For millions of years, man and his pre-human ancestors have fought a struggle for survival against the very germs that destroyed the Martians. "By the toll of a billion deaths," he concludes, "man has bought his birthright of the earth."

H. G. Wells has cleverly woven his own theories about evolution and natural selection into recent scientific observations about germs by Pasteur, Chaveau, Buchner, and Metschnikoff to produce the most striking conclusion of any novel produced in the last two hundred years. The Martians are not destroyed by man's technology, which in the nineteenth century (and probably just as true today) was far inferior to that of the invading army, but by a simple micro-organism. No other work of science fiction or mainstream literature has so deftly dealt with an adversary as this. In his struggle for existence, man has acquired certain immunities against harmful microorganisms, and any visitors from another planet would not be able to resist even the most common of germs that we seem to take for granted. Was it the flu, small pox, diphtheria, or the common cold that killed the Martians? Wells does not confide in us other than to say that, when one alien's body was finally autopsied, no bacteria except those already known to scientists were found. We may never be able to thank those microscopic allies that sought to overthrow the Martians, but we can be grateful for the acquired immunity that each cough and sniffle and sneeze has guaranteed us.

In the wake of the overwhelming success of Wells's *The War of the Worlds*, the inevitable sequels and rip-offs followed. In fact, the novel was such a success in the United States when it was serialized in *Cosmopolitan* (in 1898) that it inspired the very first sequel. Written by Garrett P. Serviss, a journalist and amateur astronomer, "Edison's Conquest of

Mars" sent a battalion of Earthmen to Mars to redress some of the havoc caused by the rampaging Martians. The Martians are eventually defeated on their own turf, their cities are destroyed, and both a British and American flag are raised. The story appeared in the *New York Evening Journal* in the Spring of 1898, and was immensely popular. Of course, in addition to this sequel (and others), Wells's novel has been subsequently imitated and copied, parodied and lampooned, serialized in various other media, broadcast (in America with the most startling effect), and adapted for music and film.

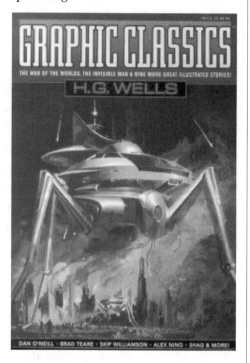

As a result of the novel's instant appeal, Charles Graves and E. V. Lucas, two of Britain's leading humorists, wrote "The War of the Wenuses" (1898). The poem was dedicated to H. G. Wells, and featured yet another invasion from space with a decidedly different kind of adversary. Apparently, the women of Venus have tired of their impotent male counterparts, and decide to travel to Earth to find human lovers. Their striking beauty quickly bewitches every male who comes into contact with them. Earth women soon form a resistance, and counterstrike with their own sexual wiles, sending the Wenuses packing back to their own planet. Wells was flattered by the parody, but chose to write his own follow-up of sorts with *The First Men in the Moon* (1901). Instead of sexy sirens from Venus, H. G. Wells sent two astronauts, Bedford and Cavor, as hapless emissaries to the Selenites who dwell in the Moon. Unfortunately, the bacteria from his Earth visitor's cold wipes out the Selenites's advanced but stagnant civilization.

In 1962, following a long, successful tradition of packaging trading cards with bubblegum, Topps Incorporated issued a fifty-five card set that updated Wells's story to the paranoid Fifties, called "Mars Attacks!" The bubblegum cards told the familiar story of an invasion from Mars and how individual humans responded to the attack. Each card featured a lurid illustration by artists Norm Saunders and Bob Powell, a short caption with lurid titles like "Burning Flesh" or "Destroying a Dog," and a continuing storyline by Len Brown and Woody Gelman. When parents objected to the gory violence and gruesome depictions, Topps removed the cards from the market-only to make the infamous card set more valuable on the collector's market. Thirty years later, the set was re-issued with additional cards, and reached a whole new audience with its very graphic portrayal of an attack from Mars.

Yet another kind of sequel to *The War of the Worlds* was imagined by John Christopher (the pseudonym for prolific author Samuel Youd). Christopher's *The Tripod Trilogy*, which included *The White Mountains* (1967), *The City of Gold and Lead* (1967) and *The Pool of Fire* (1968), depicted a future world in which the Martians (called here Masters) had not succumbed to Earth's bacteria and still roam the planet in giant Tripods that rule the land with an iron tentacle. Every person who reaches puberty is "capped" with a mind-control device, and serves the Masters. The three books, which were released as juvenile fiction, follow the adventures of Will and Henry Parker and Beanpole as they traverse the world of the Tripods, and fight to free humanity from the tyranny of the Masters.

Wade and Manly Wade Wellman revisited the Martian invasion through the eyes of Sherlock Holmes with "The Adventure of the Martian Client" (*The Magazine of Fantasy and Science Fiction*, 1969), which was later expanded into the novel, *Sherlock Holmes' War of the Worlds* (1970). When Holmes acquires a crystal egg into which alien scenes are transmitted from the red planet, he takes it to be examined by Professor Challenger. The two discover the interplanetary war is imminent, and take steps to fight the Martians with their superior intellects. In 1973, Marvel Comics brought the Martians back to Earth with an immunity to disease in *Amazing Adventures 18*. Equipped with protection against nuclear and biological weapons, the blood-thirsty aliens conquered the entire planet in a matter of days. Twenty years later, a specially-trained warrior Killraven and his comrades fight a gorilla war with the Martians. In 1978, Jeff Wayne wrote original music for a "War of the Worlds" album from Columbia that also featured the vocal talents of Richard Burton and Julie Covington. And the Martians tried again in George H. Smith's *The Second War of the Worlds* (1980).

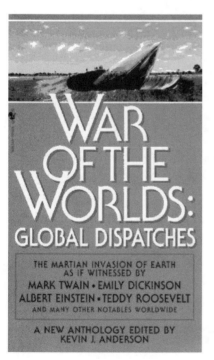

More recently, Star Trek scribe J. M. Dillard wrote a novelization of the pilot for the short-lived "War of the Worlds" television series, titled *War of the Worlds: The Resurrection* (1988), and Kevin J. Anderson edited an anthology, titled *War of the Worlds: Global Dispatches* (1996), in which nineteen authors, including Connie Willis, Dave Wolverton, and Walter Jon Williams, re-imagine H.

G. Wells's frightening tale of a Martian invasion through the perspectives of various historical figures. And finally, Alan Moore's second volume of *The League of Extraordinary Gentleman* (2003) finds Allan Quatermain, Mina Harker, Captain Nemo, the Invisible Man, and Dr. Jekyll all fighting to protect the British Empire when alien invaders from Mars mercilessly attack London. Using their various skills and intellect, the League goes about preparing a defense against the invasion, but when the Invisible Man joins the Martian's cause, all appears to be lost. Now, as one of the members dies a horrific death, the League turns to the legendary Dr. Moreau as their last desperate hope. We can only hope that future re-imaginings of *The War of the Worlds* will be as imaginative as H. G. Wells's seminal work of science fiction enters its second century of publication.

Checklist for *The War of the Worlds* Comic Books

Amazing Adventures #18-39: War of the Worlds, featuring Killraven. (May, 1973-November, 1976). Marvel Comics Group. Regular Series. Writers: Gerry Conway, Roy Thomas, Marv Wolfman, Don McGregor, and Bill Mantlo. Pencilers: Neal Adams, Howard Chaykin, Gene Colan, Herb Trimpe, Keith Giffen, and P. Craig Russell.

Classics Illustrated #124: The War of the Worlds (January, 1955). The Gilberton Company. Production: Jerry Iger Shop. 56 Pages.

Classics Illustrated #SG60: The War of the Worlds (March, 1998). Acclaim Books.

Killraven: The War of the Worlds #1-6 (February, 2001-May 2003). Marvel Comics Group. One-shots and Limited Series.

The League of Extraordinary Gentlemen, Volume 2: The War of the Worlds (October, 2004). DC Comics. One-Shot and 6-Issue Limited Series. Writer: Alan Moore. Artwork: Kevin O'Neill.

Marvel Graphic Novel #7: War of the Worlds, featuring Killraven (August, 1983). Marvel Comics Group. Regular Series. Writer: Don McGregor. Penciler: P. Craig Russell.

Pocket Classics #24: The War of the Worlds (September, 1984). Academic Inc. Publications. 68 Pages.

Superman: War of the Worlds (Summer, 1999). DC Comics. One-shot.

CHAPTER THREE: THE RADIO BROADCAST

This is Orson Welles. A few years ago, people were frightened by my "War of the Worlds" broadcast which, I must say, seems pretty tame considering what has happened to our world since. We weren't as innocent as we meant to be when we did the Martian broadcast. We were fed up with the way in which everything that came over this new magic box, the radio, was being swallowed. . . . So, in a way, our broadcast was an assault on the credibility of that machine. We wanted people to understand that they shouldn't take any opinion predigested, and they shouldn't swallow everything that came through the tap, whether it was radio or not.

—Orson Welles, October 1955

On Sunday, October 30, 1938, the day before Halloween, millions of Americans tuned into a popular radio program that featured plays directed by, and often starring, a twenty-three year-old Orson Welles. His "Mercury Theatre on the Air" was not the highest-rated program between 8:00 and 9:00 P.M. on Sunday evenings. That distinction belonged to the "Chase and Sanborn Hour," which featured Edgar Bergen and his dummy Charlie McCarthy. The medium of radio was still in its infancy at the time, and most listeners believed what they heard over the airwaves, even the ventriloquist's claim that his dummy was actually talking. Welles's radio program was a prestige show with high production values and consistently good performances that appealed to a smarter, though somewhat smaller, audience. The Mercury Theatre's presentation that evening was an adaptation of H. G. Wells's science fiction novel, *The War of the Worlds*, about an invasion from Mars. But rather than adapt the book as a period piece, which would have been faithful to the source material, Welles updated the story to the modern day, and instructed Howard Koch to write the radio play so that it would sound like a news broadcast about an actual Martian invasion—a technique that, presumably, was intended to heighten the dramatic effect for his listeners. So, when the program began that Sunday evening, audience members who had either missed or did not listen to the introduction panicked thinking they were listening to actual news bulletins about invading Martians spreading death and destruction in New Jersey and New York. That mass hysteria disrupted households, interrupted religious services, created traffic jams, clogged communications systems, and generally created a panic that disabled America.

So how, and why, did this all happen? Why didn't radio listeners change channels to get another perspective on the events that were unfolding at Grover's Mill, New Jersey? And how was it that a science fiction novel written forty years earlier could so captivate a whole new generation of fans?

Less than seventy years ago, when television was still at the experimental stage and motion pictures required an evening out, radio was the medium that most people sought for entertainment and news. In 1935, three out of four families owned a radio set, and approximately eight million sets were sold each year. Most who listened to radio did not know how powerful the medium was, and simply accepted the information that was broadcast as truth. Ironically, the new and exciting form of entertainment and news was less than a dozen years old. The big radio networks, NBC and CBS, had only been in existence for a decade when Orson Welles made his famous broadcast, and they were responsible for filling with the airwaves with a vast amount of material that was completely new and experimental. At the same time, Americans were connecting for the first time with news events that were happening all over the globe. They could tune into Roosevelt's "fireside chats," follow the gripping saga of the Lindbergh baby kidnapping, experience the Hindenburg crash, or listen to the rantings of Hitler and Mussolini as fascism spread through Europe.

With this experimental, new medium, Welles and his troupe of players captured lightning in a bottle, and dramatically proved that people lacked a basic understanding of the power of radio. Little did he realize, at the time, that his career would be forever changed by that night that panicked America.

Orson Welles

Born George Orson Welles to Richard Head Welles and Beatrice Ives in Kenosha, Wisconsin, on May 6, 1915, his middle-class family often boasted they could trace their lineage back to the Mayflower. Whether that family boast was true or not has always been a matter of fierce debate for Wellesian scholars, but what is certainly true is that Orson's childhood was anything but normal. His boyhood was characterized by much travel and upheaval. Always one step ahead of the bill collectors, his family moved from city to city in the Midwest, eventually settling in Chicago. His alcoholic father, who was a dreamer and would-be inventor, was not inclined to hold down an ordinary job for any great length of time, and he was always borrowing money to pay his debts. His mother, once an accomplished pia-

nist and a suffragette, soon grew tired of her husband's alcohol abuse, and left him in 1919; she subsequently died in 1924, and her death, which the nine-year-old Orson witnessed first hand, traumatized him for years to come.

By every account, the young Welles found formal education very tedious, and seized every opportunity to go into his own fantasy worlds. But then in 1926, when his father and a close family friend, Dr. Maurice Bernstein (a man whom Welles immortalized in "Citizen Kane"), enrolled him in the progressive Todd School in Woodstock, Illinois, he met Roger Hill, the school's revered headmaster. Hill encouraged Orson to channel his energies into theater, and soon the eleven-year-old was writing, directing and acting in his own plays at the Todd School. He also made his first film, entitled "Hearts of Age," a four-minute short featuring Virginia Nicholson, another Todd student who would later become Orson Welles's first wife.

When his father died in 1930, he became the ward of Dr. Bernstein, and at the age of 15, he began traveling the world, visiting France, Italy, England, Germany, and Asia. Orson graduated from the Todd School in 1931, and despite many offers from colleges, he left for Ireland to work at the Gate Theatre. After a year of working behind the scenes and occasionally acting, he went to Spain to fight in the bullring, but ended up writing pulp fiction in order to support himself. He returned to the U.S., and enrolled in classes at the Chicago Art Institute. He also continued to direct and perform in local theater, and eventually met writers Thornton Wilder and Alexander Woollcott, who in turn introduced him to the actress Katharine Cornell, then scouting for actors for her company.

After a series of impressive roles, including Tybalt in a Broadway production of "Romeo and Juliet," he met producer, writer and actor John Houseman. Houseman cast Welles in the play "Panic," and not long after made him a $1000 a week offer to perform on the radio. Orson Welles was just 20 years of age! He soon became a fixture on radio as the ominous voice of "The Shadow." By 1937, he and Houseman founded "The Mercury Theater on the Air," and began staging a great range of classic books in the medium, including of course, "The War Of The Worlds."

Welles soon turned to motion pictures because he felt that the possibilities of the screen were limitless. His first and probably greatest film was "Citizen Kane" (1941), a commercial failure which cost RKO $150,000, but is still regarded by many as the best film ever made because it was a technically brilliant piece of filmmaking. Unfortunately, because the story borrowed so liberally from the real-life escapades of media magnate William Randolph Hurst, nearly every newspaper in the country panned the feature at the behest of the newspaper baron. Never one to avoid controversy, Welles reveled in the threatened lawsuits and media bias, but cost the studio dearly.

Then, in 1942, after completing work on his second film, "The Magnificent Ambersons," Welles took a trip to South America to film a documentary. When he returned, he discovered that his new feature had been re-cut by the studio and released against his wishes. Welles was outraged at RKO, but knew there was very little that he could do. This marked the beginning of the end for his Hollywood career.

Many of his next films were commercial failures, and he exiled himself to Europe in 1948. He spent many years working largely for others in order to finance his own pet projects, but continued to make a name for himself with several excellent Shakespearean adaptations, including "Othello" and "The Chimes At Midnight," which are considered among the Bard's best cinematic features. In 1956, he directed "Touch of Evil" (1958); it also failed in the U.S., but won a prize at the 1958 Brussels World's Fair. In the 1960s and 1970s, he took on mostly character roles, including the villain in the James Bond spoof "Casino Royale" (1967) and as the national spokesman for a well-known wine. In 1975, in spite of all his box-office failures, he received the American Film Institute's Lifetime Achievement Award, and in 1984, the Directors Guild of America gave him its highest honor, the D.W. Griffith Award. He died on October 10th, 1985 in Los Angeles, and his ashes were buried in Malaga, Spain. His reputation as a filmmaker has climbed steadily ever since, but in many ways, his career was always overshadowed by his "War of the Worlds" broadcast.

The Mercury Theatre on the Air

The finest in radio drama to emerge from the era of radio in the 1930's and 1940's was "The Mercury Theatre on the Air," a show featuring the acclaimed New York drama company founded by Orson Welles and John Houseman. As a drama company, the Mercury Theatre had initial success producing Marc Blitzstein's controversial labor union opera, "The Cradle Will Rock," for the Federal Theatre Project in June of 1937. In November, they introduced an inventive adaptation of William Shakespeare's "Julius Caesar," written by Welles, set in contemporary Fascist Italy. The production created so much controversy that lines of patrons cued up for their next offering, a voodoo-themed "Macbeth," and public recognition soon followed. When the company turned to radio, Welles had already established a niche with his frequent appearances on "The March of Time" and his radio dramatizations of "The Shadow," a seven-part adaptation of Victor Hugo's "Les Misérables," and other notable works.

In 1938, "The Mercury Theatre on the Air" was born, with most of the actors and crew from the stage productions lending their talent to radio. The hour-long program was scheduled by the CBS radio network as a summer replacement for the Lux Radio Theater, but proved so popular that it became a regular fixture on the network. Originally programmed for nine weeks, the network extended its run into the fall, moving the show from its Monday night spot to a Sunday night time slot opposite "The Chase and

Sanborn Show," a variety show featuring Edgar Bergen and Charlie McCarthy." Most episodes of "The Mercury Theatre on the Air" dramatized many works of classic and contemporary literature. The very first radio production was an adaptation of Bram Stoker's "Dracula," with Welles playing both Count Dracula and Doctor Seward. Other adaptations included "Treasure Island," "A Tale of Two Cities," "The Thirty-Nine Steps," "Abraham Lincoln," "The Man Who Was Thursday," and "The Count of Monte Cristo." John Houseman wrote many of the early scripts for the series himself, then turned the job over to Howard Koch at the beginning of October. Bernard Herrman conducted music for the program.

During its brief run, the company featured an impressive array of talents, including Agnes Moorehead, Martin Gabel, Alice Frost, Ray Collins, Virginia Welles (Mrs. Orson Welles), and Everett Sloane. The early shows were praised by critics, but the Crossley ratings never reached beyond a dismal 5.4. CBS executives knew they had a worthwhile prestige program on their roster, and stuck by "The Mercury Theatre on the Air" despite its low ratings. The one broadcast that changed the ratings was the October 30, 1938, adaptation of H. G. Wells's *The War of the Worlds*. The huge fury created by the broadcast generated significant publicity, and soon the fledging series became one of the radio's top-rated shows, proving to the Campbell Soup Company that people were listening. On December 9, 1938, "The Mercury Theatre on the Air" became "The Campbell Playhouse," and the 9pm Friday time slot formerly held by "The Hollywood Hotel" became theirs. Ratings shot to an impressive 14.4, and the show became one of radio's must-hear programs.

Of course, Orson Welles had become a huge celebrity, thanks to the "War of the Worlds" broadcast, and soon signed a contract with RKO to make "Citizen Kane." For the balance of the season, Welles split his time between New York and Hollywood. His bi-coastal lifestyle helped enlist new talent for the radio show from among the motion picture industry, including Margaret Sullivan, Katherine Hepburn, Helen Hayes, Lionel Barrymore, and Laurence Olivier. In the show's second season, "The Campbell Playhouse" moved from New York to Hollywood in order to accommodate Welles and the other Mercury Players who were working on "Citizen Kane." Now directed by George Zachary (with creative input by Welles) and scripted by John Houseman and Willis Cooper, the series continued to produce top-notch radio drama with an impressive array of guest stars, including Randolph Scott, Frank Morgan, Fred Allen, Miriam Hopkins, and Humphrey Bogart.

"The Campbell Playhouse" continued after Welles's departure on March 31, 1940, but never reached the level of inventiveness or overall quality that had marked its tenure under the young Orson Welles. Certainly, the show never eclipsed the furor created by the "War of the Worlds" broadcast.

The Broadcast

The infamous "War of the Worlds" broadcast began innocuously enough with a radio announcer stating, "The Columbia Broadcasting System and its affiliated stations present Orson Welles and the Mercury Theatre on the Air in *The War of the Worlds* by H. G. Wells." Mr. Welles opened the program with a description of the series of which it was a part, and then the show began with Welles as himself, setting the scene for his radio listeners: "We know now that in the early years of the twentieth century this world was being watched closely by intelligences greater than man's and yet as mortal as his own...We know now that as human beings busied themselves about their various concerns they were scrutinized and studied, per-

haps almost as narrowly as a man with a microscope might scrutinize the transient creatures that swarm and multiply in a drop of water. With infinite complacence people went to and fro over the earth about their little affairs, serene in the assurance of their dominion over this small, spinning fragment of solar driftwood which, by chance or design, man has inherited out of the dark mystery of Time and Space. Yet across an immense ethereal gulf, minds that are to our minds as ours are to the beasts in the jungle, intellects vast, cool and unsympathetic, regarded this earth with envious eyes and slowly and surely drew their plans against us. In the thirty-ninth year of the twentieth century came the great disillusionment. It was near the end of October. Business was better. The war scare was over. More men were back at work. Sales were picking up. On this particular evening, October 30th, the Crosley service estimated that thirty-two million people were listening in on radios…"

As Welles finished his introduction, a weather report faded in, stating that it came from the Government Weather Bureau. The official sounding weather report was quickly followed by an announcer remarking that the program would be continued from the Meridian Room in the Hotel Park Plaza in downtown New York with "the music of Ramón Raquello and his orchestra." The Spanish-themed "La Cumparsita" started playing, with people tangoing to the music. Actually, the broadcast was all done from the studio, but the script led people to believe that there were announcers, orchestras, newscasters and scientists on the air from a variety of locations.

For a few moments, dance music played as part of the program. Then there was a "break in" with a "flash" or special bulletin from the Intercontinental Radio News announcing that Professor Farrell at the Mount Jennings Observatory in Chicago, Illinois, had seen a series of incandescent gas explosions on the planet Mars. The second announcer stated, "The spectroscope indicates the gas to be hydrogen and moving towards the earth with enormous velocity. Professor Pierson of the Observatory at Princeton confirms Farrell's observation, and describes the phenomenon as, quote, 'like a jet of blue flame shot from a gun,' unquote. We now return you to the music of Ramón Raquello…" The dance music resumed until it was interrupted yet again, this time by a news update: "Ladies and gentlemen, following on the news given in our bulletin a moment ago, the Government Meteorological Bureau has requested the large observatories of the country to keep an astronomical watch on any further disturbances occurring on the planet Mars. Due to the unusual nature of this occurrence, we have arranged an interview with a noted astronomer, Professor Pierson, who will give us his views on this event. In a few moments we will take you to the Princeton Observatory at Princeton, New Jersey…" Koch's clever script specifically attempts to make everything sound real as if the events were happening right at the moment of the interruption. In fact, near the beginning of his interview with Pierson, Newsman Carl Phillips, tells the radio listeners that he "may be interrupted by telephone or other communications. During this period he is in constant touch with the astronomical centers of the world . . . Professor, may I begin our questions?" Of course, this interview was being staged in the studio, and was not actually happening on location, but for all intents and purposes, the radio listeners thought it was real.

During the interview, Phillips tells the audience that Professor Pierson had just been handed a note, which was then shared with the audience. The note stated that a huge shock "of almost earthquake intensity" occurred near Princeton. Professor Pierson believes it might be a meteorite. Another news bulletin announced, "It is reported that at 8:50 p.m. a huge, flaming object, believed to be a meteorite, fell on a farm in the neighborhood of Grover's Mill, New Jersey, twenty-two miles from Trenton. The flash in the sky was visible within a radius of several hundred miles and the noise of the impact was heard as far north as Elizabeth. We have dispatched a special mobile unit to the scene, and will have our commentator, Carl Phillips, give you a word picture of the scene as soon as he can reach there from Princeton. In the meantime, we take you to the Hotel Martinet in Brooklyn, where Bobby Millette and his orchestra are offering a program of dance music." Carl Phillips then resumed his reporting from Grover's Mill. Again, no one listening to the program bothered to question the very short time that it took the reporter to reach his new location. Part of the reason was that the musical interludes seemed to the radio audience to last longer than they actually were.

At the site, the reporter stated, "Ladies and gentlemen, this is Carl Phillips again, out of the Wilmuth farm, Grover's Mill, New Jersey. Professor Pierson and myself made the eleven miles from Princeton in ten minutes. Well, I... hardly know where to begin, to paint for you a word picture of the strange scene…The ground is covered with splinters of a tree it must have struck on its way down. What I can see of the object itself doesn't look very much like a meteor, at least not the meteors I've seen. It looks more like a huge cylinder…" The meteor turns out to be a 30-yard wide metal cylinder that is making a hissing sound. Most of the people at the site, including Farmer Wilmuth, keep their distance from the cylinder, until one man tries to touch it and is chased away by police. Then the top began to "rotate like a screw." Phillips reported that he thought the cylinder was hollow, and a few breaths later, proclaimed, "Good heavens, something's wriggling out of the shadow like a gray snake. Now it's another one, and another one, and another one! They look like tentacles to me. I

can see the thing's body now. It's large, large as a bear and it glistens like wet leather. But that face, it... Ladies and gentlemen, it's indescribable. I can hardly force myself to keep looking at it, so awful. The eyes are black and gleam like a serpent. The mouth is V-shaped with saliva dripping from its rimless lips that seem to quiver and pulsate. The monster or whatever it is can hardly move. It seems weighed down by... possibly gravity or something. The thing's... rising up now, and the crowd falls back now. They've seen plenty. This is the most extraordinary experience, ladies and gentlemen. I can't find words... I'll pull this microphone with me as I talk. I'll have to stop the description until I can take a new position. Hold on, will you please, I'll be right back in a minute..." People at the crash site began to panic at the site of the invaders from Mars, but before the state police or Phillips can react, the Martians unleash their "heat-ray" weapon, and kill everyone (except presumably Professor Pierson) on the New Jersey site.

For an excruciating few seconds, silence. When the Announcer finally acknowledged that Phillips's microphone was dead, he reported: "Ladies and gentlemen, due to circumstances beyond our control, we are unable to continue the broadcast from Grover's Mill. Evidently there's some difficulty with our field transmission. However, we will return to that point at the earliest opportunity..." Listeners were led to believe his eyewitness account had been cut off. Then a second report was issued from the studio, stating that at least forty people, including six state troopers, were killed in a field east of the village, their bodies burned and distorted beyond all possible recognition. As the radio play unfolded, more new bulletins and scene broadcasts followed, reporting that the "meteor" near Princeton had been joined by others. General Montgomery Smith who commanded the state militia at Trenton ordered his troops into the field to join up with local law enforcement and fire departments in Mercer County in order to contain the Martians, while Captain Lansing and seven thousand armed men closed in on the first cylinder. All of Mercer and Middlesex counties were now under martial law.

Despite the fantastic nature of the events that were occurring in the small New Jersey town, the program seemed very real. As members of the audience sat on the edge of their collective seats, actors playing news announcers, officials and other roles one would expect to hear in a news report, continued to describe the landing of an invasion force from Mars. The situation became more and more grim as radio listeners were told that the Martians' "heat ray" obliterated Lansing's men. Then the "Secretary of the Interior," who sounded like President Franklin Roosevelt (purposely), addressed the nation: "Citizens of the nation: I shall not try to conceal the gravity of the situation that confronts the country, nor the concern of your government in protecting the lives and property of its people. However, I wish to impress upon you - private citizens and public officials, all of you - the urgent need of calm and resourceful action. Fortunately, this formidable enemy is still confined to a comparatively small area, and we may place our faith in the military forces to keep them there.

In the meantime placing our faith in God we must continue the performance of our duties each and every one of us, so that we may confront this destructive adversary with a nation united, courageous, and consecrated to the preservation of human supremacy on this earth. I thank you." While his assurances that the military would do whatever was necessary to repel the advancing Martian armies were meant to calm listeners, the mayhem continued. Additional radio reports stated that the U.S. Army was engaged in pitched battles with the Martians up and down the East Coast, and finally, the announcer declared that New York City was being evacuated.

From the roof of Broadcasting Building in New York City, the announcer described the scene in Manhattan: "I'm speaking from the roof of Broadcasting Building, New York City. The bells you hear are ringing to warn the people to evacuate the city as the Martians approach. Estimated in last two hours three million people have moved out along the roads to the north... Hutchison River Parkway still kept open for motor traffic. Avoid bridges to Long Island... hopelessly jammed. All communication with Jersey shore closed ten minutes ago. No more defenses. Our army is... wiped out... artillery, air force, everything wiped out. This may be the last broadcast. We'll stay here to the end..."

The first half of the broadcast ends famously after the last reporter reporting from the top of a building collapses from the poison gas, and a radio operator is heard desperately calling out "2X2L calling CQ... Isn't there anyone on the air? Isn't there anyone on the air? Isn't there ... anyone?"

At the half-way point, approximately forty minutes into the broadcast, Welles was still directing from his center podium, feverishly curing actors and sound effects when there was a bang at the studio door. CBS executive Taylor Davidson demanded that Welles break into the program to calm down all of the scared listeners. He responded: "They're sacred? Good! They're supposed to be scared!" Davidson insisted on a brief commercial break, during which the announcer stated, "You are listening to a CBS presentation of Orson Welles and the Mercury Theatre on the Air in an original dramatization of *The War of the Worlds* by H. G. Wells. The performance will continue after a brief intermission. This is the Columbia Broadcasting System." But by that time, no disclaimer could calm radio listeners. Most Americans who had heard the first part of the broadcast were already panicked.

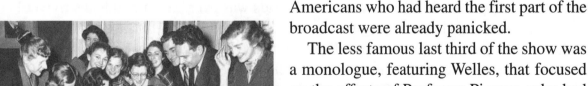

The less famous last third of the show was a monologue, featuring Welles, that focused on the efforts of Professor Pierson, who had earlier commented on the strange Martian explosions, to reach New York and other human survivors. His monologue began: "As I set down these notes on paper, I'm obsessed by the thought that I may be the last living man on Earth. I have been hiding in this empty house near Grover's Mill - a small island of daylight cut off by the black smoke from the rest of the world. All that happened before the arrival of these monstrous creatures in the world now seems part of another life... a life that has no continuity with the present, furtive existence of the lonely derelict who pencils these words on the back of some astronomical notes bearing the signature of Richard Pierson. I look down at my blackened hands, my torn shoes, my tattered clothes, and I... try to connect them with a professor who lives at Princeton, and who on the night of October 30th, glimpsed through his telescope an orange splash of light on a distant planet. My wife, my colleagues, my students, my books, my observatory, my... my world... where are they? Did they ever exist? Am I Richard Pierson? What day is it? Do days exist without calendars? Does time pass when there are no human hands left to wind the clocks?... In writing down my daily life I tell myself I shall preserve human history between the dark covers of this little book that was meant to record the movements of the stars, but... to write I must live, and to live, I must eat... I find moldy bread in the kitchen, and an orange not too spoiled to swallow. I keep watch at the window. From time to time I catch sight of a... Martian above the black smoke. The smoke still holds the house in its black coil, but... at length there is a hissing sound and suddenly I see a Martian mounted on his machine, spraying the air with a jet of steam, as if to dissipate the smoke. I watch in a corner as his huge metal legs nearly brush against the house. Exhausted by terror, I fall asleep…"

Pierson's ramblings on the radio sounded to the average listener like a very real and accurate account of what a survivor might have encountered on his journey into the Martian stronghold. He met a Stranger (formerly an Artilleryman) hiding in the shadows who had lost his mind, and walked along in the dark through the Holland Tunnel. Eventually, Pierson reported: "I climbed a small hill above the pond at Sixtieth Street and from there I could see, standing in a silent row along the mall, nineteen of those great metal Titans, their cowls empty, their steel arms hanging listlessly by their sides. I looked in vain for the monsters that inhabit those machines. Suddenly, my eyes were attracted to the immense flock of black birds that hovered directly below me. They circled to the ground, and there before my eyes, stark and silent, lay the Martians, with the hungry birds pecking and tearing brown shreds of flesh from their dead bodies." The Martians had succumbed to human bacteria, and were dying off in large numbers. The war of the worlds was over…mankind had survived!

Welles, who had been playing the role of Professor Pierson, broke character at the end of his monologue in order to assure listeners that the broadcast was nothing more than a Halloween prank. He said, "This is Orson Welles, ladies and gentlemen, out of character to assure you that 'The War of The Worlds' has no further significance than as the holiday offering it was intended to be. The Mercury Theatre's own radio version of dressing up in a sheet and jumping out of a bush and saying Boo! Starting now, we couldn't soap all your windows and steal all your garden gates by tomorrow night... so we did the best next thing. We annihilated the world before your very ears, and utterly destroyed the C. B. S. You will be relieved, I hope, to learn that we didn't mean it, and that both institutions are still open for business. So goodbye everybody, and remember please, for the next day or so, the terrible lesson you learned tonight. That grinning, glowing, globular invader of your living room is an inhabitant of the pumpkin patch, and if your doorbell rings and nobody's there, that was no Martian... it's Halloween." But by then, as the last cords of the Mercury Theatre theme played out across the airwaves, the damage had already been done.

With word that a crush of reporters and law enforcement officials were waiting in the lobby of the Columbia Broadcasting Building, Orson Welles and his crew made their way out of the back of the studio. The next day, however, Welles put on an innocent face, and met with the press. "We are deeply shocked and deeply regretful," he stated. When asked if he had purposely created the panic for publicity purposes, he said, "Oh, no, no, no, no."

The Panic

The broadcast reached a huge audience, demonstrating the enormous reach of radio at that time. Approximately six million people heard it, and out of this number, estimates suggest that almost one million people panicked. Revisionist historians place that number lower (in the hundreds of thousands), and blame the media for pumping up the story in the weeks that followed, but that would not account for the hundreds of reports that came in on the night of the broadcast that showed thousands of people engaged in the mass hysteria. Though the program began with the announcement that the broadcast was a radio dramatization of the H. G. Wells novel, most of those who panicked hadn't tuned in early enough to hear the opening credits.

Recent research suggests that many panicked listeners missed the show's disclaimers because they were tuned into the very popular "Chase and Sanborn Hour," featuring Edgar Bergen and his dummy Charlie McCarthy. On this particular Sunday evening, Madeline Carroll was the guest host on the NBC show, and the first ten minutes opened with the usual Edgar Bergen and Charlie McCarthy monologue. Sometime between 8:09 and 8:12 P.M., EST, a musical number featuring Nelson Eddy began, and an estimated one to two million listeners tuned the dial, like they did every Sunday, and were captivated by Carl Phillips's eyewitness report. Not surprisingly, Welles and Koch timed that segment to occur at the exact moment when listeners were expected to be channel surfing. They wanted these listeners to be shocked to hear another station carrying news alerts warning of an invasion of Martians attacking Earth, but they didn't expect it would cause a panic.

All across the United States, listeners reacted. Thousands of people called CBS in New York, and jammed the phone lines in and out of the Columbia Broadcasting System. Others contacted their local newspapers and police officials in confusion over the realism of the simulated news bulletins. Many sought first to verify the reports. But large numbers of others, obviously in a state of terror, asked what civil defense procedures they should follow in order to safeguard themselves against the Martians. Some wanted to know if they would be safe from the poison gas in their cellars; others wanted to know how they could protect their children from the "death

rays," and still others worried about family members living in London and Paris. So many calls came into newspapers and official offices that the Associated Press investigated the rumors and sent out a disclaimer at 8:48 P.M.: "Queries to newspapers from radio listeners throughout the United States tonight, regarding a reported meteor fall which killed a number of New Jerseyites, are the result of a studio dramatization. The A. P." Similarly, police teletype systems dispatched notices to all its radio cars in the New York and New Jersey areas that the event was imaginary.

Those notices didn't reach many of the broadcast listeners, however. Some people flocked to the "scene" of the events at Grover's Mill, New Jersey, hoping to catch a glimpse of the Martians, while still others went looking to cash in on the "meteorite" that had supposedly fallen. Dr. Arthur F. Buddington, chairman of the Department of Geology, and Dr. Harry Hess, Professor of Geology, received the first alarming reports at Princeton University in a form that indicated the meteor had fallen less than five miles away. They armed themselves with the necessary equipment and set out to find a specimen. All they found was a group of sightseers, searching like themselves for the meteor.

In Newark, blanketed across a single block at Heddon Terrace and Hawthorne Avenue, more than twenty families rushed out of their houses with wet handkerchiefs and towels over their faces to flee from what they believed was to be a gas raid. Some even began moving household furniture. Throughout New York families left their homes, some fleeing to near-by parks. Across the Hudson, thousands of New Yorkers began a mass exodus to Westchester and Connecticut for safety. At St. Michael's Hospital in Newark, fifteen people were treated for shock and hysteria, a scene repeated throughout tri-state area medical facilities. Some people claimed that the radio show had nearly given them a heart attack. Many in the New England area loaded up their vehicles with personal belongings and fled their homes. In other areas of the country, notably the South, people went to churches to pray, while others grabbed their rifles and mobilized small groups of militia. People improvised gas masks. Miscarriages and early births were reported all up and down the East Coast. Deaths, too, were reported but never confirmed. Many people were hysterical. They all thought the end of the world was near.

The Aftermath

In the aftermath of the broadcast and subsequent panic, the public was outraged with Orson Welles and his "Mercury Theatre on the Air." They accused him of purposely manipulating the medium of radio as some sort of elaborate publicity stunt. Many people threatened to sue Welles and the Columbia Broadcasting System. But CBS insisted that the network was blameless. Executives explained that listeners were reminded throughout the broadcast that it was only a performance, nothing more. Senators and Congressmen, many of whom had been just as frightened as the most gullible listeners, issued public condemnations about the broadcast, and demanded legislative action. Senator Clyde L. Herring, a Democrat from the state of Iowa, publicly told the press that he planned to introduce to Congress a bill which would control "such abuses as was heard over the radio last night. . . Radio has no more right to present programs like that than someone has in knocking on your door and screaming." He felt that all future radio broadcasts should be reviewed by the government before broadcast presentation, a proposal that was even more frightening than an invasion from space.

Finally, the Federal Communications Commission intervened. One week after the broadcast, Chairman Frank R. McNinch convened a hearing to discuss the use of the newspaper term "flash" on radio programs. He interviewed most of the principles involved, and talked with several experts. After listening to hours of testimony and reviewing all of the transcripts, he declared that he would withhold judgment of the program until later, saying: "The widespread public reaction to this broadcast, as indicated by the press, is another demonstration of the power and force of radio and points out again the serious responsibility of those who are licensed to operate stations." Welles and his "Mercury Theatre" players escaped punishment, but not public censure, and CBS had to promise never again to use the "we interrupt this program" device for dramatic purposes.

Princeton University Professor Hadley Cantril published the only academic study of the "War of the Worlds" broadcast. Cantril interviewed residents of Grover's Mill and many others who had listened to the broadcast. In his "Invasion From Mars: A Study in the Psychology of Panic" (1966), he concluded that there was a distinct relationship between the power and effectiveness of a broadcast of this kind and the reaction of the audience. He also determined a strong connection between the use of the media and the impact of propaganda on willing minds. His thesis remains to this day one of the most significant sociological and psychological studies of radio.

Amazingly enough, the "War of the Worlds" script was rewritten to apply to other locations and rebroadcast, with similar results. In 1944, a broadcast in Santiago, Chile resulted in panic, including the mobilization of troops by the governor. On February 12, 1949, in Quito, Ecuador, the broadcast panicked thousands of listeners. Leonardo Paez, the program director, and Eduardo Alcaraz, the station's director, were looking for something new and exciting to do on the air. Their radio station was nestled at the foot of Mount Pichindra, in the fertile Andean valley, but it was a long way from New York and CBS. They had heard of Orson Wells's famous program, and Paez and Alcaraz drew up a script that took advantage of the locales around Quito. But when the show aired on Saturday, February 12, 1949, the radio listeners rioted. They were so enraged at the deception by Radio Quito that they set fire to the radio station and the offices of *El Comercio*, the capital's leading newspaper. Their actions resulted in the death of twenty people and property damage estimated at $350,000. Three radio executives who were responsible for the broadcast were arrested and tried. On February 8, 1955, The Lux Radio Theater (NBC) broadcast the radio version of the 1953 George Pal film, featuring Dana Andrews as Professor Clayton Forester and Pat Crowley as Sylvia Van Buren. Lux Theater had been doing radio versions of Hollywood movies since 1936. The setting, like the film version, moved the invasion to

sunny Southern California, and the time period was updated so that the Army could use nuclear weapons to fight the invaders. But the dramatization was inferior to Koch's highly original script, and failed to make a ripple.

Recreations of the original "War of the Worlds" broadcast in 1988 and 1994 by Otherworld Media and L.A. TheatreWorks, respectively, ignited the public's interest in nostalgia but achieved little more. Most old-time listeners of radio were thrilled to hear actors like Jason Robards, Steve Allen, and Hector Elizondo in the Fiftieth Anniversary Production, just as "Star Trek" fans delighted to hear Leonard Nimoy, Gates McFadden, Armin Shimmerman, and Brent Spiner in the John de Lancie-directed 1994 production. But neither had the impact of the original by Welles and the Mercury Theatre players. What radio program could ever top that infamous broadcast?

The Night That Panicked America

In 1975, ABC television tried to set the record straight with a television movie inspired by the events of the broadcast. Directed and produced by Joseph Sargent, "The Night that Panicked America" tells the true story of the night that Orson Welles (played by Paul Shenar) and the players of the Mercury Theater set out to dramatize *The War of the Worlds* by H. G. Wells, and in turn scared an entire nation with their alien invasion. The tale as written by Nicholas Meyer mixes elements of the broadcast with a number of fictional vignettes charting the terrified reaction of the public. The movie functions at its considerable best when set at the Columbia Broadcast Studio in New York City, with the build up and behind the scenes action really ratcheting up the tension and suspense. (In 1987, Woody Allen's "Radio Days" relied on this same technique to spoof the Welles panic broadcast.)

On the sixtieth anniversary of the broadcast, Melissa Jo Peltier and W. W. Weiner released "Martian Mania: The True Story of the *War of the Worlds*" (1998). Hosted by Academy Award winner James Cameron, this one-hour special commemorated the infamous 1938 Orson Welles broadcast that panicked America. Peltier relied on old newsreel footage, re-created scenes, eyewitness testimony, and celebrity interviews to tell the "never-before-told" true story of "War of the Worlds." Her documentary concludes that when it was all over, there was devastation and outrage. Not at the renegade Martians, but at the man who unleashed an unprecedented hoax on an unsuspecting public, Orson Welles. As a result of his radio broadcast, lives were transformed, laws were changed, and the world would never be quite the same again.

For the record, Edward R. Murrow also hosted a television special that examined the impact of the "War of the Worlds" broadcast. On the twentieth anniversary (October 27, 1958), CBS television broadcast "The Night America Trembled," featuring newsreel footage and interviews with most of the principles involved. Despite the fact that many of the Mercury Theatre players were involved, Welles declined participation, and later commented that Murrow had inaccurately portrayed him.

The Legacy of Orson Welles and the Radio Broadcast

So, was the "War of the Worlds" broadcast part of some elaborate publicity stunt to advance the career of Orson Welles? Probably not. Or, was it merely the confluence of several mighty forces, including the emergence of a brand new and untested medium, the creative talents of one man and his extraordinary collaborators, and the innocence of a people still living in relative isolation from the rest of the world, all colliding together at one point in history? Yes, probably!

Over the years, Welles has offered conflicting accounts of the events that October evening 1938, and has even tried to take credit for planning what happened after the broadcast. But newsreel footage from the time clearly demonstrates that he was as confused and frightened by the events himself. He has never publicly apologized for his part in the panic. Many years after the event Welles claimed he had "merrily anticipated" the kind of response the program drew, while being astonished by its intensity. He said, "We weren't as innocent as we meant to be when we did the Martian broadcast. We were fed up with the way in which everything that came over this new magic box, the radio, was being swallowed. . . . So, in a way, our broadcast was an assault on the credibility of that machine." Despite this statement, it seems likely that none of the cast or crew of the Mercury Theatre really had any inkling of what effect the show would have before it aired. The broadcast remains a significant event in the history of communications, and remains a testament to Welles as a showman and the skill and dedication of his cast and crew.

Two years after the broadcast, on October 28, 1940, H. G. Wells and Orson Welles met for the first time, and discussed the radio show on Radio KTSA in San Antonio. At first, the author of the original novel had been critical of the dramatization, stating that it "was made with a liberty that amounts to a complete rewriting and made the novel an entirely different story." But his attitude soon mellowed when he met the radio celebrity for an interview on live radio. Wells admitted his surprise that Americans had reacted in the way they did to his famous story, while Orson Welles joked politely about the matter. Ultimately, Wells expressed his appreciation for the broadcast because it had boosted sales of one of his older and more obscure titles.

The notoriety of the "War of the Worlds" broadcast certainly gave the boy genius the capital and publicity he needed to mount his motion picture debut, "Citizen Kane." Most critics still regard that epic as the greatest American film of all time. Scriptwriter Howard Koch wrote many movies, including his Oscar-winning screenplay for "Casablanca," the second most popular American film after "Kane." John Houseman turned from producing to acting, and earned an Academy-Award nomination for his role of Professor Kingsfield in "The Paper Chase." And many of the other Mercury players went onto long and distinguished careers as character actors in film and on television.

For a long time, the good people of Grover's Mill, New Jersey, grumbled about how they were portrayed in the broadcast, and felt that the work of Welles and Koch was a mean-spirited joke played specifically on them. With time, however, the legend of the Martian invasion grew more remote; old-timers who had heard the broadcast and responded in panic died off, and a whole new generation joked about their parents and grandparents. For the 50th anniversary of the "War of the Worlds" broadcast in 1988, the citizens of West Windsor Township erected a bronze plaque at Van Nest Park to commemorate Welles, his fictional aliens, and a frightened family huddled around a radio set.

One of the guest speakers at the three-day event was Howard Koch. But instead of being ridiculed by the people of Grover's Mill as a hoaxer, he was celebrated as a pioneer of the science fiction genre. Koch admitted that he had done the men from Mars a grave "injustice" by depicting them as murderous invaders. "I believe," he said, "if ever living beings arrive at Grover's Mill from another planet, they will have the wisdom to come in peace and friendship."

While most critics and historians agree that a similar panic could not happen in today's world of instant news and global communications, one might be surprised to learn what happened in Madrid, Spain, in September 1996. Hundreds of people were panicked by television "news" broadcasts depicting giant flying saucers hovering over landmarks in the United States and around the world. The segments turned out to be clever advertisements for a new version of *The War of the Worlds*, titled "Independence Day."

The War of the Worlds (1938). CBS/The Mercury Theatre on the Air, Radio: 50 minutes. Director and Producer: Orson Welles. Writers: Howard Koch, Paul Stewart, and John Houseman. Based upon The War of the Worlds by H. G. Wells. Associate Producer: Paul Stewart. CBS Production Supervisor: Davidson Taylor. Script Editor: John Houseman. Music Supervisor: Bernard Herrmann. Sound Effects Technicians: Ora Nichols, Ray Kremer and Jim Rogan. Sound Engineer: John Dietz. Announcer: Dan Seymour. Cast: Orson Welles (Professor Richard Pierson), Frank Readick (Carl Phillips, Operator 2X2L), Ray Collins (Wilmuth, Harry McDonald, rooftop announcer), Paul Stewart (New York weather announcer, studio announcer #3), Carl Frank (studio announcer #2, stranger), Kenny Delmar (Captain Lansing, Secretary of the Interior, Bayonne radio operator, policeman), Richard Wilson (Brigadier General Montgomery Smith, Langham Field operator, voice of Newark), William Alland (Meridian Room announcer, gunner), Stefan Schnabel (observer), William Herz (operator 8X3R), and Howard Smith (Misc. Voices). Available on Compact Disc.

CHAPTER FOUR: GROVER'S MILL

Fake 'War' on Radio Spreads Panic Over U.S. *A radio dramatization of H. G. Wells's "War of the Worlds"—which thousands of people misunderstood as a news broadcast of a current catastrophe in New Jersey—created almost unbelievable scenes of terror in New York, New Jersey, the South and as far west as San Francisco between 8 and 9 o'clock last night. The panic started when an announcer suddenly interrupted the program of a dance orchestra—which was part of the dramatization—to "flash" an imaginary bulletin that a mysterious "meteor" had struck New Jersey, lighting the heavens for miles around. A few seconds later, the announced "flashed" the tidings that weird monsters were swarming out of the mass of metal—which was not a meteor but a tube-like car from Mars —and were destroying hundreds of people with death-ray guns...*
                        —George Dixon, New York Daily News (10-31-1938)

Located just off a lonely country road, a few miles from Princeton University, in West Windsor Township, New Jersey, a solitary marker on a children's field of dreams commemorates the first landing site of the Martian Invasion. What Martian Invasion?—readers might ask. Most people forget that, long before the War in Iraq or even the Second World War, Martian war machines invaded our living rooms on October 30th, 1938, through the (then) popular medium of radio, and a young Orson Welles and his Mercury Theatre players were responsible for a panic that was as real to Americans in the 1930s as the fear most of us experienced on 9/11. Welles and playwright Howard Koch wanted the beachhead for their fictional invasion to be a real place in the United States. And Koch, after setting a pencil point down on a New Jersey map with his eyes closed, selected the sleepy backwater of Grover's Mill.

"I liked the sound," he later recalled. "It had an authentic ring."

"The War of the Worlds" broadcast, which was loosely based on H.G. Wells' Victorian novel, began at 9 p.m. (EST) on the Sunday evening before Halloween with the chilling

DEDICATED BY THE CITIZENS OF WEST WINDSOR ON THE OCCASION OF THE 50th ANNIVERSARY OF THE WAR OF THE WORLDS BROADCAST — OCTOBER 29, 1988.

words: "In the early years of the twentieth century, intelligences greater than man's . . . regarded this earth with envious eyes." By the end of the hour between four million people (Hooper poll) and twelve million (Gallup) had tuned into the CBS program, and over a million of the listeners, believing it was real, readied themselves for the end of the world.

"Most every year for the nearly seventy years (since the broadcast), curious visitors and members of the press have asked us to recount the time when this community was panicked by invaders from Mars," explained Douglas R. Forrester, former mayor and chairman of the local committee responsible for the monument. Forrester is no relation to the Dr. Clayton Forrester who fought the Martians in the 1953 film by George Pal. "One of the

reasons we endeavored to present the commemoration was to set the record straight: the good people of Grover's Mill and West Windsor responded the same way other listening audiences responded. Some were perplexed, some were amused and some were alarmed. We wanted to turn what some have considered an awkward moment in our history into something charitable and worthwhile."

The thirty-seven acres that make up Grover's Mill Pond were generously donated by the Dey Family in 1976 in order that the historic site would be maintained and enhanced for future generations. Less than ten years later, after wading through tons of legal red-tape, a group called the New Jersey Conservation Foundation announced that the site would be officially preserved. Forrester and others founded the "War of the Worlds" (WOW) Commemorative Committee in 1986 to prepare a fitting celebration for the fiftieth anniversary of that famous broadcast in 1988. Celebrities Howard Koch, Garrison

Keillor, Irwin Corey, the Amazing Kreskin and the entire cast of the short-lived television series "War of the Worlds" were all invited to take part in the four-day event, which included a parade, a twenty-five mile race, a fireworks extravaganza (at nearby Mercer County Park), a masquerade party and a re-enactment of the radio play at Princeton University. On October 29, 1988, the citizens of West Windsor Township dedicated a monument to the memory of the Martian Invasion.

With its own sense of irony, Howard Koch delivered the keynote speech. He started by apologizing to the Martians for the grave "injustice" he had done them by making them into murderous invaders. "I believe," he said, "if ever living beings arrive at Grover's Mill from another planet, they will have the wisdom to come in peace and friendship."

The bronze monument, which was sculpted by Jay Warren, depicts a skyscraper-high Martian war machine in the upper right corner; in the left center, a brilliant, twenty-three year-old Orson Welles stands in front of a microphone, and in the lower two-thirds, a fairly typical family listens to the broadcast on the radio. Today, like most monuments that overlook bloody battlefields of our nation's past, the six-foot-tall and three-foot-wide marker stands in the middle of a small field of dreams where children play baseball or climb on monkey bars, lovers stroll along a wooded path, and ducks frolic in a small pond. Its solitary visage not only reminds us of the notorious broadcast that panicked Americans but also recalls the fateful night when America lost its innocence. That singular radio program forever changed the way people think about their sources of news, information and entertainment.

Even though it's been almost seventy years since the Martians first "landed," the peaceful tranquility of Grover's Mill Pond easily

On the evening of October 30, 1938, Orson Welles and the Mercury Theatre presented a dramatization of H.G. Wells' *The War of the Worlds* as adapted by Howard Koch. This was to become a landmark in broadcast history, provoking continuing thought about media responsibility, social psychology and civil defense. For a brief time as many as one million people throughout the country believed that Martians had invaded the earth, beginning with Grover's Mill, New Jersey.

gives way to the imagination, and conjures images of towering war machines. Listen closely and you just might hear the sounds of their pistons as they lumber into view.

The Martian landing site marker is located in West Windsor Township, New Jersey. Take Exit Eight from the New Jersey Turnpike and follow Route 571 through the small hamlet of Hightstown to Princeton Junction. Just prior to the overpass, which takes you into Princeton, turn right onto Cranbury Road, and travel approximately eight-tenths of a mile. Grover's Mill Pond is the first right past Clarksville Road.

The "War of the Worlds" monument today.

CHAPTER FIVE: THE 1953 FILM

Whenever a Hollywood producer brings out a new motion picture in which he has tampered with the plot of a well-known novel or play, he's inviting criticism. If for one moment you think the challenge of modernizing Wells's story was child's play, just take a scrap of paper and list the commonplace inventions and scientific discoveries which we utilize in our daily living that were utterly nonexistent when Wells wrote his story. There were no airplanes, atom bombs or tanks with which to fight the Martian machines at the time he wrote his tale. His readers followed his story on a flight of imagination. Our audience comes to the theater today conversant with the terms: nucelar physics, atomic fission, gravitational fields and space platforms. Even the children play with space helmets and ray guns and are even more familiar with such expressions as "blast off" than their elders. We took a risk when we made the H. G. Wells classic, "War of the Worlds," but inasmuch as none of us connected with it have been dodging any verbal tomatoes since, I take it that the audiences approve.
—George Pal, Astounding Science Fiction (October 1953)

One of the first, big-budget Hollywood films produced during the science fiction boom of the 1950's, "The War of the Worlds" (1953) told the spectacular and exciting tale of an alien invasion through the eyes of a handful of people who become caught up in the action. At a time when the world was poised on the brink of nuclear annihilation and one man's crusade to end the Communist infiltration of American culture spread fear, panic and paranoia, the motion picture tapped right into the pulse of middle America with its realistic portrayal of an interplanetary war. Produced by George Pal, who had already made "Destination Moon" (1950) and "When Worlds Collide" (1951) and would later helm "The Time Machine" (1960), "Atlantis the Lost Continent" (1961), and "The Seven Faces of Dr. Lao" (1964), "The War of the Worlds" not only reflected our anxieties of atomic war and the maelstrom of events surrounding the "Red Scare" but also showed that science fiction was an adult medium of ideas and ideals. The Paramount Pictures production became one of the

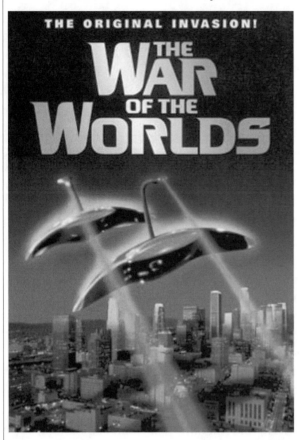

most successful films of its day, and is still highly regarded by fans as one of the greatest science fiction films ever made.

Origins

Although the 1950's produced the greatest number of science fiction films of any other decade (to date), the genre of science fiction was far from a proven box office favorite when the decade first began. In fact, there had been only a handful of successful science fiction films made in the first fifty years of the Twentieth Century, and most of those had been made overseas in Europe. Science fiction had been first characterized by the trick photography of Georges Melies with the French fantasy, "A Trip to the Moon," in 1902. Other short films-mostly whimsical comedies that relied on numerous camera tricks to fool audiences into thinking they were taking a journey to the stars or under the sea-came and went, with little fanfare in the two decades that followed. Following World War I, filmmakers in Germany experimented with exaggerated sets, extravagant costumes, and far-out ideas to create some of the first Expressionist films. Films like "The Cabinet of Dr. Caligari" (1919), "Algol" (1920), "Metropolis" (1926), "Alraune" (1928), and "The Girl in the Moon" (1929) represented the first serious attempts at using science fiction as a medium to discuss the ills of the day, including fascism, conformity, and the threat of technology out of control. In 1936, England's "Things to Come," based on the

novel by H. G. Wells, relied on elegant and expensive special effects to depict a world after a devastating final war and the efforts of a group of men to take a rocketship to the stars. By the late Thirties and early Forties, however, science fiction was relegated to low budget pot boilers and kiddy fare, as in serials like "The Phantom Empire" (1935), "Flash Gordon" (1936) and "Buck Rogers" (1939) and in films like "King Kong" (1933) and "Dr. Cyclops" (1940).

While the science fiction film was largely undistinguished in the first five decades of the Twentieth Century, science fiction's literary legacy had been squandered on low budget pulps by the 1950s. The promise of Mary Shelley's *Frankenstein, or the Modern Prometheus* (1818) and H. G. Wells's *The War of the Worlds* (1898), which had established science fiction as a literary art-form of distinction in the Nineteenth Century, had given way to the best-selling potboilers of Edgar Rice Burroughs and H. Rider Haggard. By the 1920s, a group of talented writers, including Abraham Merritt, Ray Cummings, and Murray Leinster, were competing with Burroughs and Haggard in the very lucrative market of science fiction, but the genre which had begun as an exploration of scientific inquiry and extrapolation quickly became an outlet for action and adventure. Lurid tales of extraterrestrial conquest, rampaging robots, and nearly naked

women being carried off by monstrous creatures were what readers (mostly young, male readers) clamored for in the magazines of the day.

Hugo Gernsback responded to the demands of the marketplace with the first all-science fiction magazine, *Amazing Stories*, in April 1926; but as an editor, he also tried to shape the genre by insisting that each story have a "scientific content." Manuscripts poured into Gernsback's offices from A. Hyatt Verrill, Miles Breuer, David Keller, E.E. "Doc"

Smith, and Jack Williamson, and soon he was printing some of the best speculative fiction since Shelley and Wells. But other editors of the day, including Harry Bates, favored science fiction stories that told action-packed adventures, and *Astounding Stories of Super Science* was born. *Astounding*, first published in January 1930, featured the work of Cummings and Leinster, as well as new writers like Edmund Hamilton, S.P. Meek, Stanley Weinbaum, and John W.

Campbell (writing as Don A. Stuart). Other magazines, including *Wonder Stories, Marvel Science Stories, Thrilling Wonder, Astonishing Stories*, and *Planet Stories*, were published, and many new authors, including Isaac Asimov, L. Ron Hubbard, Robert Heinlein, L. Sprague De Camp, and A.E. Van Vogt, appeared. With very few exceptions, most of the work was less than literary, and the quest for a thoughtful and intelligent treatment of science took backseat to a thrilling adventure tale set on another world. To the public at large, science fiction was a juvenile art-form, just a cut above the comic book.

The few literary works of science fiction explored many social issues beyond the purview of science and technology. Issues related to bigotry, prejudice, paranoia, fascism, political corruption, sexuality, psychology and the power of the mind showed up in works like Asimov's "Nightfall" (Astounding 1941), Lewis Padgett's "Mimsy Were the Borogroves" (Astounding 1943), Heinlein's "The Roads Must Roll" (Astounding 1940), and other stories. Instead of fearsome alien monsters, Weinbaum's "Martian Odyssey" (Wonder 1934) introduced audiences to a creature with a life and a purpose all its own; instead of mindless rampaging robots, Campbell wrote about automatons still dutifully tending machines long after man's demise in "Twilight" (Astounding 1934) and "Night" (Astounding 1935), and encouraged Asimov to carve a set of commandments that every robot must follow. But for each thoughtful and intelligent story, a dozen others that focused on the more lurid and juvenile elements of the genre characterized the work of literary science fiction at the time.

Enter George Pal

So, when, early in the winter of 1951, Producer George Pal arrived at Paramount Pictures, and started looking for a follow-up to his successful "Destination Moon" (1950), science fiction was still considered a second-rate genre by most of the studio executives. Both "The Day the Earth Stood Still" and "The Thing" had not yet been released, and the science fiction boom of the Fifties was still a couple of years away from happening. Pal knew that he faced an uphill battle, but he was really no stranger to adversity and hardship.

George Pal was born in Cegled, Hungary, in 1908, and studied architecture at the Budapest Academy of Art. When he graduated in 1928, he found work as an architect limited, and rather than joining the swelling ranks of the unemployed, he took a job as an artist and animator at Budapest's Hunnia Film Studio. He subsequently married his childhood sweetheart, Zsoka Grandjean, and settled into life. However, as the Great Depression swept from America into Europe, Pal found it increasingly difficult to support he and his wife, and sought a better-paying job elsewhere. In 1931, he and his wife moved to Berlin so that he could go to work as an animator at the huge UFA studio. Within a few months, he was given charge of the studio's cartoon department, and began producing lots of children's programming.

In 1933, when the Hungarian-born Pal fell under the scrutiny of Hitler's secret police, he and his wife escaped to Prague, Czechnoslovakia, and then, later Paris, where he went to work making cartoons for Philips Radio of Holland. The executives at Philips liked his work so much that they convinced him to move to Holland, and open up his own studio for them. Once there, he met an American animator named Dave Bader, and the two collaborated on a brand new, experimental form of three-dimensional animation using puppets. They called their features "puppetoons," a word formed by combining puppet and cartoon. With war in Europe imminent, Pal and his wife immigrated to the United States in 1939, and he set up shop in Hollywood, California, producing a series of animated shorts called "Madcap Models" for Barney Balaban of Paramount Pictures. Between 1941 and 1947, George Pal Productions made over forty puppetoons for the studio. He received six Academy Award nominations, and was voted a special Oscar in 1943 for his unique contributions to the field of animation.

George Pal soon became interested in making live action films, and with the backing of Peter Rathvon, a former chief at RKO and then head of the independent Eagle-Lion Pictures, he made "The Great Rupert" (1949), with Jimmy Durante and a talking squirrel (really just another animated puppet), and "Destination Moon" (1950), the most successful science fiction of its day. Paramount Pictures lured Pal back onto the studio lot with the promise of a two-picture deal, and permitted him enormous latitude with his choice of projects. The producer decided to find a science fiction story to make into a motion picture, and turned to the best-selling *When Worlds Collide* (1933) by Edwin Balmer and Philip Wylie for his source material. Then, while working on the film version with director Rudolph Maté, Pal took a look through Paramount's script archive, and found a pile of un-produced scripts for *The War of the Worlds*. He saw great potential in the idea, even though he discarded most of the scripts, and approached Paramount with the project.

Paramount and *The War of the Worlds*

The War of the Worlds by H. G. Wells was first serialized in *Pearson's Magazine* in 1897, then later published in book form in January of 1898, and solidified the author's reputation as a master of "scientific romances." While Wells himself was a fan of motion pictures and had written a number of scripts and screen treatments as part of his fifty-year career, he had long since dismissed the likelihood of his most famous novel ever being made into a movie. He knew the enormous scope of his book would make the cost of a film prohibitively expensive. So, when Paramount Pictures sought to purchase his novel in 1925 for Cecil B. DeMille, Wells gladly sold the studio executives at Paramount the rights in perpetuity.

In 1926, the studio announced the start of production on a big-screen adaptation of *The War of the Worlds* by DeMille as his follow-up to the enormously successful 1923 version of "The Ten Commandments." The silent film was to be shot partially in color using the same 2-strip Technicolor process that had been used on previous films with the remainder of the picture in Black & White. Shortly after Paramount Pictures' official announcement, *The New York Times* leaked a story that Arzen Doscerepy, a famous German technical expert who had been producing movies in Berlin, had been hired to complete the film's special effects. *The Times* reported that he had "spent two years perfecting devices and mechanisms which will make Wells's Martians walk and spray death around the world." Doscerepy's work was very similar to the stop-motion animation that Willis O'Brien had employed to make dinosaurs come to life in "The Lost World" (1925) and other films. Unfortunately, DeMille could not come up with a script that he liked, and he left the project in pre-production.

Four years later, Jesse L. Lasky, the man who produced Hollywood's first feature film (in a barn) and one of the 36 founders of the Academy of Motion Picture Arts and Sciences,

gained control of Paramount. He looked at all of the properties owned by the studio, and thought *The War of the Worlds* had the most potential for success. Lasky offered the Wells property to renowned Russian director Sergei Eisenstein, who had made "The Battleship Potemkin" (1925). Another script was prepared for yet another silent version of the film, but as pre-production on the special effects dragged into its fourth month, Eisenstein withdrew to make "Que Viva Mexico" (1931), a film he never completed. Hollywood pioneer Jesse Lasky shelved the project, claiming the story was impossible to make with all of the special effects.

In 1934, Alfred Hitchcock, who was a very well-respected director in England but yet-unknown in the United States, approached Wells, and tried to persuade the science fiction author to let him make the film version. At the time, Wells was hard at work writing the screenplay to "Things to Come" (1936). He liked Hitchcock's take on the story, but confessed that he had assigned all of his rights in perpetuity - an unlimited amount of time - to Paramount. Hitchcock did not pursue the project any further, and turned his attention to "The Thirty-Nine Steps" (1935).

Not long after Orson Welles rose to prominence with his "War of the Worlds" radio broadcast on October 30, 1938, Paramount pressured him with offers to make the Wells's story his first feature film. But he wanted no part of it as he already had plans to make "Citizen Kane" (1941) at RKO. After Welles declined Paramount's offer, *The War of the Worlds* was almost made several other times at the studio, but never got past the script phase. Over the years, several screen treatments and five different scripts were produced under the auspices of various personalities at the studio. So, when George Pal expressed interest in the project, Paramount executives were more than pleased to give him the green light to make the movie.

Updating the Genius of H. G. Wells

After reading all of the various drafts in the Paramount script archive, Pal selected Barré Lyndon to pen a new version. Lyndon had never written a science fiction film before, but he had just finished co-writing DeMille's circus extravaganza "The Greatest Show On Earth" (1952), and he knew how to think in grand terms. He also collected Wells memorabilia, and possessed considerable respect for the material. Together with Lyndon and director Byron Haskin, the three began to craft the tale, working to produce a movie that, above all else, would attempt to portray as realistically as possible the details of an alien invasion. In adapting the 1898 novel to the screen, Barré Lyndon made a number of improvements over the original story while still maintaining the spirit of H. G. Wells. One of the first changes was updating the time frame of the story to a more contemporary setting. Since audiences were conversant with terms like nuclear physics, atomic fission, and gravitational

fields, he felt that it was imperative man fought the Martian machines with the current weapons at his disposal. Airplanes, tanks, and atomic bombs - which would have seemed fantastic in Wells's day - became the means by which humanity struck back against the invading armies. The next change was moving the setting from London to Southern California. From a practical standpoint, the city of Los Angeles and its immediate suburbs were more easily accessible than Great Britain. And with all of the recent sightings of flying saucers in the area, the western part of the United States seemed like an ideal locale to mount an invasion.

Since the narrator in Wells's novel is never identified by name, Lyndon made him Major Bradley, a career soldier who becomes separated from his wife and family during the first attack. Pal preferred that he become a scientist, and Lyndon replaced his original lead with Clayton Forrester, a nuclear physicist from Pacific Tech. The vice president in charge of production, Don Hartman felt their protagonist needed a "love interest" to sell the picture, and demanded that they get rid of the wife and child. Reluctantly, Pal asked Lyndon to create the character of Sylvia Van Buren. Barré Lyndon also took great pains to avoid all of the clichés and stereotypes associated with invading aliens; in far too many science fiction stories, beginning as far back as H. G. Wells's *War of the Worlds* (1898), aliens brought only death and destruction in their conquest of Earth. Lyndon wanted to humanize the story by focusing more on the people and how they reacted with fear and paranoia to the menace. Pal agreed, but with each page of script devoted to the more human elements in the story, that meant money and less time spent on advancing the Martian invasion.

Another victim of cost (and the available technical expertise of the time) was the look of the Martian war machines. Lyndon's early drafts made them look like the tripods from the original novel, and early production drawings also maintained this same look. But the difficulties of stop-motion animation in making the tripod machines come to life made it apparent that a fresh approach was needed.

When Lyndon submitted his final screenplay on June 7, 1951, Hartman decried it as a "piece of crap" to Pal, and threw it in the trashcan. The curse of those other earlier productions seemed to have been visited upon George Pal. Undaunted, Pal enlisted the help of his friend and colleague Cecil B. DeMille, and went to the head of the studio, Frank Freeman, with his project. Freeman listened to Hartman's objections, and then told Pal to make his film any way he wanted.

The Screen Story

Following a brief prologue (read by Paul Frees) which details the history of modern warfare and the ever increasingly destructive power of modern weapons, a second narrative (read by Sir Cedric Hardwicke) describes how the Martians "regarded the Earth with envious eyes." Their civilization had exhausted all of its natural resources, and they looked for a new world to exploit. That precipitates a two-and-a-half minute "grand tour" of the solar system (which curiously omits Venus), ending with the Martian focus on our own green and inviting planet.

At the time of Earth's nearest orbital approach to Mars, a meteorite shoots through the evening sky, and plunges to the ground near the small California town of Linda Rosa. Residents watch the meteor crash into Pine Summit, and skid sideways, touching off a number of small brush fires. After the local fire-fighters contain the blaze, Sheriff Bogany (Walter Sande) seeks the help of three Pacific Tech scientists who are fishing in the area. Dr. Clayton Forrester (Gene Barry), one of the scientists, decides to take a look at the fallen meteor.

Meanwhile, news of the meteorite has spread rapidly through town, and many of the residents have gathered around the pit where the meteorite is still steaming. They discuss the economic benefits that a discovery of this kind can have on tourism for their little town.

Forrester, who is a well-known nuclear physicist, arrives at the site, and meets Sylvia Van Buren (Ann Robinson) and her uncle, Pastor Matthew Collins (Lewis Martin), the local minister. At first, Van Buren does not recognize Forrester for the famed scientist that he is, and prattles on about her own educational background and her job teaching Library Science at USC. But then, as others seek his opinion (particularly when his Geiger counter starts clicking), she realizes her mistake, and sets her sights on making his better acquaintance. Forrester is encouraged to stay, and agrees to attend a square dance with her.

While most of the townspeople attend their local dance, three residents remain behind to watch the meteorite. Suddenly, a section of the rock unscrews, and from inside the hollowed meteor, a long-necked, cobra-headed probe snakes out. The "thing" regards the three local townspeople with momentary curiosity as they attempt to make "first contact" by waving white flags of friendship, and then vaporizes them with a powerful and deadly

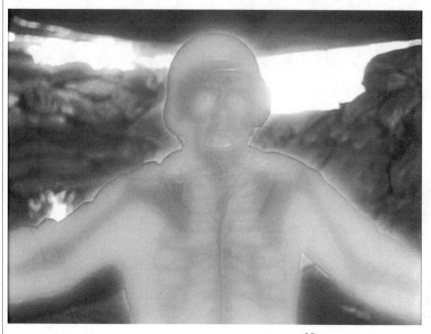

Heat-Ray. All at once, the lights and power in the town go out, and every clock and wristwatch stops. Forrester and the local sheriff decide to investigate the site of the meteorite, and find the charred remains of the three men. They then watch as three Martian war machines, topped with snake-like proboscises, and riding on what appear to be anti-gravity beams emerge from the pit. One of the machines fires its Heat-Ray and destroys the sheriff's car as Forrester and the sheriff dive for cover. When a second meteorite streaks through the sky overhead, they conclude that this is no longer a matter for the local police, and call in the military.

Quickly mobilized, the Army dispatches hundreds of soldiers in troop transports, tanks, and field artillery to the valley that shelters the Martian machines. General Mann (Les Tremayne) orders his men to contain the invaders at all costs, while Pastor Collins feels compelled to talk peaceably with them. He believes that technologically advanced creatures like the Martians must be closer to God. With his Bible in hand, reciting the twenty-third Psalm, Collins approaches the trio of machines, and is instantly vaporized by their Heat-Rays. Mann orders a full-scale reprisal, but their weapons are no match for the superior ones of the marauding invaders. The army, military experts, and bystanders are quickly pulverized, and the rampage of destruction begins.

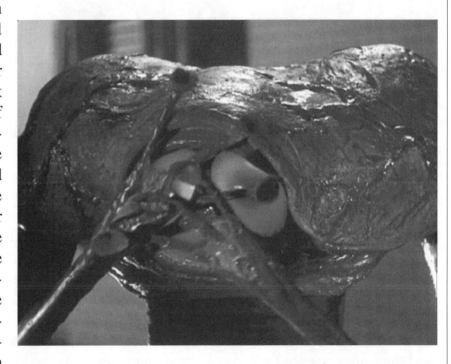

Forrester and Van Buren escape in a small plane, but are forced down by the Martian war machines as they attack and destroy a squadron of military jets that have engaged them. They take refuge in an abandoned farmhouse, and are trapped when another meteorite crashes into the homesite. Cornered in the ruined house, they manage to glimpse one of the aliens. The Martians appear to be small, humanoid-shaped creatures with bulbous heads, and single eyes with three lenses (red, blue and green) in the center of their foreheads. Forrester is forced to strike one with a wooden post when it gets too close, and then also severs one of its electronic probes. Taking the severed probe with them and a sample of the Martian's blood, they escape just moments before the invaders destroy the farmhouse.

Mid-way through the film, Sir Cedric Hardwicke's narrative resumes detailing the rout of humanity. By showing us scenes depicting the destruction of Earth's greatest cities, including London, Paris, and New Deli, we understand the extent of the Martians' power as they sweep across the world. Man seems utterly helpless before the superior firepower of the alien menace. (Ironically, New York and Washington D.C. are spared the destructive wrath of the Martians.)

Meanwhile, the military under the command of General Mann has not been idle, and is preparing to drop an atomic bomb on the Martian war machines. But when the most destructive force on Earth fails to make even a dent in their force shields, man's best efforts seem totally futile, and the onslaught continues. "Guns, tanks, Bombs... they're like toys against them," Mann exclaims, and defers to the scientists to find a way to stop them.

At Pacific Tech, Forrester and his colleagues examine the blood sample he took from the Martian, and advocates a biological approach to defeating them since "we can't beat their machines." But before they can get very far with their research, the Martian war machines approach the city of Los Angeles, and force their evacuation. Mass panic breaks out as residents of the great metropolis loose all manner of hope and reason, and become an irrational mob. They smash Forrester's invaluable research, and steal his truck. Left behind, he wanders through the empty streets as the Martians begin their final assault on the city.

Eventually, Forrester finds Van Buren huddling with other survivors in a small church. The sounds of destruction grow nearer and near, and just when all appears lost, until an unearthly silence drops over the city. The machines have fallen to earth, their creatures struck down by Earthly germs for which they have no immunity. Sir Cedric Hardwicke's narrative concludes, "The Martians had no resistance to the bacteria in our atmosphere... And thus, after science fails man in its supreme test, it is the littlest things that God in His wisdom had put upon the Earth that save mankind."

Production Details

Shortly after George Pal received Freeman's assurance that he could make any film he wanted, he met with his first choice for a director, Byron Haskin. Haskin, then a journeyman director, had begun his career as a cameraman at Pathé in 1920, then worked as an assistant director for Selznick Productions. In the 1930's, he had been instrumental in the development of sound film technology, and then worked for twenty years as head of Warner Brothers Special Effects Department. His directorial debut was Disney's live-action version of "Treasure Island"(1950), and within the space of three years, he made four other films. He was just completing "Denver and Rio Grande" (1952) when Pal first approached him with the idea to film *The War of the Worlds*. Byron Haskin liked Pal's take on the classic

science fiction novel, and agreed to make the film. "War of the Worlds" marked the beginning of a creative association with Pal that lasted nearly twenty years. Haskin made three more films with Pal, including "The Naked Jungle" (1954), "Conquest of Space" (1955), and "The Power" (1968). Together they collaborated on every aspect of the production. They met with Lyndon to discuss the script; they prepared a budget of

$2,000,000 for the Paramount executives, and they gathered the right cast and crew together for their picture.

Producer George Pal and director Byron Haskin carefully selected each member of the cast to bring their science fiction film to life. At first, they considered Lee Marvin for the pivotal role of Clayton Forrester, but then thankfully they reconsidered. Pal felt the role should be played better by an actor who was not overly familiar to American audiences, and selected the handsome, young Broadway actor Paramount had just put under contract, Gene Barry. (While waiting for shooting to begin, Barry made the sci-fi quickie "The Atomic City," 1952.) For the part of his love interest, Sylvia Van Buren, the college professor who

taught Library Sciences at USC, a twenty-four-year-old contract player Ann Robinson was given the nod. Her only experience was a bit part in George Stevens' "A Place in the Sun" (1951). Tall, curvaceous, and sophisticated, Robinson was perfect as the intellectual girl-next-door; unfortunately, the part called for the actress to do a great deal of screaming, and that diminished the credibility of her character.

Les Tremayne, the versatile star of both stage and radio dramas, was chosen for his authoritative presence and impressive "radio voice" to play the role of the hardened military leader, General Mann.

For the role of the narrator, Pal approached his friend and colleague Cecil B. DeMille, but he was busy promoting "The Greatest Show on Earth" (1952). Demille recommended Sir Cedric Hardwicke. Hardwicke, one of the great character actors of the stage and cinema, had been working in the industry since his debut in 1912. He saw military service in World War One, and was knighted by King George V in 1934 for his distinguished work on stage and in films. He played Theotocopulos opposite Raymond Massey and Ralph Richardson in "Things To Come" (1936), written for the screen by H. G. Wells, and appeared in a hundred other films. Pal later observed that it was somehow appropriate that an Englishman (of the stature of Hardwicke) should narrate a picture based upon a book written by Wells. They rounded out the cast with Lewis Martin as Pastor Collins, and populated the city of Linda Rosa with character actors like Bill Phipps, Jack Krushchen, and Paul Birch.

On the production side, Pal and Haskin agreed to employ George Barnes as the cinematographer. Barnes was renowned throughout the industry for his excellent skills with the camera, and since the production was going to be filmed with a special 3-strip Technicolor process, he was essential to the team. Barnes also had knowledge of the new technique of shooting with two camera lenses and thereby blending the images together to create a three-dimensional effect. At one point, George Pal discussed the possibility of shooting the final third of the movie in 3-D with Haskin and Barnes. When the humans don their protective goggles, during the sequence in which the atomic bomb is used unsuccessfully against the Martians, Pal wanted audience members to put on their 3-D glasses. But Don Hartman at Paramount believed that 3-D was nothing more than a passing fancy, and this time Freeman agreed with him. Thankfully, the idea was discarded as too gimmicky.

Art directors Hal Pereira and Albert Nozaki were brought aboard to design most of the hardware in the film and to provide hundreds of sketches to storyboard the script shot-by-shot. The brilliant Al Nozaki, a Japanese-American artist and draftsman who had spent a year in an internment camp in California during World War Two, had been Pal's art director on "When Worlds Collide," so it came as no surprise that he would turn to the same person to conceptualize the Martian war machines. Pal had tried unsuccessfully to work Wells's original concept of the Tripod machines into the production, but when he realized that they "just didn't look right," he turned to Nozaki to come up with another design. While acknowledging the public's hysteria about flying saucers, the design is, in fact, quite original. His Martian war machines look like manta rays with a fluid, almost organic feel of metallic copper. The first view of its appendage as it rises from the still smoldering cylinder is a chilling one; then, as its cobra-like neck swivels and focuses on the advancing army, any further thoughts of a Tripod machine were completely forgotten. (These same Martian war machines make a return engagement in Byron Haskin's 1964 "Robinson Crusoe on Mars.") Artist Chesley Bonestell, who had worked with Pal on "Destination Moon" and "When

Worlds Collide," was called upon to render the paintings of the other planets in the Solar System.

The Martian was also designed by Albert Nozaki. Nozaki went back to the original story, and from Wells's description of the alien invader, he dreamed up the notion of an octopus-like being with a single, Cyclopean eye.

Makeup artist Charles Gemora, who had become famous as the gorilla in "Ingagi" (1943), built the Martian out of papier-maché and sheet rubber. Pal warned Gemora not to make the alien look too much like a man in a rubber suit, but in the end that was the only design he approved. When the producer was looking around for someone to wear the costume, he remembered that Gemora was short in stature, and hired him for the few brief shots of the Martian. Haskin was not entirely pleased with the finished product, and kept the alien invader isolated in the shadows as much as possible. In the end that turned out to be the best decision in the whole film. The Martian truly looks menacing and decidedly alien because we never really see him fully.

Gordon Jennings and his five-man crew, including Paul Lerpae, Wallace Kelly, Ivyl Banks, Jan Domela, and Irmin Roberts, were given the formidable task of creating the film's special photographic effects. They relied on many conventional optical and matte-work effects, including a traveling matte shot for the Martian cylinder's crash landing outside Linda Rosa. Other optical effects, including the Martian's destructive Heat-Ray, were added in postproduction using double-printing techniques that were fairly commonplace at the time. Then Jennings and his team were charged with bringing the Nozaki's Martian war machines to life. Originally, George Pal wanted them to "walk" on visible electronic beams of light as a kind of tribute to Wells's Tripod machines. Jennings first tried to use electrical sparks that emanated from the three holes at the bottom of the machine, but this was quickly abandoned for fear of starting a fire. The shot of the first war machine emerging from the gully has this effect, but no others. After trying several other techniques, they decided to forego this idea altogether. During filming, however, the actors were still under the impression that they were dealing with the walking Tripod machines of the book. Barry's dialogue in the farm-house scene reveals this overlooked detail: "There's a machine standing right next to us."

For the highlight of the film, in which the Martian war machines totally destroy the city of Los Angeles, Jennings and his crew cleared Stage 18 on the Paramount lot, and built four huge miniature sets with sky backings. The miniature of the Los Angeles City Hall was over eight feet tall itself. Then, with the help of eight-one year-old Walter Hoffman who placed all of the explosive charges, they rolled several high-speed cameras (filming at approximately four time normal speed) and created cinema magic with their special photographic effects. (The six-minute sequence was so extraordinarily real that it later showed up in other science fiction films, in particular an episode of the television series "V," 1984.) To capture the sequences in which the Martian war machines "die," Jennings shot them crashing into telegraph poles in order to hide the suspension wires with the telegraph wires. Other sequences in the film, including the one with the Northrop YB-49, also known as the Flying Wing, relied on stock footage. More than $1,400,000 of the film's total budget of $2,000,000 was spent on the extensive and elaborate special effects.

Principal Photography

Production on "War of the Worlds" began on December 1, 1951, and principal photography took approximately six weeks to complete, with the crew working six out of seven

days. Filming was halted briefly, two days into production, when Paramount discovered their filming rights to the novel had only included the rights to make a silent film. It was quickly resolved through the kind permission of H. G. Wells's estate. Frank Wells, the author's son, settled the problem, selling them the "talkie" rights for an additional $7,000.

Contrary to popular opinion, the film was shot almost entirely on the backlot at Paramount Pictures, not Washington, D.C., London, or even Los Angeles. Still shots of Bunker Hill in Los Angeles were matched to one of the streets on the backlot, and even the little town of Linda Rosa was created on one of the soundstages. The interior of the deserted farmhouse, Forrester's lab at Pacific Tech, and the dance hall where Forrester square-dances with the local residents were also built at the studio. That beautifully atmospheric set where the residents of Linda Rosa find the first Martian cylinder was created on the same backlot where so many Westerns had been made.

A second-unit film crew, under the direction of Michael D. Moore, was dispatched to Florence, Arizona, forty-five miles southwest of Phoenix in December 1951 to shoot location scenes that would later be incorporated into the sequences Haskin shot on the backlot. Moore was given unprecedented access to military machines and equipment by the Arizona National Guard. He literally mobilized a small army, including jeeps, tanks, weapons carrier, and trucks, for the climatic battle against the Martians. Meanwhile, Haskin and another crew filmed briefly in Los Angeles at the First United Methodist Church on Franklin Avenue in Hollywood and at St. Brendan's Catholic Church on Van Ness Avenue. They then shot the evacuation of the threatened city at the United States District Court Building on Spring Street and at City Hall, and a part of Hill Street early one Sunday morning. Other portions of the mass exodus were filmed on an unopened segment of the Hollywood Freeway. In the hilly terrain overlooking Simi Valley, Haskin gathered hundreds of extras for the scenes in which onlookers watch the atomic bomb explosion that fails to stop the Martian advance. Principal photography wrapped in mid-February 1952.

The Film's Release and Aftermath

"The War of the Worlds" premiered in Hollywood on February 20, 1953, and then later opened in New York City on August 13,

1953. Two weeks later, on August 26, 1953, debuted in cities and towns all around the country to brisk box office business and glowing reviews. *The New York Times* declared that it was "for all of its improbabilities, an imaginatively conceived, professionally turned adventure which makes excellent use of Technicolor, special effects by a crew of experts, and impressively drawn backgrounds... Gene Barry, as the scientist, and the cast behave naturally, considering the circumstances." *Variety* wrote that it was "by far the best of Hollywood's recent flights into science fiction." Several critics also saw the film's allegorical message buried under its blockbuster surface, and commented about it in their critical commentaries. And Moira Walsh, writing in *America*, called the film a "surprisingly pertinent and updated science-fiction account of an invasion from Mars... Its technicolored special effects (by the late Gordon Jennings) are superlative and its scientific explanations are lucid and convincing. By comparison, its handling of earthy matters, such as mass panic, boy-meets-girl (yes, even here!), and a well-intentioned but rather sappy affirmation of religious faith, is rather flat and small in conception."

"The War of the Worlds" went onto become one of Paramount Pictures' big box office successes in 1953, besting the similarly themed "Invaders from Mars," "Magnetic Monster," and "Donovan's Brain." The film was nominated for three Academy Awards, including honors for Best Film Editing, Best Sound Recording, and Best Special Effects, and won Gordon Jennings a posthumous Oscar for Special Effects at the 1954 ceremony. Later, when it played on network television for the first time, it garnered the highest ratings of any motion picture shown up to that time. Subsequent showings on television and re-releases at the theaters have made the film one of the most popular and best loved science fiction classics of the decade of the 1950s.

Critical Commentary

The world of 1953 may seem as distant and remote to most contemporary science fiction fans as the Great Depression or Antebellum South or Colonial America, but it was out of that time and place, slightly more than fifty years ago, that the American science fiction film was born. Prior to the de-

LA GUERRA DEI MONDI

GEORGE PAL · BYRON HASKIN · BARRÉ LYNDON
H. G. WELLS "IL TERRORE VIENE DA MARTE" | TECHNICOLOR
UN FILM PARAMOUNT · CINEMA INTERNATIONAL CORPORATION

cade of the Fifties, the science fiction film was nothing more than an import from France or Germany or Great Britain, a novelty, or a live-action cartoon. But after World War II, the Nazi death camps, the atomic bombing of Hiroshima and Nagasaki, the world changed, and the far-fetched stories of pulp writers didn't seem so far fetched. Front-page news stories about the recovery of a flying saucer in Roswell, New Mexico, or the arrest of Julius and Ethel Rosenberg for selling atomic secrets to the Soviet Union, or the outbreak of war in Korea, or the declaration of Senator Joe McCarthy in Wheeling, West Virginia, that he had a list of 205 "card-carrying" members of the Communist Party, which might have seemed like fantasy a few years before, were now topics of everyday conversation. The world of the 1950s was not the quaint little portrait of "Ozzie and Harriet" or "Father Knows Best" that was used to sell products for the tobacco companies or the automotive industry, but rather a vast canvas of fear, anxiety, prejudice, and paranoia. No other art-form quite reflected that world as vividly or as thoughtfully or as truthfully as the science fiction film that was produced in Hollywood at the time.

Films like "Destination Moon" (1950), "Rocketship X-M" (1950), and "Flight to Mars" (1951) pointed the way to the stars, and proclaimed our hopeful aspirations for a better tomorrow, while others like "Five" (1951), "The Thing (from Another World)" (1951), and "Invasion of the Body Snatchers" (1956) penetrated the façade of optimism to reveal our greatest fears of nuclear annihilation, Communist infiltration, and the loss of personal identity and freedom. Still others like "Them!" (1954), "The Beginning of the End" (1957), "The Incredible Shrinking Man"(1957), and "The Fly" (1958) examined the role of technology as it quickly advanced and outpaced man's ability to control and harness it and the other marvels of science. Few of the motion pictures could be labeled masterpieces, in the true sense of the word, and yet a surprising number of the science fiction films that were released in the Fifties still retain tremendous power and meaning to this day.

"The War of the Worlds" was the epitome the science fiction film of the decade of the 1950s. The motion picture was not only suspenseful and immensely entertaining, but also thoughtful and highly provocative. As an allegory, the film held up a great, big mirror on the world in order to capture the reflection of its life and times, and explored many controversial themes, including fear, anxiety, paranoia, mass panic and the mob mentality, and interplanetary war. While on the surface "The War of the Worlds" may have appeared to have been just another science fiction movie in the current box office cycle, its message could not have been louder or more profound.

On the threshold of man's greatest adventure into space, he had also discovered a force so terrifying that if used by both sides in a third world war it spelled certain doom for the entire planet. The fear of atomic war was very real to Americans (and the rest of the world) in 1953. Just four years earlier, the Soviet Union had detonated its first nuclear bomb, igniting the fuse on a cold war that would smolder and burn for another thirty-five years. Both the United States and the Soviet Union knew that if the one side struck first there would still be enough bombs to totally obliterate the other; the balance of terror was called "mutually assured destruction" (or mad, for short), but that didn't prevent either side from experimenting with the Hydrogen bomb or producing enough weapons of mass destruction to destroy the world many times over. Ironically, the United States and the Soviet Union and all of the other nations of the world must band together in

"War of the Worlds" to fight the Martian menace. President Ronald Reagan, a former actor from the movies of the Forties and Fifties, suggested in 1984 that one of the only ways the nations of the world would ultimately band together was to fight a common enemy from space.

Atomic war was simply unthinkable, and thankfully, the United States and the Soviet Union stepped away from the brink of total destruction in order to peacefully co-exist with each other. Both countries eventually did end their nuclear arms proliferation, and became allies in the war on terrorism. In the film, the two nations turn their weapons of mass destruction on the Martians, and attempt to stop the marauding invaders with a taste of their own medicine. Unfortunately, the atomic bomb fails to stop them. Pal and Lyndon seem to suggest that technology, in and of itself, was not good or bad-it was how man chose to employ that technology that determined its nature. In the Fifties, scientists and learned scholars recognized the dual nature of the atom: When used as a weapon, it was a force of frighteningly destructive power; when used as a power source, the atom had many peaceful uses as well.

The film also confronts the decade's fear of the unknown and its prejudices towards strangers by challenging the very pretenses and lies middle America embraced in place of the truth. While the white-bread, all-American Nelsons and Andersons of tvland were supposed to reflect the cosmopolitan make-up and moral decency of every home in the country, the truth was that they reflected only a very small percentage of America. Most families struggled to make ends meet on single-salary incomes which were well below the seemingly luxurious lifestyles depicted on television; they paid taxes, and grumbled about supporting entitlement programs; they built bomb shelters and worried about what the godless Communists might do if they ever gained a statistical superiority in nuclear warheads; they kept to themselves in small, segregated communities, and sent their children to the same schools that they had attended when they were children; they never ventured far away from their homes, even on vacation, and distrusted everyone who looked or sounded or worshipped differently from them. The reality was that Middle America was composed of fearful, anxious people who mistrusted strangers and even the neighbor down the street that they didn't know. True, they had fought and won a war against fascism and had survived one of the greatest financial upheavals in human history, but their complacency in accepting the lie about America had also allowed others to strip away their civil liberties in the name of patriotism and bring them to the brink of nuclear annihilation.

Lyndon's screenplay seems to reinforce that myth about Middle America, and in doing so, reveals a great deal about us at that time. When the first Martian cylinder crashes outside Linda Rosa, the residents all gather around the pit where the meteorite is still steaming, and discuss the economic benefits that a discovery of this kind can have on tourism for their little town. One of them suggests they charge admission, while another says that they can sell hotdogs and beer. Pastor Collins, the local minister and conscience of the town, wants them to build picnic benches so that families will be able to enjoy the site together. The members of the community, including Sheriff Bogany, Buck Monahan (Ralph Dumke) and Salvatore (Jack Kruschen), are meant to represent a microcosm of Small Town, America. They are white, middle-class citizens (with one having only the slightest hint of a Hispanic background), and no individuals of color and any other ethnic background are represented. Their reaction is also indicative of how real people in the 1950s would have reacted to these extraordinary circumstances. The fairy tale world of television families, like "Ozzie and Harriet" and "Father Knows Best," had many believing that racism and bigotry didn't exist in the Fifties, but that simply wasn't true. Similarly, the film's portrayal of the media, with its exploitative rhetoric, also showed how the liberal press of the day seized upon any story to boost its circulation even if it meant throwing a city, or the world, into a panic.

The decade's fear of strangers also meant a fear of the individual whose often unpopular and idiosyncratic views represented a threat to the complacency and conformity of centrist America. Those who did not share the popular view or failed to toe the party line were labeled as Communists, even if they had no affiliation at all with the Communist Party. Scientists, intellectuals, writers and free thinkers were all suspected as being subversive. There was no middle ground in the Us-versus-Them mentality of the 1950s. So, when the Martians arrive and start obliterating everything in sight, only Pastor Collins, a man of God, has the courage to confront them with his Bible held high in his hands. While most would agree with his sentiments that peace was preferable to violence and aggression, the popular belief was that peace was only obtainable through strength and the mutually assured destruction of the enemy if war broke out. Ironically, when the military runs out of options to fight the Martians, they must turn to the scientists - in particular, Clayton Forrester - to build them a bigger and better weapon to destroy the enemy. Like Einstein and Oppenheimer, Forrester is a scientist and therefore suspect, and yet, as a nuclear physicist, he also represents one of the scientists that had made the bomb. "War of the Worlds" seems to make heroes out of religious fools and scientists because they were willing to put themselves on the line at a time when the world needs them the most.

And finally, the film addresses the issue of fear and mass panic. When Forrester is pulled forcibly from his truck by the frightened mob and they destroy the research materials that may be used against the Martians, he shouts gravely, "You fools! You destroy yourselves!" But no one is listening...the madness of mob violence has replaced all forms of reason. Slightly more than ten years earlier, President Franklin Delano Roosevelt reminded people (following the attack on Pearl Harbor): "The only thing we have to fear is fear itself..." Forrester as an intellectual knows that fear is an emotion that can be controlled, but left unchecked, it grows into paranoia, hatred and mass hysteria. That same madness had brought the decade of the 1950s to the brink of destruction, and Lyndon was telling us there was a better way.

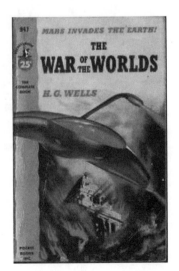

Even to this day, "War of the Worlds" remains a gripping, suspense-filled, and entertaining film to watch, despite its sentimental ending. Gordon Jenning's special effects are superb, and surprisingly hold up very well fifty years later. While the Wells's novel considerably more thought-provoking than the screen affair, Haskin and Pal make a credible presentation.

The winning formula behind "War of the Worlds" was copied many times during the Fifties and early Sixties. Like the marauding invaders from Mars, many other aliens attacked the Earth in films as diverse as "Invaders from Mars" (1953), "Robot Monster" (1953), "Killers from Space" (1954), "Target Earth" (1954), "Earth Versus the Flying Saucers" (1955), "Invasion of the Body Snatchers" (1956), "Plan Nine from Outer Space" (1956), "Kronos" (1957), "The Monolith Monsters" (1957), "Battle in Outer Space" (1959), and many, many others. That formula was re-discovered in the Nineties, and triggered a whole new wave of alien invasion films, including "The Puppet Masters" (1994), "Independence Day" (1996), "Mars Attacks!" (1996), "Starship Troopers" (1997), and "The X-Files: Fight the Future" (1998). In each case, science fiction played an important role not only in entertaining us but also helping us confront our deepest fears and anxieties.

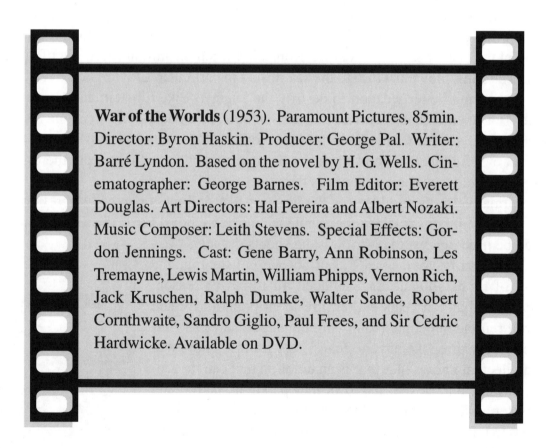

War of the Worlds (1953). Paramount Pictures, 85min. Director: Byron Haskin. Producer: George Pal. Writer: Barré Lyndon. Based on the novel by H. G. Wells. Cinematographer: George Barnes. Film Editor: Everett Douglas. Art Directors: Hal Pereira and Albert Nozaki. Music Composer: Leith Stevens. Special Effects: Gordon Jennings. Cast: Gene Barry, Ann Robinson, Les Tremayne, Lewis Martin, William Phipps, Vernon Rich, Jack Kruschen, Ralph Dumke, Walter Sande, Robert Cornthwaite, Sandro Giglio, Paul Frees, and Sir Cedric Hardwicke. Available on DVD.

CHAPTER SIX: THE JEFF WAYNE ALBUM

Take a look around you at the world you've loved so well,
And bid the aging empire of man a last farewell
It may not sound like heaven but at least it isn't hell
It's a brave new world with just a handful of men,
We'll start, we'll start all over again!
All over again! All over again! All over again!
—The Artilleryman, The War of the Worlds, 1978

In 1978, forty years after the infamous radio broadcast, musician and songwriter Jeff Wayne produced a rock musical version of the H. G. Wells novel, with Richard Burton as the album's narrator. Wayne's rock opera harkens back to the Victorian setting that Wells had originally intended for his story, and includes many of the original locations and scenes. Most people who were only familiar with the George Pal film or the Mercury Theatre version were pleasantly surprised to learn that the story was far more exciting and detailed than they ever imagined. Produced by Columbia Records, the recording which is finally available on compact disc featured singers like Justin Hayward (of the Moody Blues), David Essex (from "Godspell"), Thin Lizzy's Phil Lynott and Julie Covington and musicians like Jo Partridge, Herbie Flowers, Chris Spedding, and Jeff Wayne himself. No other music could have imagined "The War of the Worlds" with such amazing moods, atmospherics and sound effects, and orchestration better than the album that Wayne produced. Nearly thirty years after its initial release, it still sounds just as fresh and exciting as it did back then. A real classic!

When the album was first released in 1978, the science fiction genre was exploding, thanks to the success of "Star Wars" and "Close Encounters of the Third Kind," as well as the forthcoming "Superman: The Movie" and "Star Trek: The Motion Picture." And somewhere into that period, Jeff Wayne imagined an all-new version of H.G. Wells's *The War of the Worlds*. But not as a movie or a television show, but rather as a rock album with lyrics and orchestration from the top performers of the day.

"I really had no idea that anyone would ever buy it, whether it would even be released," confesses Wayne, the man who brought a disco groove to the might of the Martian war machine. "CBS [Records] didn't even have an obligation to release it. Two days after it came out it entered the charts and then began to spread around the world, and that's when I started to realize that this was something that was really reaching a lot of people. We just had a vision. And it was a vision that stayed on course."

It was a vision that has sustained him well. Two decades after the triumphant, demonic cry of 'Ulla!' first subjugated the charts, Wayne's musical rendering of *The War of the Worlds* remains a genuine pop phenomenon, tirelessly reissued, remixed and even, intriguingly, reincarnated as a computer game.

"I Was Never a Science Fiction Fanatic..."

"I was never a science fiction fanatic," admits Wayne. "I think the genre offered a lot of possibilities musically, a lot of space to fill in. I found *War of the Worlds* an exciting story. It was full of clean, big images and I liked the way that Wells brought in other topics built around a science fiction concept. Part of the attraction was that it was set on Earth, in Victorian England, and you were seeing this very modern technology, the machines that the Martians brought, through human eyes in the nineteenth century."

Wayne's endlessly popular soundscape of screaming gentlefolk and pitiless Red Planet conquerors proved a personal triumph, too. Originally forsaking journalism for a career as a composer, he soon found himself pigeonholed as a producer and arranger. "It was my father who reminded me of what I set out to do. While I was doing some things like TV themes and the odd film, I hadn't actually done a complete piece, perhaps built around a story. So we agreed to try and find a story that I could hear sound to and would be a natural platform for me. And so we set out, just reading lots of different books. The War of the Worlds was the first and only book that I read that I could really hear sound all the way through on the first reading. I don't know if it's because the book itself isn't that long, or simply the fact that it was never written as a novel - I later discovered that H.G. Wells originally wrote it as an episodic piece in a magazine, and so it was very well segmented, always leaving the reader wanting more for next week's issue. Wells' estate still owned everything except the book and feature film rights, so we met up with them and told them what was in our minds, to create a musical interpretation based on the novel."

The Coming of the Martians

The album kicks off with "Eve of the War" (vocals by Justin Hayward), which essentially describes the first Martian cylinder landing on earth. The cylinder is opened in "Horsell Common and the Heat Ray," which features guitar by Jo Partridge. "The Artilleryman and the Fighting Machine" has Wells's "the journalist" encounter the young soldier, and witnesses the Martian war machines for the first time. Hayward's ballad "Forever Autumn" is next up, chronicling the journalist's reaction at finding the home of the woman in his life, Carrie, empty. His tragedy turns to joy, however, in "Thunder Child" when he learns that Carrie is alive and aboard a steamer that is being protected by the war ship *Thunder Child* against the Martians. Unfortunately, Earth falls to the reign of the alien invaders from Mars.

"The Red Weed" has the journalist exploring what is happening to the planet and finding a growth of the red plant life that gives Mars its color. In "The Spirit of Man" he meets Parson Nathaniel, who is absolutely convinced that the Martians are actually from hell, and his wife, Beth. During the course of this song, a Martian cylinder arrives, which results in Beth's death and Parson's abduction. With no choice, the journalist heads back to London in "The Red Weed, Part 2." There he re-encounters the Artilleryman in "Brave New World," who sings about starting an underground society. Pessimism is replaced by a sense of optimism in "The Eve of the War," in which hope is restored as the Martians begin to fall victim to bacteria on earth.

Things are wrapped up in the two-part "Epilogue." In the first part, the journalist details the rebuilding of society in the aftermath of the Martians. The situation is a little more enigmatic in part two, when it's revealed that an earth mission to Mars has gone missing and mysterious flares are started to be released from the planet.

Explains Wayne. "I started going through the book over and over again, underlining bits that I thought were going to wind up as a script element, or were ideas within the story that needed to be interpreted thematically, whether as a song or a motif. The object was to have two soundscapes. When it was human you were hearing more of the symphonic string section. Everything else was either the band or synthesizers, but the strings were live and they were scored to represent more of the human landscape. When it became much more electronic and aggressive you were looking at it through the eyes of the Martians. It was a subtle thing, but it was like a ping-pong match between human and alien, batting back and forth. The object was not to lose sight that this was to be a musical work, not a talking album that had an underscore."

In an age of "Saturday Night Fever," record companies were surely jittery at the commercial prospects of a science fiction concept album? "I don't really think, even when I did the deal, that anybody had any idea what I was going to do," smiles Wayne. "They didn't hear a note of it until I handed it in. What I did know was that I wanted the music to be with all the honesty and integrity I could come up with as a musician. I also didn't want it to be a rose in the middle of the desert, where it was considered some pearl that nobody knew about. Even though I planned the album as continuous play, I knew that I wanted to have singles, so I always kept my eye on that side."

Naturally, certain elements of Wells's tale had to be discarded in the recording studio in order to fit the format of the album. "The novel is pretty much divided in half between the journalist, who then arrives in London, and his brother, who in fact has the fiancee. We didn't want to create two characters, so the journalist became the one thread all the way through. The journalist was our narrator, the person who glued it all together, recounting how he survived this Martian invasion."

Enter Richard Burton

Intoning the tale was the majestic voice of the late Richard Burton. A coup, surely? "We were looking for someone with a voice you felt confident with the moment you heard it," declares Wayne, revealing that the dulcet hellraiser topped a wish list that included Ralph Richardson and John Gielgud. "We discovered he was appearing in New York in 'Equus,' and the second we found that out we knew we could reach him. All we had to do was write him a letter at the stage door. And so I sent him a letter of introduction and the first few pages of the script, so that he could see the spirit of it, and literally within a day or two of receiving our little package his agent called and said Richard would love to do it.

"What I didn't know until later," he continues, "was that he was an avid reader, and that he would ask his wife, Suzy Hunt, to go out and buy him lots of books to read on matinee days and in between acts 1 and 2. It turned out that a week or so before my letter arrived he had finished reading *The War of the Worlds*. We never knew this until we were working together. It was one of those amazing coincidences."

Surely Burton came with a formidable reputation, accrued from years of Tinseltown mischief? "He was totally professional," states Wayne, fondly recalling the eternally driven

Welshman. "He took directions superbly. I remember him walking into the studio and the way that he just had a presence and a charisma around him. His voice boomed. His natural speaking voice was as you heard it, and he could project it louder or softer. It was a glorious voice." And showcased to perfection as the "needle" hits the very first groove. "The funny thing is I actually wrote a piece to accompany Richard's first speech. As soon as I heard his voice I said 'There's nothing that can be better than just this voice on its own'. Everyone on the production agreed, and so out went this entire piece of music that I'd written and recorded."

RICHARD BURTON — DAVID ESSEX — JUSTIN HAYWARD — JEFF WAYNE

The Best of the Best

Wayne assembled a diverse troupe of thespians, warblers and rockers for the project, from Glam era chum David Essex to stage star Julie Covington and Moody Blue Justin Hayward. "There were certain clear cut characters in the story. I knew I had to create vocal impressions from the people who were performing them, because obviously it wasn't an audio-visual piece. Everything was for the listener. And so the people who played the parts were very much aligned with how I could hear the vocal performances." Even Thin Lizzy frontman Phil Lynott found himself thrusting a crucifix at the tripods. "Phil played the role of Parson Nathaniel, who was slightly bonkers and thought that the Martians were the Devil and only he, as a man of the cloth, could exorcise them and save our souls. I wanted a voice that was more rock and manic. Phil was very definitely rock and roll, he lived life to the full in every aspect, but when you got to know him you realized that he was a real gentle soul and a poet. I still have a book of his poetry that he gave to me at the end of the production."

Was there anyone he chased in vain for the record? "There were a couple of people that we approached that actually came in and started work in advance of their managers concluding a deal with us. Carlos Santana came in to play guitar and was actually recording in the studio before he suddenly got pulled out by his manager. They were asking for more money than we were getting from CBS for the whole project, and the rest was my savings, so there was a limit to what we could afford. There was also a point when Phil went on tour and he hadn't finished his role. We were suddenly running out of time and Paul Rodgers from Bad Company wanted to have a go at it, which he actually did. He was great - then he had to come in and do some acting, and suddenly we couldn't get him on the phone!"

"Ulla!"

As anyone ever foolish enough to don headphones in the dark will tell you, *The War of the Worlds* could be a totally petrifying piece of vinyl, forever scarring a generation still recovering from the Smurfs. Perhaps it was the death screams in the grooves, the ravens pecking at red Martian flesh in the sleeve booklet or simply the distorted shrieks of "Ulla!" that left icicles in our bloodstreams. Not so much a concept album; more a rite of passage.

"I've had a few people come up to me and say that," laughs Wayne, still seemingly oblivious to all the bloodcurdling laid at his door. "It wasn't a horror record in the sense of trying to scare, although there were elements within it where I knew that, through sound, I could bring the listener into my world and convince them that this was really happening. The sound that I created for the Martians - 'Ulla!' - was an H.G. Wells world. I knew that would create an image in the listener's mind, whether the Martians were terrifying the Earth or dying at the end, and hopefully it did create a bit of a chill..."

How closely involved was he with the album's memorable imagery?

"Absolutely involved, but my father had certain roles within the development and production. My stepmother adapted the script. She was a professional writer, and so my dad was the link between her and me. Because he had been a performer as well as a writer he had the ability to communicate between musician and writer. It was the same in the development of the paintings. He had done some painting of his own and was able to find the right art director, who introduced us to the painters - he would give them a briefing as to what the canvas would encompass, each major moment within the story. My father was, again, a good buffer between me trying to get my ideas out of the painters and art director."

Surely the only album in history to boast its own officially licensed poster magazine, Jeff Wayne's Musical Version of "War of the Worlds" spent an epic six years hogging the upper reaches of the charts, spawning the hit singles "Forever Autumn" and "The Eve of the War."

How does Wayne explain such commercial wildfire?

"Hopefully I got something right in the grooves," he shrugs, sitting within playing distance of the very grand piano that brought him the fabled opening chords of the Martian onslaught. "It was launched at the London Planetarium and we were fortunate to attract a lot of the media. By having the media behind you, you have a tremendous head start. And the marketing people got behind it and it all integrated."

And 1978 was, again, a science fiction goldrush. Timing was obviously on Wayne's side. "I'm sure you're right," he nods. "I'm sure there's an element of that. Science fiction, which today is the biggest genre in the world, has always existed, so there's always been a core following of people who live science fiction and fantasy. Those two films probably took it to a modern audience with technology and quality film making that helped spread the word in that respect."

Sequels and Other Projects

Given the project's success, it does seem surprising that there has never been a sequel, or for that matter a prequel which explains why the Martians decided to conquer Earth in the first place. "I considered it, and indeed I was asked to by several record companies," says Wayne. "I just felt that *The War of the Worlds* was the classic story and that should be that. Today everything has sequels and it's probably a little more logical. We left the possibility of a sequel open in that rather tongue-in-cheek way that we ended the record, where it jumps to modern times and suddenly the Martians are at it again and the album suddenly cuts off dead. So it's always there to do."

He admits that he was, briefly, tempted by the notion of adapting one of Wells' many other stories. "Once 'War of the Worlds' established itself I was sent by one of Wells' publishers first editions of everything he ever wrote and there are some really good stories in there which maybe one day I'll have a go with. *The Time Machine* is always one that comes up, but you'll probably find that the rights have already been sold off. With any book that's still in copyright the big media companies are out there very quickly buying everything up. With this one I just got very lucky."

If not a sequel, has the possibility of a big screen incarnation ever been pursued? Anyone with a half decent turntable and a smidgin of imagination could see that this is a remarkably cinematic piece of musical storytelling, surely begging for the widescreen makeover. "I know," sighs Wayne. "The feature film rights are controlled by Paramount Pictures, who made the 1950s film. For the time its technology was very good, but it didn't really bear much reflection on the H.G. Wells story, no more than 'Independence Day,' which is an absolute carbon copy of the story but set in a different time frame with more modern technology interpreting the story. I'd love to see H.G. Wells's vision and my musical version on the screen, because I think that's an entertainment possibility that would really make its mark on the cinema."

In 1979, executives at Paramount Pictures initially approached Wayne with the possibility of making a big screen version of the musical, but the project never materialized. Not surprisingly, when approached at that time to direct the film, Spielberg himself thought it would have made an incredible motion picture. "We tried to develop a film project with Paramount, but they're a big corporation, and musicals are not necessarily always the big successes that they could be," he remarked. "We've just never been able to get it together with them, although we've had great success in a lot of other media and the album keeps selling and the singles keep getting reinterpreted. My vision has remained for over 20 years of how it would be done as a film and now there are all these things which have grown up in that world of technology which would make it that much more exciting. The vision is still as clear to me today as it was all that time ago."

While the promise of a multiplex invasion remains frustratingly out of reach, Wayne's vision still fired a computer game, one that conjures all the familiar, richly atmospheric imagery of a nineteenth century enslaved by the strutting Martian hordes.

"The technology has changed to the point where I thought it was a natural time to reinvestigate the computer industry," says Wayne, patently delighted to see his baby stake a claim in another medium. "There's two formats and I think the hook is that it's a two CD set and you can choose to play it through either the eyes of the Martians or the humans. The Martians bring a huge range of machines, each with a different function. There's the Red Weed, as we discovered on the album, and there's also the Black Dust, which is almost like a chemical agent that smothers from above, like a cloud. There's also something called the Flying Machine, which H.G. Wells created, along with a few new machines. All these things became natural weapons against the humans, but you can win from both sides, you just have to plan your missions and figure out how. It's limitless, it really is, and I don't think that anyone will ever duplicate playing the game the same way twice."

As Wayne recalls, his involvement in the game goes back to the gestation period of the original album. "I was introduced to the game's distributor and most of the people thereknew my album better than I did. I was stunned by how much they were into it, and so we found ourselves going down very similar paths as to how to interpret it. We hooked up with a development company who knew how to create games and who also loved the album. I think that really was the main starting point - the technology existed and people were enthusiastic about staying true to the album and the story. It was an evolution. Every time we took a big step and got something done, you'd think 'Gosh, that's great, that's different.'"

Wayne relished the chance to revisit his musical score for the video game. "Coming back to it was actually pretty fresh for me, especially hearing other people's input as to how the music should be interpreted. There are segments of this game scored as if for the big screen," he notes. "It's recorded in surround sound and it's epic in places. It's scored accurately to the footage and it all comes together like a big screen picture. Apart from the scored sequences, we recorded 30 minutes of sound for each CD. It's like doing a whole album again, taking all the compositions and reinterpreting them as moods, mostly with club grooves. The player can actually choose the mood they want to play the game in - if you're in a moreaggressive mood then you've got some aggressive tracks and if you want a little more of anambient feel then you've got some tracks on there too, from both sides, Martian and human."

Cradling a coffee in his home recording studio, surrounded by an original record shop mobile of a Martian fighting machine and assorted foreign pressings of "The War of the Worlds," Wayne reflects on his own, personal piece of global subjugation. "I get royalty statements to this day, and I'm surprised that it chugs on each year, with a reasonable amount of sales all over the place. I guess as a recording artist and as a composer, that stands out as my most commercial success, something I'll always be proud of. It was a family production and I made friends on it that I've stayed in touch with to this day, so it represents a great time in my life. 'The War of the Worlds' will always stand out as a very happy moment in time for me. I'll always be proud of it."

The 2005 Re-Launch of Jeff Wayne's "The War of the Worlds"

In the winter of 2005, Jeff Wayne and Sony Entertainment UK signed a multi-project contract to develop properties related to his musical version of "The War of the Worlds," including an international re-launch of the album. Since its initial release in 1978, the album has produced in excess of 12 million records in worldwide sales, and garnered a cult following among music fans that rivals "Star Trek" fandom. With a remix in SACD 5.1 Surround Sound and re-packaging in a number of new, exciting formats, the multi-award winning album will reach a whole new generation of fans. The re-launch project represents a major priority both domestically and internationally, including the United States, and involves all of Sony's marketing and public relations staff in key territories. In fact, Sony Music is counting on the album to be its crown jewel in virtually every market in the world.

Timed to coincide with news of the album re-launch came confirmation that a $48million CGI-animated film, based on Wayne's musical interpretation of H.G. Wells classic story and set in Victorian England, would also be produced by Sony. Fans have been clamoring for years for such a project. Ironically, a joint venture between Wayne and Paramount Pictures to produce a musical film version with Steven Spielberg in 1979 never got beyond the discussion phase; but at the time, Spielberg remarked that it would make a "unique and visionary film." Now, over twenty-five years later, Wayne's team has already completed a script, storyboards, and an original prequel which explains why the Martians were forced to leave their planet to invade Earth. His company has also produced footage as part of its research and development into using state-of-the-art CGI and Motion Capture technology.

Science fiction fans who attended the four-day Collectormania 7 in Great Britain from April 29 to May 2, 2005, were among the first to see some five minutes of footage from "Jeff Wayne's The War of the Worlds" movie at the Milton Keyes convention center. Those who saw the footage, synchronized with Wayne's award-winning music, claimed that it was "awesome" and "spectacular." Just imagine, for a moment, the music and lyrics of "Forever Autumn" cued to the exodus of sad, weary people fleeing the cities from the Martians, or "Thunder Child" timed to images of the armada fleeing from the coast of England, and then the big battle. Regrettably, the CGI film is still, at least, three years away from its debut in the summer of 2008.

Several other projects in development based on Wayne's musical work, however, will reach fans a bit sooner. Two of those projects include a major Theme Park attraction and a large scale multi-media live touring show, which will include some 20 minutes of animation from Wayne's CGI film. Additionally, the album re-launch on June 20, 2005, will also see the launch of an official website celebrating "Jeff Wayne's The War of the Worlds" with all sorts of new and exciting merchandise. New versions of Playstation and PC computer games, which have already enjoyed lots of success, will reach commercial markets, as well as a new comic book.

"These are interesting time for 'The War of the Worlds,'" Wayne remarked from Los Angeles, while holding meetings with various companies (including Paramount Pictures) related to his album. "There is no doubt that its profile in its different forms is going to be spectacular."

When asked to comment on the rival productions, he would only say, "From what I understand, the Cruise/Spielberg production will be set in more contemporary times, probably the USA, unlike my Musical Version which is set as H.G. Wells wrote it - in Victorian England. The excitement to me was always that through the eyes of humanity in the 1890's, as opposed to today, a superior force from another planet was far more terrifying and would be far more difficult to defend against." He had no comments to make about the Timothy Hines film.

While the H.G. Wells story remains in the public domain in the United States and certain other territories, Jeff Wayne owns all worldwide rights to his musical version. He also maintains certain ancillary rights to the original 1898 novel including merchandising, soundtrack and commercial tie-ins, across Europe and much of South America. Viacom Consumer Products and its subsidiary Paramount Pictures own the feature film rights in those same territories.

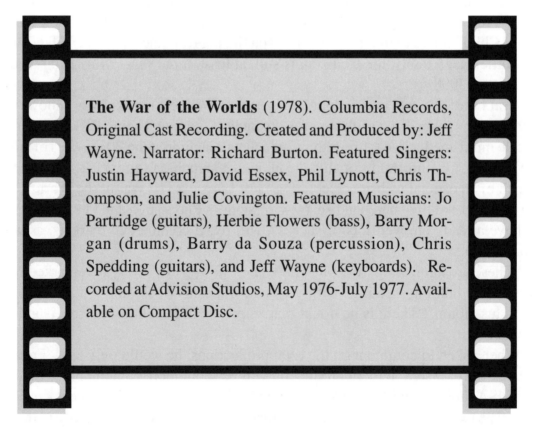

The War of the Worlds (1978). Columbia Records, Original Cast Recording. Created and Produced by: Jeff Wayne. Narrator: Richard Burton. Featured Singers: Justin Hayward, David Essex, Phil Lynott, Chris Thompson, and Julie Covington. Featured Musicians: Jo Partridge (guitars), Herbie Flowers (bass), Barry Morgan (drums), Barry da Souza (percussion), Chris Spedding (guitars), and Jeff Wayne (keyboards). Recorded at Advision Studios, May 1976-July 1977. Available on Compact Disc.

CHAPTER SEVEN: THE TELEVISION SERIES

As cockroaches are to man, so is humanity to the invaders when the "War of the Worlds" begins, and we wanted to carry that theme from the novel and [George Pal's] film forward into the present day. The aliens could make a pretty good case that we are lousy managers of this planet, and their position is that they could do a better job... But since the aliens lack the advanced technological hardware of the 1953 movie, they have to rely on less obvious methods of conquering our planet. If we wanted our aliens to pollute the New York water supply, we could take out a nice section of the city. In subtle ways, they'll try to infiltrate governments. They could, through their technology, increase the danger of acid rain. Through civil unrest or ecological disaster, they could upset the balance, weakening mankind's ability to resist their main invasion, which is only a few years distant.
-Greg Strangis, Producer, December 1988

Thirty-five years after the enormous success of George Pal's adaptation of "The War of the Worlds," Paramount Pictures and creative producer Greg Strangis joined forces to launch a new Martian invasion in 1988. Thanks (in part) to the success of "Star Trek: The Next Generation" and "Friday the 13th: The Series," both shows syndicated by Paramount, this new television series was intended as a quasi-sequel to the 1953 movie and even the 1938 Orson Welles radio broadcast. Regrettably, the series was hampered right from the start by the rather weak premise that a form of blanket amnesia had wiped out all our collective memories of the 1953 attack. What most people remembered was a hoax, similar to the radio broadcast, but not the actual invasion. To have engineered a direct sequel to the Pal film would have required the creative staff to have envisioned a completely different history for our planet from 1953 to modern times, and American television in the late eighties was not about innovation but rather formula. Strangis and creative consultant Herbert Wright decided right from the beginning that it would be far easier from a production standpoint to leave the world as readily recognizable to the average television audience than to create something very new. With a budget of less than $680,000 per episode, they relied on familiar ideas borrowed from 'Invasion of the Body Snatchers" (1956) and "The Invaders" (1967) rather than stage a full-scale battle each week. Most viewers accepted the blanket amnesia storyline, and followed the cast somewhat faithfully through the first season of production. Still, the task to make the show a successful one was very daunting at first.

The Creative Force

The creative force behind the show was producer/writer Greg Strangis. Strangis had been a successful television writer and producer for shows like "Love, American Style" (1969), "Happy Days" (1974), "Eight Is Enough" (1977) and "Falcon Crest" (1981) when he signed on as a creative consultant on the first season of "Star Trek: The Next Generation" (1987). His impact on the update of Gene Roddenberry's classic 1960's series lead to his opportunity to make "War of the Worlds" into a weekly series for Paramount. He had some serious aspirations for the show, seeing it as an opportunity to highlight our poor treatment of the planet, and that the aliens might simply be our destined replacements in the natural scheme of things. "The aliens could make a pretty good case," he stated in a 1988 magazine interview, "that we are lousy managers of this planet, and their position is that they could do a better job." He and his writing staff worked to make the first season relevant to the problems that we humans faced, with episodes focusing on drug addiction, global warming, runaway children, and abortion.

Strangis and his crew filmed most of the first season in Toronto, Canada, to take advantage of the favorable exchange rates between the United States and its northern neighbor. "For years," Greg Strangis commented in 1988, "Los Angeles was every location in the world. Hollywood never left Hollywood. But Toronto lends itself to many different looks, if you're willing to use your imagination."

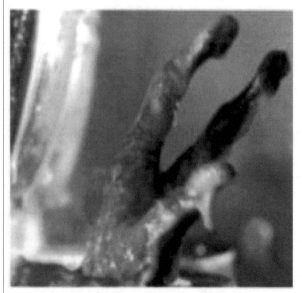

In addition to moving the production to Canada, Strangis hired Herbert Wright from "Star Trek: The Next Generation" to act as his creative consultant on the show. The writer and producer of such television shows as "Night Gallery" (1970), "Hunter" (1984), "Stingray" (1986), and "Star Trek," Wright was the right man for the enormous task of bringing the new series to life. He felt the show was the right forum to teach the public about less obvious trends and developments in the world. "Physicists," he explained in a 1988 interview, "have now arrived at the same place that yogis, gurus, and great Zen masters reached 2,000 years ago, namely knowing that

Earth is one living organism. Just a short five years ago, this idea was considered ridiculous. For me, this is a blending of the scientific and the spiritual." Part of that blending meant for Wright that each episode title of the new series would have a Biblical reference, and would merge the science of the day with a very real New Age component.

While Strangis and Wright collaborated on the story arc for the first season, they relied on the creative talents of Bill Sturgeon and his FX team to bring their alien invaders to life every week. Sturgeon, the veteran of numerous horror and science fiction films including "The Howling" (1981), "An American Werewolf in London" (1981), and "The Thing" (1982), created hundreds of makeup prosthetics in order to transform actors into alien zombies. "We designed appliances that we can fit on just about anybody," he explained. "Most of them are latex, but we're using a lot of gelatin because it's quick."

The Leading Players

The ensemble of characters that must lead the fight for Earth against the nearly invisible alien invaders were cast only a few weeks before shooting began in Toronto in April 1988. Jared Martin, who played the lead in "Fantastic Journey" (1973), was hired to play renowned astrophysicist Dr. Harrison Blackwood. According to the back-story, his parents died in the 1953 invasion, and he was raised as the foster son of Dr. Clayton Forrester (the character played by Gene Barry) and Sylvia Van Buren (Ann Robinson), who appeared in the original movie and several television episodes. Martin was called at his home in New York two days before the start of principle photography to take over the role when another actor bowed out, and leaped at the chance to play ostensibly the lead in the ensemble cast.

"He's a wonderful character," Martin commented enthusiastically during a 1988 press junket, "because he's many-faceted. He's intelligent, charming, sexy, athletic and adventuresome. He has a wonderful sense of humor. He's a leading man. He's a scientist, an astrophysicist. Blackwood's eccentric, in that he doesn't use the so-called scientific method. He's highly intuitive, given to spur-of-the-moment, instinctive things—great leaps of faith and reason. His office is a shambles, like a kid's place, full of toys and odd things."

Also leading the battle against the aliens was microbiologist Dr. Suzanne McCullough, as played by Lynda Mason Green. A working mother, McCullough has a twelve-year-old daughter named Debi (Rachel Blanchard), and multiple degrees from Harvard and MIT.

"She's an extremely highly educated woman," Green remarked. "As a woman in a male-dominated profession, there's a certain amount of over-compensating, over-achiever in her. She's committed to the discipline and its regimen, very, very precise about her process, moreso than she might be in another environment."

The military's liaison from the Pentagon was the commander of an elite squad of Delta soldiers, half-Cherokee Lt. Colonel Paul Ironhorse. Played by Vietnam veteran Richard Chavez, who essayed a similar role in "Predator" (1987), the character gave Blackwood's team military muscle and combat strategy. Ironhorse was very different from the other members. "He is a graduate of West Point," Chavez explained. "He is very straight-forward as far as his military bearing is concerned. He can fly anything that flies, drive anything that drives, shoot anything that shoots, and handle any edged weapon. He usually wants to go in and shoot the aliens up, or call an air strike. But the scientists are always saying we can't do this and we can't do hat."

Rounding out the team was Norton Drake, played by Canadian actor Phil Akin. He is a lifetime friend of Harrison Blackwood's, and as a paraplegic, he is restricted to a wheel-chair; but his restrictions do not prevent him from being an invaluable member of the team with his background in computers and communications. "I'm trying to get away from the image of the nerd computer freak," Akin said. "I want a more active image. He doesn't let his disability get him down. He has his own van, what I call the 'shaggin wagon,' carpeted and stuffed with computer and communications equipment so he gets around and does stuff. He's not stuck in a lab all of the time."

Of course, no war between the worlds would be complete without the opposing forces, the invading aliens. These aliens, who are identified early on in the series as Mor-Taxians not Martians, are totally ruthless as they strive to strengthen their foothold on Earth. Led by a trinity of leaders known as the Advocacy (Isle Van Glatz, Richard Comar, and Michael Rudder), there was not a creepier group of monsters on television or at the movies. Clad in black leather suits full of coolant to keep their bodies from sucumbing to the same radiation that protects them from our germs, the three members of the Advocacy exuded menace and absolute control. They dispatched other aliens to take over the bodies of humans, and resume their plan to conquer the planet. However, because of the rapid effects of radiation poisoning, the invaders are constantly forced to take over new human bodies. So, much like "The Invasion of the Body Snatchers" (1956), television viewers were never quite certain where they might appear. Of course, when killed, the bodies dissolved into a slimy mess with some great special effects. Their invasion by stealth made them nearly unbeatable, and featured many episodes that ended on a downbeat note.

Season One

When the two-hour pilot episode, "Resurrection," first aired on October 10, 1988, the formulaic pattern was set for the series. "In 1953, Earth experienced a War of the Worlds," the promotional ads stated. "Common bacteria stopped the aliens, but it didn't kill them. Instead, the aliens lapsed into a state of deep hibernation. Now the aliens have been resurrected, more terrifying than before. In 1953, aliens started taking over the world. Today, they're taking over our bodies." The stored remains of the alien invaders (no longer referred to as Martians) are re-activated by irradiated toxins during a terrorist strike on a nuclear waste dump. Released from their containers, the aliens kill the terrorists and "absorb" their bodies; they then set out to reclaim their weapons and Martian war machines from a top secret Air Force base (presumably Area 51 at Groom Lake, Nevada). By the end of the first episode, Blackwood and his team had prevented the aliens from re-activating a cache of mothballed weapons warehoused alongside other forbidden objects (including the Ark of the Covenant from "Raiders of the Lost Ark," 1981). But the alien invaders had not given up…they had merely changed their tactics to fight a cold war with the humans. Subsequently, each week the resurrected invaders relied on their superior intellects and their stealth to carry out their mission to prepare for a new invasion.

Clearly, the aliens needed to be tracked down and destroyed, and so, week after week, Blackwood and his elite team were given the task. The episodes that followed were consistently good, especially the brilliant "An Eye For An Eye," in which the Orson Welles 1938 radio broadcast was woven into the series mythology to considerable effect. Almost always, there was a real feeling of dread to the episodes, as victory was never entirely certain, and often the aliens won. However, because the production values were not especially high and the aliens were bereft of their technology, the actual "war of the worlds" was more like the skirmish of the week. With ratings that continued to sink, the series appeared destined for cancellation after the first season.

Season Two

Ratings were not good enough for Paramount to justify a second season, but when Frank Mancuso Jr., the creative force behind "Friday the 13th: The Series" (1988), came forward with an idea, the executives listened to him. What emerged was a whole new show built around several of the original characters, battling a new wave of alien enemies called the Morthren. Season Two was dubbed "War of the Worlds: The Second Invasion," and began explosively on October 2, 1989 with the deaths of Ironhorse and Drake and a reshuffling of the members of the Blackwood team. With the aid of a maverick ex-soldier, Kincaid (Adrian Paul), the remaining trio of Harrison, Suzanne and Debi take to the road, and eventually set up a new base in an abandoned military bunker. Meanwhile, newly-arrived Morthrens, under the leadership of a powerful military commander Malzor (Denis Forest), destroy the old Advocacy, and prepare Earth for colonization by their people. These chilling new invaders can also create clones of humans to take the place of real people to do their bidding. Predictably, the Morthren fight a cold war with Blackwood's team, each week attempting to gain a foothold on the planet. In the final episode, Malzor's personal ambitions were exposed by his own people, and he died in a climatic shoot-out. The Morthrens agree to call off their impending invasion.

The second-season episodes were not as bad as generally considered, but the changes to the mythology of the show were jarring and not well explained. Mancuso and his writing team never fully explain why the Earth is a run-down place, suffering economic disaster and environmental blight. The new, entirely different set of aliens were interesting, but not particularly compelling enough to jettison those aliens from the first season. Thankfully, an actual resolution to the plotline was provided when the series was cancelled at the end of second season.

We wonder what might have happened, given today's level of digital effects, had Strangis or Mancuso decided to fight a real "war of the worlds" each week with the fate of the planet hanging in the balance.

Season One Episode Guide:
Episode 1: "The Resurrection" (Pilot-2 Hour Feature-length)
Airdate: October 3, 1988
Writer: Greg Strangis
Director: Colin Chilvers
Regular Cast: Jared Martin (Harrison Blackwood), Lynda Mason Green (Suzanne McCullough), Richard Chaves (Paul Ironhorse), and Philip Akin (Norton Drake).
Guest Cast: John Vernon (General Wilson), Rachel Blanchard (Debi McCullough), Corrinne Conley (Mrs. Pennyworth), Larry Reynolds (Tom Kensington), Isle Van Glatz (Urick/Advocate #2), Richard Comar (Chambers/Advocate #1), Michael Rudder (Einhorn/Advocate #3), Frank Pellegrino, Gwynneth Walsh (Charlotte), Eugene Clark (Gordon Reynolds), Desmond Ellis, Martin Neufeld, Ric Sarabia, Jack Mather, Harry Booker, David Hughes and Donald Tripe.
Plot: Thirty-five years after the events of "The War of the Worlds" (1953), most people have forgotten the Martian Invasion. They have returned to their daily jobs and resumed their daily struggles. Tensions between the various governments on Earth have been re-ignited, and the threat of global war remains a very real possibility. A terrorist group, representing one of the various war-like factions, raid a nuclear waste disposal site at Fort Jericho. But when the terrorists attempt to steal enough plutonium to make a nuclear bomb, the remains of the alien invaders are reactivated by the radiation. The aliens kill the terror-

ists and take over their bodies. They then send a transmission to Mor-Tax, with the hopes of igniting a new "war of the worlds." Harrison Blackwood (adopted son of Dr. Clayton Forrester) and his assistant Norton Drake discover the source of the alien transmissions, and together with newly hired microbiologist, Suzanne McCullough, discover the aliens from 1953 have been freed from their containers at Fort Jericho. Meanwhile, Colonel Ironhorse and his Delta Squad are in pursuit of the terrorists who raided the waste dump. The two teams are brought together by General Wilson to fight the aliens. The aliens have but one objective: Hangar 15 at a top secret Air Force base where their ships from the 1953 invasion are stored. (Also, the "Ark of the Covenant" from "Raiders of the Lost Ark" (1981) is stored in the same hangar.) Harrison's team manages to plant bombs on the ships before the aliens arrive, and prevent them from escaping with the valuable space craft which explode as they are about to attack. The aliens slip away, and vow to fight a covert battle with the humans until their Mor-Tax reinforcements can arrive.

Memorable Quotes:

Harrison: In 1953, we experienced what can only be described as a War of the Worlds. If it weren't for common, every day bacteria attacking the aliens' immune systems, they would have won this war, and you and I would not be having this conversation.

Suzanne: But we are having this conversation, which I don't want. So I fail to see your point.

Harrison: My point is that even though the bacteria stopped the aliens, I don't think it killed them!

Suzanne: Excuse me, but I think you have been sitting too close to your television set.

Episode 2: "The Walls Of Jericho"
Airdate: October 10, 1988
Writer: Forrest Van Buren
Director: Colin Chilvers
Guest Cast: John Vernon (General Wilson), Rachel Blanchard (Debi McCullough), Corrinne Conley (Mrs. Pennyworth), Larry Reynolds (Tom Kensington), Isle Van Glatz (Urick/Advocate #3), Richard Comar (Chambers/Advocate #1), Michael Rudder (Einhorn/Advocate #3), and Mark Humphrey.
Plot: Dr. Harrison Blackwood struggles to convince General Wilson and Ironhorse that the alien threat is not over, even though it appears that they died in the previous episode. The aliens are, in fact, still alive; the radiation that killed the deadly bacteria is slowly destroying their human host bodies. They start a crime spree to gather items needed to slow the radiation poisoning including a stockpile of liquid nitrogen. The three members of the Advocacy begin wearing their radiation suits, and vow "To Life Immortal." Also, Blackwood discusses "selective-amnesia" theory which is used to explain the world's apparent loss of memory of the original invasion.
Memorable Quotes:
Ironhorse: All right, you've worn me down. I'll go with you. But you've got to promise me one thing: if you're wrong, you're going to get the hell out of my life and stay out.
Harrison: I won't even send you a Christmas card.

Episode 3: "Thy Kingdom Come"
Airdate: October 17, 1988
Writer: Herbert Wright
Director: Winrich Kolbe
Guest Cast: Ann Robinson (Sylvia Van Buren), Richard Comar (as Advocate #1) Ilse von Glatz (as Advocate #2) Michael Rudder (as Advocate #3), and Alar Aedma (as Alien Hunter)
Plot: Harrison Blackwood contacts Sylvia Van Buren, his stepmother and a survivor of the 1953 alien invasion, in order to find out how much she knows about his adoptive father Clayton Forrester's work. But she has been confined to Whitewood Mental Health Care Center because of psychic visions about aliens. With her help, they track the aliens to Montana, and ultimately Canada and the Ontario Federal Reserve where a lake is being used to help revive more aliens.
Memorable Quotes:
Ironhorse: Wolfjaw, Montana. That's Indian Territory.
Harrison: It looks like we got aliens moving into the neighborhood. Let's go.
Ironhorse: Great. First the white man, now aliens.

Episode 4 : "A Multitude Of Idols"
Airdate: October 24, 1988
Writer: Tom Lazarus

Director: Neill Fearnley
Guest Cast: Rachel Blanchard (Debi McCullough), Corinne Conely (Mrs Pennyworth), Michelle Scarabelli (Elise Conway), Neil Vipond, Ray James, Van Flores and Garfield Andrews.
Plot: In the small, abandoned town of Beeton, the aliens are using more nuclear waste to revive more aliens, and then are using busloads of churchgoers as the new host bodies. When a local reporter stumbles on the alien scheme to steal radioactive waste and actually captures an alien possession on film, Blackwood and his team move into action. But by the time reinforcements arrive, the aliens are gone.
Memorable Quotes:
Harrison: Gone. They're all gone.
Suzanne: We did everything we could.
Harrison: That's not good enough, Suzanne.
Ironhorse: He's right. We keep loosing like this, we're dead meat on this planet.

Episode 5: "Eye For An Eye"
Airdate: October 31, 1988
Writer: Tom Lazarus
Director: Mark Sobel
Guest Cast: Rachel Blanchard (Debi McCullough), Jeff Corey (Francis Flannery), Jack Ammon (Sam), John Ireland (Harv), Mark Holmes (Red), Kevin Rushto (Dog), Sergio Galli (Biker #1), Jack Jessop and Rita Tuckett.
Plot: Citizens of the small town of Grover's Mill, New Jersey, celebrate the 50th anniversary of the 1938 radio broadcast of a Martian invasion, unaware that the "Martians" were real and that the Military covered up the alien reconnaissance mission to prevent a mass panic. Aliens posing as bikers arrive looking for a spaceship that crashed in the town 50 years earlier. When they recover a death ray, Harrison Blackwood and his team along with the help of the towns folk defeat the aliens before they can use it to cause mass damage to the surrounding populace.
Memorable Quotes:
Harv/alien: You are but fungus before us.
Harrison: If we can just open up a dialogue -
Harv/alien: There can be no dialogue with fungus. Only death.

Episode 6: "The Second Seal"
Airdate: November 7, 1988
Writer: Patrick Barry
Director: Neill Fearnley
Guest Cast: Greg Morris (General Masters), Lynne Griffin (Amanda Burke), Michael McKeever, James Kidnie, Kirk Dunn and Miriam Newhouse.
Plot: A number of secret military files from the 1953 invasion, encoded by Clayton Forrester

under the name "Operation Deep Ice," are discovered by Norton and access is granted to Harrison and his team. The aliens are also interested in getting the files as they include the burial sites of 10,000 aliens.

Memorable Quotes:

Ironhorse: I hate to interrupt this cozy conversation, but could someone please call me an ambulance?

Suzanne: You're an ambulance. Sorry.

Episode 7: "Goliath Is My Name"

Airdate: November 14, 1988

Writer: Tom Lazarus

Director: George Bloomfield

Guest Cast: Rachel Blanchard (Debi McCullough), Corinne Conely (Mrs Pennyworth), Jeremy Ratchford (Student), Eric Bruskotter (Jefferson), Jason Blicker, Hume Baugh, Carolyn Dunn, Kelly Rowan and James Kee.

Plot: When a friend of Suzanne's is murdered at a college campus, Blackwood's team investigates, and discovers the aliens are involved. They are attempting to steal vials of a deadly virus from a research lab which will help them eliminate the human race. A war game gets out of hand as the aliens attempt to infiltrate the campus.

Memorable Quotes:

Advocate #2: We can rely on the self-destructive nature of the primitives.

Advocate #3: It is our greatest ally.

Advocate #1: And our greatest enemy. This is truly a filthy place.

Episode 8: "To Heal The Leper"

Airdate: November 21, 1988

Writer: David Tynan

Director: William Fruet

Guest Cast: Ann Robinson (Sylvia Van Buren), Paul Boretsky (Leo), Kim Coates (Scott), Guylaine St Onge (Beth) and Neil Dainard.

Plot: When one of the Advocacy succumbs to the chicken pox, the Advocacy travels to a power station and begins collecting human brains. They secure the required brains and take over the Lyndon Power station blacking out the entire area. Harrison Blackwood sees his step-mother Sylvia Van Buren recovered from her mental breakdown, but is almost captured by the aliens.

Memorable Quotes:

Ironhorse: Maybe they - they've gone back to where they came from.

Harrison: How? Walk?

Episode 9: "The Good Samaritan"

Airdate: December 26, 1988

Writer: Sylvia Clayton
Director: Paul Tucker
Guest Cast: Rachel Blanchard (Debi McCullough), Corinne Conely (Mrs Pennyworth), Lori Hallier (Teri), Warren Davis (Franklin) and Alex Cord (Marcus Madison Mason).
Plot: Marcus Mason, a greedy and womanizing businessman, invents a new grain which is resistant to climate, pestilence and radiation. Because he has created it to be resistant to radiation, Suzanne contacts him in an attempt to learn about it for the fight against the aliens. The aliens also want to use the grain to spread a deadly toxin killing those who eat it, and take Mason hostage.
Memorable Quotes:
[After Harrison burns his hand.]
Ironhorse: Are you okay?
Harrison: I think my violin-playing days are probably over.
Ironhorse: You play the violin?
Harrison: It's something I've always been meaning to do.

Episode 10: "Epiphany"
Airdate: January 2, 1989
Writer: Sylvia Van Buren
Director: Neill Fearnley
Cast: Deborah Wakeham (Katya) and Patrick MacNee (Valery).
Plot: The aliens plot a nuclear holocaust, deliberately planting a nuclear device near the location of sensitive peace talks between the Soviets and the U.S. When Katya, a Soviet scientist, wants to defect, her old flame Harrison Blackwood assists, and then learns the consequences of his interference.
Memorable Quotes:
Ironhorse: It's so small.
Katya: Just how big do you like your bombs?

Episode 11: "Among The Philistines"
Airdate: January 9, 1989
Writer: Patrick Barry
Director: William Fruet
Guest Cast: Rachel Blanchard (Debi McCullough), Corinne Conely (Mrs Pennyworth), Cedric Smith (Adrian Bouchard), David

Calderisi and Gregory Cross.

Plot: A language expert who has started to break the alien transmissions code is revealed to be an alien infiltrator. Adrian then reveals that the aliens are from Mor-Tax, and that there are millions on their way to Earth.

Memorable Quotes:

Ironhorse: You understand the need for maintaining the secrecy of our location.

Adrian: Of course. Anyway, I like being blindfolded in the back of a van. It's my idea of a good time.

Episode 12: "Choirs Of Angels"

Airdate: January 16, 1989

Writer: Dumford King

Director: Herbert Wright

Guest Cast: Rachel Blanchard (Debi McCullough), Corinne Conely (Mrs Pennyworth), Jan Rubes (Von Deer), Billy Thorpe (Billy Carlos), John Novak (Alien #1), Alex Carter (Alien #2) and Heidi Von Palleske (Alien #3).

Plot: Members of Blackwood's team stumble onto two new alien plots simultaneously... a scheme to place subliminal messages in the music of a popular rock star to create an army of slaves, and the creation of an antidote that will enable the aliens to shed their protective clothing and survive in Earth's atmosphere. But Harrison also becomes a pawn in the alien's game, and must fight the "lies" they have planted.

Memorable Quote:

Ironhorse: It reminds me of the 60's. You remember? "Paul is dead."

Episode 13: "Dust To Dust"

Airdate: January 23, 1989

Writer: Richard Krzemien

Director: George Bloomfield

Guest Cast: Ivan Naranjo (Joseph), Eric Schweig (Darrow), Robin Sewell (Grace), Elias Zarou (Kirk), Joseph Zeigler (Pat), Linda Goranson (Connie) and R D Reid.

Plot: When an archeologist steals a Native American headdress (with an apparent alien artifact), both the Blackwood team and the aliens take notice. The Morthren crystal leads them to an ancient Indian burial ground and the remains of an abandoned Martian saucer thousands of years old.

Memorable Quotes:

Ironhorse: My grandfather used to disappear for, like, four or five days. We used to tell my grandmother that he was going off to see the Spirits. I think - I think he had a girl-friend in the next alley, though.

Episode 14: "He Feedeth Among The Lilies"

Airdate: January 30, 1989

Writer: Tom Lazarus

Director: George Bloomfield

Guest Cast: Cynthia Belliveau (Karen), Larry Mannell (Doctor), Bonnie Gruen (Nurse), Andrea Nevitt (The Aide), Maria Del Mar, Carole Galloway, Graham Batchelor and Myron Senkus.

Plot: The scientists discover that the aliens are abducting humans to perform experiments on them to unravel the secrets of the human immune system. One of these unfortunate victims is a beautiful woman for whom Dr. Blackwood has fallen in love.

Memorable Quotes:

Norton: Who's Karen McKinney?

Harrison: She's the Stanford grad who spent a couple of years in the Amazon with the aboriginal tribes, recording their music. She has a very inquisitive mind, Norton.

Norton: And how beautiful is she?

Suzanne: She's very beautiful!

Harrison: She's very beautiful.

Norton: And where do I sign up?

Episode 15: "The Prodigal Son"

Airdate: February 6, 1989

Writer: Herbert Wright and Patrick Barry

Director: George McCowan

Guest Cast: John Colicos (Quinn), James Purcell (McGinnis), Jim Yip (Hwang), Randall Carpenter (Margo) and Robert Morelli (Fitzpatrick).

Plot: On his way to a United Nations briefing, Harrison Blackwood meets hermit artist Quinn, an alien who has survived in human form since the 1953 invasion. While his fellow aliens are attempting to track down, kill and dissect for study, he kidnaps Blackwood, and delivers his own personal ultimatum to the UN.

Memorable Quotes:

Harrison: Quinn, if you have any information about aliens, tell me.

Quinn: Oh, I'll tell you, Harry, but just about one. I'll tell you all about one who did not fall to the bacteria in the great invasion, one who was stranded alone 35 long, lonely years on a hostile *alien* planet... called Earth.

Harrison: You're an alien.

Quinn: Oh, no, Harry. *You're* the alien.

Episode 16: "The Meek Shall Inherit"

Airdate: February 12, 1989

Writer: D.C. Fontana

Director: William Fruet

Guest Cast: Ann Robinson (Sylvia Van Buren), Diana Reis (Molly), Sam Malkin (Pollito), Michael Copeman (Dayton), John Gilbert (Sensky), Gene Mack (Bull) and Steve Perni

Plot: The aliens attempt to destroy Earth's communications network by knocking out global phone links. Meanwhile, the witness to their operation, a homeless woman, is sent to the same asylum as the psychic Sylvia Van Buren. The two flee the sanitarium in an effort to warn Blackwood and his team.

Memorable Quotes:

Stavrakos: Don't you believe that life on other planets is possible, sir?

Ironhorse: Don't you believe in the swamp-gas theory, corporal? Project Bluebook - it wasn't good enough for you? I suppose if aliens were to invade this planet you'd be the first one to pick up a weapon and start shooting.

Stavrakos: Don't think I'd be the first, colonel, but I'm sure I wouldn't be the last. Last time I checked, this planet was ours.

Episode 17: "Unto Us A Child Is Born"
Airdate: February 20, 1989
Writer: David Braff
Director: George McCowan
Guest Cast: Brent Carver (Jesse), Geoffrey Bowes (Colin), Clark Johnson (Young), Amber-Lea Weston (Nancy), Peter Boretski and Martha Irving.
Plot: When an alien takes the body of a pregnant woman, the body goes into labor and gives birth to a half-human, half-alien mutant. The alien decides to seize the baby for experimentation, but Blackwood and his team are on his trail to prevent the hybrid child from falling into the hands of the Advocacy.
Memorable Quotes:

Ironhorse: "You're saying we have some kind of half-breed on our hands here?"

Harrison: "A monster. Half human, half alien."

Episode 18: "The Last Supper"
Airdate: March 6, 1989
Writer: Tom Lazarus
Director: George McCowan
Guest Cast: Efrain Figueroa (Morales), Suzanne Coy (Dr Menathong), Colm Feore (Argochev), Barry Kennedy (Raymond) and James Hong (Soo Tak).
Plot: The scientists organize a top secret meeting with representatives from each world power at a high security location to discuss strategy... but the aliens still discover the site and launch an attack... with the aid of their agent inside. (This episode is a clip show with reused footage from the 1953 film and various episodes.)
Memorable Quotes:

Harrison: The most frightening thing of all, they've absolutely no regard for human life. Not since Nazi, Germany has the world witnessed such callous and brutal treatment of human beings. They mutilate, they maim... To them, we're an inferior species and they treat us like one.

Episode 19: "Vengeance Is Mine"
Airdate: April 17, 1989
Writer: Arnold Margolin
Director: George Bloomfield
Guest Cast: Denis Forest (Martin Cole), Carolyn Dunn (Sarah), Don Allison (Milton), Roger Montgomery (Henchman), Alannah Myles (Samantha) and Bernard Behrens (Psychiatrist).
Plot: Ironhorse is appalled to discover that he has killed an innocent civilian in a battle with two aliens, mistaking their hostage for a third invader. He cannot seem to get over his mistake, and becomes distant from the rest of the group who are trying to track down the aliens and whatever their new plot may be. Meanwhile, the dead woman's husband Martin seeks his own form of justice.
Memorable Quotes:
[Martin takes out a shotgun.]
Ironhorse: What the hell are you going to do?
Martin: What the Bible tells me to.

Episode 20: "My Soul To Keep"
Airdate: April 24, 1989
Writer: John Kubichan
Director: William Fruet
Guest Cast: Michael Parks (Cash McCullough) and John Colicos (Quinn).
Plot: The scientists are plagued by Suzanne's journalist ex-husband, who is spying on them as they search for a nest of alien eggs.
Memorable Quotes:
Advocate #2: These humans are treacherous.
Advocate #3: We'll be doing a great service for the entire universe to kill each and every one of these revolting human beings.
Advocate #1: Death to all humans!

Episode 21: "So Shall Ye Reap"
Airdate: May 1, 1989
Writer:Michael McCormack
Director: George Bloomfield
Guest Cast: Dixie Seatle (Teri

Novak), Angelos Rizacos (Young Alien Aide), Jill Jacobson (Envoy), Peter Mac Neill (Director), Jonathan Welsh (Jack Sawyer), Shelly-Lynn Owens (Streetwalker) and Isabelle Mejias.

Plot: The aliens try to perfect a drug that will cause human beings to act out their violent impulses, and test it on local vagrants. When the team learns of the drug, they impersonate DEA agents to obtain a sample. But Blackwood and his people are arrested by the police.

Memorable Quotes:

Director: If I return to the caverns now, the Advocacy will execute me.
Envoy: Don't be so pessimistic, comrade. Perhaps they'll take pity on your miserable existence. Your feeble pleas may move them so much, you might be permitted the honour of taking your own life.

Episode 22: "The Raising Of Lazarus"
Airdate: May 8, 1989
Writer: Dumford King
Director: Neill Fearnley
Guest Cast: Nicholas Coster (Dr Frederick Alexander), Thomas Hauff (Colonel Manning), Janet Bailey (Perry), Dale Wilson (Sgt Tex) and Hugh Thompson

Plot: When a shadow government agency unearths a flying saucer with an alien in suspended animation, the Pentagon informs Blackwood and his team. Unfortunately, Colonel Frederick Alexander, the leader of the agency, has different ideas about the aliens, and the deadly creature within gets loose inside the base.

Memorable Quotes:

Harrison: Norton, I have a...
Norton: Green floating weirdness?
Harrison: Green floating weirdness.

Episode 23: "The Angel Of Death"
Airdate: May 15, 1989
Writer: Herbert Wright
Director: Herbert Wright
Guest Cast: Elain Giftos (Q'Tara), Richard Blackburn (Fred), Doug Hughes (Man With Glasses), Art Nefsky (Janitor), John Evans (Jake), Rachel Stephens (Housewife).

Plot: When an alien android arrives on Earth and starts blasting away at the aliens, Blackwood and his team are suspicious. But Q'Tara announces herself to the aliens as an ally... but she has her own secret agenda.

Memorable Quotes:

[Repeated line]
Q'Tara: Remember nothing!

Season Two Episode Guide:
Episode 24: "The Second Wave"
Airdate: October 2, 1989
Writer: Michael Michaelian and Jonarthan Glassner
Director: Francis Delia
Regular Cast: Jared Martin (Harrison Blackwood), Lynda Mason Green (Suzanne McCullough), Adrian Paul (John Kincaid), Denis Forest (Malzor), Catherine Disher (Mana)
Guest Cast: Richard Chaves (Paul Ironhorse) and Philip Akin (Norton Drake).
Plot: In between seasons, the world has become a real mess; the environment has changed, and anarchy has been unleashed on the planet; basically, the whole end-of-the-world-as-we-know, with elements of "Blade Runner" thrown in for good measure. Just when it looks as if Blackwood and his team have the Mor-Tax aliens beaten, a new force of aliens arrive on Earth. These Mortherns are more deadly than the previous ones and can assume human form without needing to remain in areas of high radiation. They clone Ironhorse who kills Norton and then commits suicide. Harrison and Suzanne team up with John Kincaid, and a new "war of the worlds" begins.
Memorable Quotes:
Ironhorse Clone: You won't leave, will you? You'll stay and die because you won't leave one child behind. That's why we'll win.
Harrison: That's why you'll lose.

Episode 25: "No Direction Home"
Airdate: October 9, 1989
Writer: Nolan Powers and Thomas Baum
Director: Mark Sobel
Guest Cast: Angelo Rizacos (Father Tim), Peter Blais (Ralph) and Denise Ferguson (Helper).
Plot: Borrowing a page from "V-The Series," Blackwood's team sets up camp in a new underground bunker. Meanwhile the aliens clone Father Tim, whom they return to his mission where he cares for vagrants. The team investigates when things at the mission go wrong, and discovers the alien cloning technology.

Episode 26: "Doomsday"
Airdate: October 16, 1989
Writer: Tony DiFranco
Director: Timothy Bond
Guest Cast: Patricia Phillips (Bayda), Diana Reis (Grace), Kurt Reis (Thomas), Nathaniel Moreau (Steven), Stephen Black, Donnie Bowes and Vince Guerriero.
Plot: A heat wave, followed by a water shortage, drives everyone to the brink of desperation. The aliens block a water main and cause a bad drought to become even worse. They then engineer a series of 'miracles' in a local church before cloning the church leader. Blackwood's team becomes suspicious.

Episode 27: "Terminal Rock"
Airdate: October 23, 1989
Writer: John Groves
Director: Gabriel Pelletier
Guest Cast: Shannon Lawson (Rosa Douglas), Jaimz Woolvett (Larry), Paul Bettis (Sol) and Lawrence King (Ripper).
Plot: The aliens clone the leader of a rock group and plant subliminal messages into their music. They also manufacture brain-controlling devices which fit into human ears. The Mortherns are unaware that the Mor-Taxians tried this same plot in the first season. Oh, well! They're have to catch the repeats.

Episode 28: "Breeding Ground"
Airdate: October 30, 1989
Writer: Alan Moskowitz
Director: Armand Mastroianni
Guest Cast: Gerard Parkes (Dr. Emil Gestaine) and Helen Hughes (Kate Barrows).
Plot: While scavenging for medicine at a hospital, Blackwood discovers the aliens are incubating their young in human beings. The team tries to stop this hideous practice.

Episode 29: "Seft Of Emun"
Airdate: November 6, 1989
Writer: J.K.E. Rose
Director: William Fruet
Guest Cast: Laura Press (Seft), Illya Woloshyn (Torri) and Victoria Snow (Blade).
Plot: Seft, a high priestess of Emun, is a captive held by the Morthren. They dispatch her to collect parts to make power crystals, but she complicates the alien plot by falling in love with Harrison.

Episode 30: "Loving The Alien"
Airdate: November 13, 1989
Writer: Janet MacLean
Director: Otta Hanus
Guest Cast: Rachel Blanchard (Debi McCullough), Mira Kirshner (Jo), Eugene Glazner (Marcus) and Keram Malicki-Sanchez (Ceeto).
Plot: Debi runs away from home, and meets a young boy called Ceeto. Unfortunately, Ceeto turns out to be a runaway alien, being sought by the Mortherns.

Episode 31: "Night Moves"
Airdate: November 20, 1989
Writer: Lorne Rossman
Director: Mark Sobel
Guest Cast: Rachel Blanchard (Debi McCullough), Sally Chamberlin (Rebecca), Ken Pogue (John), Wayne Best (Paul), Dale Wilson (Roy) and Meg Hogarth (Shirley).
Plot: Suzanne takes Debi to her grandmother's farm to escape the growing civil unrest caused by the food rationing. At the farm, Researchers from the Department of Agriculture turn out to be aliens, and they have their own plans for the family homestead.

Episode 32: "Synthetic Love"
Airdate: January 15, 1990
Writer: Nancy Ann Miller
Director: Francis Belia
Guest Cast: Vlasta Vrana (Jonathan Laporte), Kathryn Rose (Rene Laporte), Sam Malkin (Mr Jimmy), and Patricia Phillips (Bayda).
Plot: Drug users are being rehabilitated and abducted by the aliens so that their brain tissue can be used for nefarious purposes. Again, the Mor-Tax aliens tried this tactic in the first season, but obviously the Morthrens were not watching.

Episode 33: "The Defector"
Airdate: January 22, 1990
Writer: Sandra Berg and Judith Berg
Director: Armand Mastroianni
Guest Cast: Charles McCaughan (Kemo), Charles Kerr (Ace), Belinda Metz (Scoggs), and Alan Feiman (Lonelyheart).
Plot: When an attempt to hack into the humans' computers goes awry, a Morthren technician (Kemo) is scarred both physically and mentally by the experience. Sentenced to death by his leaders, he runs away and meets with John Kincaid. He tries to persuade Kincaid that all he wants is peace.

Episode 34: "Time To Reap"
Airdate: January 29, 1990
Writer: Jim Trombetta
Director: Joseph Scanlan
Guest Cast: Paula Barrett (Miranda), George R Robertson (General Mann), Martha Irving and Amos Crawley.
Plot: The Eternal instructs Malzor to travel back through time to 1953 in order to try and inoculate some aliens against Earth's bacteria. Harrison and Kincaid follow him back through time and try and stop him. (All the scenes in 1953 are in black and white.)

Episode 35: "The Pied Piper"
Airdate: February 5, 1990
Writer: Nancy Ann Miller and Alan Moskowitz
Director: Allan Eastman
Guest Cast: Ron Lea (Paul Daniels), Joel Carlson (Adam), Tanja Jacobs (Miss Gholston), and Lisa Jakub (Julie).
Plot: The first-born Morthern on Earth is sent to a special school after it shows signs of emotional problems. Once at the school, however, the child uses its telepathic powers to influence the other children.

Episode 36: "The Deadliest Disease"
Airdate: February 12, 1990
Writer: Carl Binder and Wilson Coneybeare
Director: William Fruet
Guest Cast: James Purcell (Brock), Alex Karzis (Gerry), Joon B Kim (Bing), Aki Aleong (Tao), John Evans (Colonel West) and Elias Zarou.
Plot: Some of the aliens fall ill with a fatal disease. They need a new piece of technology called a med-cell to save them. However, before they can get it, it is stolen, and members of Blackwood's team want it.

Episode 37: "Path Of Lies"
Airdate: February 19, 1990
Writer: Rick Schwartz and Nancy Ann Miller
Director: Allan Eastman
Guest Cast: David Ferry (Marc Traynor), Maurice Evans (W R Samuels), Bernard Behrens (Jennings), Barbara Gordon (Bebe Gardner), Martin Doyle (Rob Numm), and Nadia Capone (Maureen).
Plot: A reporter photographs a gunfight between Harrison, Kincaid and the aliens. He threatens to expose Blackwood's team to the world, as well as reveal the alien menace. But the aliens have powerful allies, and the photographs are never used.

Episode 38: "Candle In The Night"
Airdate: April 9, 1990
Writer: Carl Binder
Director: Armand Mastroianni
Guest Cast: Rachel Blanchard (Debi McCullough), Noam Zylberman (Nate), Sandy Webster (Gunther), Gema Zamprogna, Krista Houston (Lisa), and Marlow Vella (Ralph).
Plot: Suzanne plans a surprise birthday party for her daughter Debi. Meanwhile, the aliens plan a surprise of their own as they recover a malfunctioning surveillance device, and drop in on the human's celebration.

Episode 39: "Video Messiah"
Airdate: April 16, 1990
Writer: Norman Snider
Director: Gabriel Pelletier
Guest Cast: Roy Thinnes (Van Order), Lori Hallier (Mindy Cooper), Larry Joshua (Hardy Gait), Alex Carter (Clark), Keith Knight (Bob), Angela Dohrmann (Jane), and Michael Caruana (Kurt).
Plot: The aliens use a clone of Dr. Van Order, a popular motivational speaker, to incite violence through the use of subliminal messages broadcast in television adverts. Kincaid and the rest of the team get involed when an old friend of Kincaid's is drawn into the lethal scheme.

Episode 40: "Totally Real"
Airdate: April 23, 1990
Writer: James Trombetta
Director: William Fruet
Guest Cast: Colm Feore (Nikita), Trevor Cameron Smith (David), Michael Woods (Sendac), and Belinda Metz.
Plot: The aliens are killing people using a computer game. At the same time, Harrison and Suzanne develop a drug which allows people to link telepathically.

Episode 41: "Max"
Airdate: April 30, 1990
Writer: Naomi Janzen
Director: Jorge Montesi
Guest Cast: Michael Welden (Max), Chuck Shamata (Bradley).
Plot: Max, John Kincaid's brother was killed by the aliens, and his squad get together to drink to him one year after his death. However, the aliens took the body, and turned him into a cyborg killer who is ordered to kill the rest of his squad especially his brother. After killing the rest of the squad John manages to appeal to his human side and they team up to fight the aliens sent to retrieve their malfunctioning cyborg, but Max is killed.

Episode 42: "The True Believer"
Airdate: May 7, 1990
Writer: Jim Henshaw
Director: Armand Mastroianni
Guest Cast: Timothy Webber (Thresher), Vincent Dale (Hook) and Michael Hogan (Nash).
Plot: The aliens pose as the Blackwood team and carry out petty crimes, including bank robbery and murder. The real team must convince the local authorities it is not them, but Malzor has taken over the investigation.

Episode 43: "The Obelisk"
Airdate: May 14, 1990
Writer: Rick Schwartz and Nancy Ann Miller
Director: William Fruet
Guest Cast: Rachel Blanchard (Debi McCullough), Keram Malicki-Sanchez (Ceeto), Cynthia Dale (Tila), and John Gilbert (Tallick).
Plot: With mounting Morthern losses, Malzor consults the obelisk and decides to release spores killing the planet. Harrison and Suzanne work on an antidote while Kincaid tries to find the distribution sites. Ceeto turns on Malzor taking the obelisk to Debi which reveals how they were drawn to Earth by the first atomic tests, and Malzor leading the second wave for personal revenge, stealing the obelisk and destroying their homeworld betraying them. When the other aliens are shown the truth, Malzor is killed and the war is over. This final episode tries to tie up all of the loose ends.

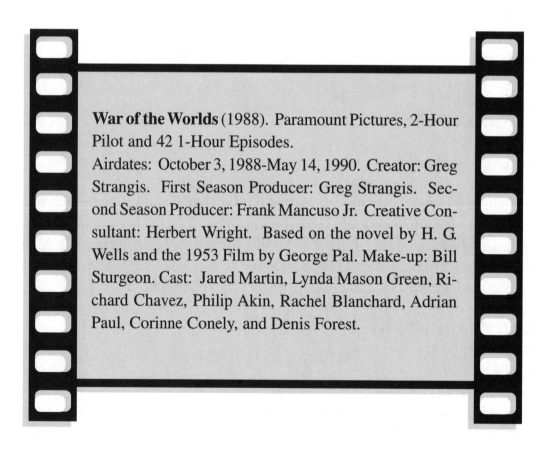

War of the Worlds (1988). Paramount Pictures, 2-Hour Pilot and 42 1-Hour Episodes.
Airdates: October 3, 1988-May 14, 1990. Creator: Greg Strangis. First Season Producer: Greg Strangis. Second Season Producer: Frank Mancuso Jr. Creative Consultant: Herbert Wright. Based on the novel by H. G. Wells and the 1953 Film by George Pal. Make-up: Bill Sturgeon. Cast: Jared Martin, Lynda Mason Green, Richard Chavez, Philip Akin, Rachel Blanchard, Adrian Paul, Corinne Conely, and Denis Forest.

CHAPTER EIGHT: THE PENDRAGON FILM

I have wanted to make The War of the Worlds my entire life. I was first introduced to it when I was eight years old, after I'd seen a movie called "The Day the Earth Stood Still." I became deeply, deeply fascinated with science fiction, and my father gave me a copy of the book, and although some of the finer, subtler points of Wells's sociological views and his views on religion were difficult for me to grasp at that time, it entirely captured my imagination. Later that same year, I heard the [1938] radio broadcast, and was entirely taken and obsessed with this idea, this story of the Martians and their fighting machines. Later I saw the 1953 version, and I can remember being disappointed that it didn't have walking machines, but still it was frightening. This is what introduced me to filmmaking, and I attempted to make my own versions from eight, nine years old. I've had my eye on The War of the Worlds ever since.
—Timothy Hines, Interview, Fall 2004

Ever since George Pal first released his modern adaptation of "The War of the Worlds" to movie houses in 1953, theatergoers and science fiction fans have hungered for a film version of the 1898 Wells novel that was faithful to the original source material. Nearly fifty years passed before anyone, in particular the world's most successful film director, expressed any interest in the material. So, when Paramount, Steven Spielberg and Tom Cruise geared up for their megabudget production of "War of the Worlds" in 2004, most every film fan thought that it would be a period piece. But alas, Spielberg and Cruise wanted to make their own modern adaptation, with equal parts of M. Night Shyamalan's "Signs" (2002) and "Independence Day" (1996) thrown into the mix for good measure. Little did anyone know that Pendragon Pictures, a small independent, was working on its own screen version of the classic alien-invasion story. Billed as "the first authentic movie adaptation," and set in Great Britain in 1898, "War of the Worlds" was shot with great stealth and secrecy under the cover title "The Great Boer War" for two and a half months in England and the Pacific Northwest by Timothy Hines with a cast of relative unknowns. In a battle of David versus Goliath, Hines beat Spielberg's production to the big screen, and produced the film that fans have been waiting to see for more than fifty years.

The War of "The War of the Worlds"

Mars taking on Earth is pretty impressive, but as a battle, that's nothing compared to an independent filmmaker who takes on Steven Spielberg. Any writing devoted to the Pendragon Pictures production should be focused on the fact that it represents the first time H.G. Wells's classic science fiction novel is accurately being adapted to the screen, with its story set in Victorian London. It should hone in on all that was accomplished given a budget somewhere in the mid 20-millions and the fact that its creators had originally planned a $42 million, modern day version before the events of September 11th caused them to rethink their plans. Instead, there seems to be no choice but to address the fact that this version of "War of the Worlds" reached theaters just prior to Steven Spielberg and Tom Cruise's mega-budget version being produced for Paramount Pictures at the same time. The bottom line was that in spring of 2004, the Paramount hype and advertising machine was at full force, but Pendragon seemed to be reaping many of the benefits.

"It's the only time in history where the world's most successful filmmaker decides to make a film that we were already in production on," offers Pendragon CEO and "War of the Worlds" writer/director Timothy Hines. "A lot of the attention that we were getting was actually based on the fact that Paramount was going to be spending $15 and $40 million in advertising for a film called 'War of the Worlds' and based on the same material called 'War of the Worlds.' Enigmatically for them, they didn't know what to do with us, because this has never happened before. Yes, there have been films that have been similar at the same time, but not two films with the same title based on the same material."

What Hines finds particularly interesting is that each time Pendragon issued a press release or updated trailer for their film, he observed that Paramount issued numerous press releases heralding their own version. "Normally you would think that would harm us," he says, somewhat amused by the whole situation, "but our website went up several thousand hits an hour because they put out press releases for people to find out about their version, but they found out about ours as well. I'm sure from their perspective, they would have liked us to take a poison pill and die. We were told by our distribution network that Paramount's ideal was that we would do all of this work on our own to get publicity and build everything up, but then somehow implode just before we were about to release, leav-

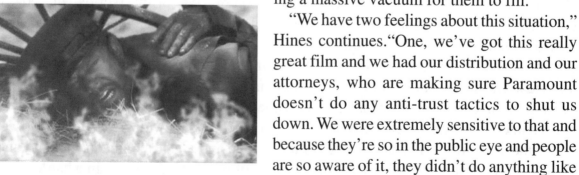

ing a massive vacuum for them to fill.

"We have two feelings about this situation," Hines continues. "One, we've got this really great film and we had our distribution and our attorneys, who are making sure Paramount doesn't do any anti-trust tactics to shut us down. We were extremely sensitive to that and because they're so in the public eye and people are so aware of it, they didn't do anything like that in an overt way. On the flip side, we wanted to get the word out that we were there and that we were not the Tom Cruise version. I didn't really want people going to the theatres thinking they're going to see Tom Cruise's 'War of the Worlds.' I wanted them to see a different version of 'War of the Worlds,' the one based on the book and what Wells conceived."

Most exciting for everyone involved was the fact that this whole situation really put Pendragon on the map, in a matter of speaking. "We're a small independent," he notes. "We've been struggling for years with a bunch of products nobody's ever heard of and barely holding on by our fingernails. But, now, you can't believe the advances and guarantees we were getting because of the Spielberg film. The distributors were anxious and we had people lining up, waiting to distribute this film. It was pretty amazing."

As the 43-year-old Hines explains it, he's spent most of his life dreaming not only of filmmaking in general, but of adapting *The War of the Worlds* in particular. To emphasize the point, he reveals that as a child he read several "making of" pieces in magazines like "Cinefantastique," and was particularly taken by images of building models that were about the size of dressers. And due to the fact that his father was an engineer, he always had access to a machine and wood-making shop, and had been taught, at age 10, how to use both properly. All he needed was the right opportunity.

"I built a bunch of dresser-sized buildings and when my parents went out, I set them up in my room," he recalls. "My parents went out and when I knew they would be out for a good long time, I doused the buildings in lighter fluid and set the city ablaze. I got my camera to film everything and a glass of water to put the fire out. Of course, I splashed the water on it and nothing happened. Pretty soon I was in the kitchen getting pans of water. I ultimately had to hook up the garden hose to put the walls out."

His parents eventually came home - naturally - and were saddled with their first impression that there might be something wrong with their son. "That's how far back it goes with me," he says. "I've always, in some form or another, been thinking about doing a version of *The War of the Worlds*. I've also always had an interest in science fiction and I've done little art films because, in a sense, that's what resources would allow me to do. I also loved Victorian dramas, watched 'Masterpiece Theater,' and saw 'Shakespeare in Love' and 'Sense and Sensibility' in theatres."

By the late 1990s, he observed that computer technology had reached a point where an aspiring filmmaker would create an independent science fiction film from their desktop. As more of an experiment, he created an independent CG-heavy film called "Bug Wars" that was shot on a $200,000 budget, which he thought would be, at best, something of a cult film. Unfortunately, distributors oversold the production "as if it was 'Aliens' done on $20 million," and it never lived up to those expectations. Nonetheless, the film did impress a number of Microsoft founders who, several connections later, led Hines to having a film-making package worth $42 million, which he felt was enough to allow him to shoot a new version of *The War of the Worlds*. He hoped it would be set in the Victorian era, as Wells had had originally intended.

Masterpiece Theater or Independence Day?

"None of these [money] guys were fans of Victorian dramas," says Hines. "At the time there was some Victorian project that came out that wasn't too successful and people were shying away from that notion of it. There was a great deal of pressure from these guys put on me to do it as an updated version." As far as he was concerned, that version had already been done in the form of "Independence Day." As a result, what he knew he needed to do was come up with a version that could satisfy the needs of both his investors and himself.

"So I wrote a version of the script that was a 'Day the Earth Stood Still' kind of thing," he offers. "The first thing these aliens do when they deploy is hit the earth with an EMP weapon to wipe out all technology. The minute I did that, I realized I could actually find a way where I cold do the original book and update it at the same time, because by taking

away all of our modern technology, everybody's on foot, everything is word of mouth, and you don't get to know what's going on in the next village or town. Then what I did was follow the book point by point by point. Even though it was updated in a modern setting, I turned the modern humans into Victorians and I followed it through. The investors were quite pleased with that version."

With financing in place, Pendragon began meeting with various studios, including Paramount, which seemed very open to the idea of talking with Hines about the project. Says the writer/director, "All of their people met with me, they absorbed a ton of information and they then essentially told me to go away."

Once Pendragon moved to the point of pre-production, they were, according to Hines, contacted by Dreamworks and told that Tom Cruise and Steven Spielberg were going to be collaborating on their own version of *The War of the Worlds*. They suggested that Hines invest his money in that project and that he would be "rewarded" later. "Sorry, but you get one life to live and this was an opportunity for me that I wasn't going to pass up."

The Tragic Events of 9/11

By September of 2001, with distribution deals falling into place, Pendragon was getting ready to begin shooting. But then the tragic events of 9/11 happened, and everything in the world changed.

"We had no choice," says Hines. "Our modern version had airplanes falling out of the sky, buildings being blown up, people running in terror. When I watched the real events unfold on TV, there was our screenplay. Not only that, but everything changed financially and the $42 million we had lined up was reduced to $8 million - all within a month." He convinced the remaining investors to allow him to shoot the other script he had written for a project called "Chrome," which was a robot slave story set in the future.. "We shot 'Chrome' in a city block-long brewery and it was beautiful," he enthuses. "It was truly ambitious and it's got 35 CGI characters and every scene is an action scene. The film is like 70% finished right now and there's a trailer for it on our website."

While he was shooting "Chrome," Hines was inspired to retool *The War of the Worlds* project back into a period piece, feeling that in a lot of ways the subject matter was more meaningful in the new climate of the world than ever before. "'War of the Worlds' is really a blueprint for survival in really complicated, difficult times. It's all about keeping your humanity together. At first, I thought this would be like therapy for me. We began rewriting and retooling and in no time we started to draw up plans again. I thought the Victorian era would be a distant enough setting that people could see this and relate to this, but it wouldn't be a story about the Iraqi War while we're in it. It would be 'All Quiet on the Western Front.' It would have these feelings, but it would be distant enough to where people could maybe accept it.

"In this story, there's a great deal of lessons to be learned; triumphs as well as dealing with loss and tragedy, which are the experiences we all have to face," he says. "We don't get a free ride; that's part of what life is. We can go to pieces or we can grow and be wiser from it. This is very much from my heart." The production team reached a point where they were ready to go, and it was decided that the completion of "Chrome," which was taking "forever," would be postponed so that "War of the Worlds" could go into production.

David Versus Goliath

Armed with a budget of approximately $25 million, a wealth of CG knowledge acquired in the interim and a cast of unknowns, they decided to move forward with the project. Interestingly, they eventually learned that certain parties they were associating themselves with actually began giving them advice that, it would later become apparent, was designed to sabotage the project and keep it downplayed in the media from the version that Spielberg and Cruise would eventually do.

"I won't go into the details," Timothy Hines states matter of factly, "but when I look back, it was a continual 'turn left off of that cliff' kind of energy. We didn't understand it then, but after we would take their advice and threw ourselves on the jagged rocks, they'd say, 'Here's what you need to do to take care of yourselves.'" To see if they were, indeed, being manipulated, Hines came up with a plan: St. Patrick's Day of 2004 was approaching, and they decided to leak to these associates that that would be the first day of shooting.

"We wanted to see what would happen," he says. "So St. Patrick's Day comes and Tom Cruise and Steven Spielberg, on St. Patrick's Day, which would have been our first day of filming, come out and make a joint public statement that they're going to start shooting 'War of the Worlds' and it's going to come out in 2006. The reason they would do that is that if it's your first day of shooting, you can't deal with it because there's no time or energy. It takes a week to get a press release out, and by the time you do that it's another publicity cycle. So we immediately shut our associate out. It was one of the biggest smoke and mirror things I've ever done in my life, but we convinced him that our production company was shutting down, and that we were just going to concentrate on the post production of 'Chrome.'"

At that point, Pendragon proceeded to very quietly have everybody involved sign non-disclosure agreements, while terminating anyone who wouldn't. And from that point forward there was no stopping them as they moved into production of the Victorian-era set adaptation of *The War of the Worlds*. Unfortunately, their former associate found out about the production when they shot a sequence involving 200 extras, and he dropped Hines an email stating that he suspected they might be going ahead.

"Within three days," Hines says with a laugh, "Tom Cruise stops making 'Mission Impossible 3,' Steven Spielberg drops his other production he was going to do about the Olympics, and they're suddenly going to fast track 'War of the Worlds.' Now one can say that this is all coincidence and that we're just paranoid. At the same time, if we are paranoid, we're not harming anyone. But why are they suddenly fast tracking the film when they were going to do it for 2006? There is no other explanation. So they started making their version and announced that they were going to start shooting in September. But we were already deep in production.

"I knew it was essential that before he began filming that we had to announce that we had finished filming," he continues. "We did so and it was the best move we ever made, because it put us in the place where we deserved to be, which was a place of integrity. We were making this movie not to be on the coattails of Steven Spielberg, but because we wanted to make 'War of the Worlds.' I had been planning on doing that for years."

From that point on, any gains Pendragon's version of the project made from the amount of money Paramount in promoting their was, a free gift from the universe that they could freely accept without any loss of integrity.

"We're not pirates," emphasizes Hines. "We can walk in the sunlight with our heads held high. They were frustrated and didn't know what to do. Every time they tried to overwhelm us with their publicity, we got the hits off that and they couldn't do anything about it. Honestly, we made jokes that they're kind of like Wile E. Coyote strapping themselves into Acme rocket shoes, and we're the Road Runner just floating along eating our little birdseed. And here comes the Paramount Coyote, shooting past us and into a wall.

"They tried to tell us we have to stop using the name 'War of the Worlds' because we're infringing on their trademark," he closes. "We immediately shot back and said, 'Not only are we not infringing on your trademark, but we've noticed that you've been kind of designing your artwork to look like ours.' If they tried an unfair competition complaint, who was there first? Who would get shot down by the courts? If they pushed too hard, they could have found themselves shut down because they were treading on the ground of a little independent."

The Cast

Unlike Spielberg, Timothy Hines selected the members of his cast from among those actors who had worked with him on "Chrome" or who had done other promising work on the British stage. For the role of the Writer, who is essentially the protagonist in the novel, Hines hired Anthony Piana. Piana spent his time preparing for the role by reading about H. G. Wells. "I read about his childhood and early parental influences that would come to shape his world," he explained, "catching insights of his own personal habits, oddities and reactions to his surroundings." He also felt the Victorian costumes helped him with the rest of the part.

Jack Clay became Piana's comrade as Ogilvy, the person who first reaches the cylinder on Horsell Common. Clay was very enthusiastic about their film version. He said, "I loved working for him [Hines] and only hope my performance half measures up to his inspiration. He is, of course, wonderfully supported and encouraged by the radiant Susan Goforth, who believes with equal passion in this project. The mounting excitement over the appearance of the film is well founded. I can only say, wow!"

For the pivotal role of the Artilleryman, Hines selected James Lathrop. Lathrop, a relative newcomer, developed the character initially out of his own military service in Saudi Arabia during Desert Storm. "As the Artilleryman enters into the battle for the first time, he is young and outwardly confident, but is quickly broken down as his fellow mates are violently killed all around him. Overall there is a wonderful arc to the character of the Artilleryman. He moves from the utter shock and horror in the massive destruction he sees all about him, to finding strength in teaching the writer how to survive, to finding a resolve in surviving in the world under the complete domination of the Martians. In the resolve of war and survival the Artilleryman never gives up, even as he loses his own perspective."

John Kaufmann had been a second unit director on "Red Betsy" (2003), "The Life" (2002), and "Tadpole" (2002) when he was tapped by Hines to play the Curate. "My character," he revealed, "has developed a rather complicated set of psychological dysfunction, amongst which is a kind of an eating disorder: When he's frightened, he deals with it by eating. Well, when you're trapped in a house surrounded by Martians, you're pretty much frightened all the time. So I would eat anything I can get my hands on. The longer we were in the house, the more pathological my eating became. We had a scene where I'm eating this big brick of moldy cheese."

Susan Goforth, who wrote the screenplay with Timothy Hines, may have seemed like an odd choice to play the very Victorian Mrs. Elphinstone as she had previously been cast as sex symbol in "Beat Angel" (2004), but she pulled off the task with a great deal of style and panache. Jamie Lynn Sease was cast as Miss Elphinstone, the young woman who, fleeing with her mother from London, becomes

caught up in the panic of the approaching Martian hordes. Darlene Sellers, best known for playing women of easy virtue in films like "The Winter of Her" (2004), "Bug Wars" (2000), "Dinosaur Island" (1994) (as a cave girl), and "California Hot Wax" (1992) (as a bikini girl), also stars.

The Theatrical Release

The Pendragon Production of "War of the Worlds" was scheduled to be released in the United States on March 25, 2005, but several weeks before its debut, the film was inexplicably delayed. With the DVD release already scheduled for June, the producer looked for an appropriate date in April or May. At the time of this writing, the film premiere was just weeks away, but no one was willing to wager against the independent production that took on the megabudget giant.

On October 30, 2004, moviegoers and fans of H. G. Wells's classic novel had the rare opportunity to examine production maquettes, stills, and original footage of the Timothy Hines film at Paul Allen's Science Fiction Museum and Hall of Fame in Seattle, Washington. The new exhibit, which will run for one year, also features dozens of book editions, radio, film and stage adaptations, and array of artists' interpretations of the Martian invasion. Sci-fi fans were not only pleased to learn about the impact of the 1898 novel on popular culture but were also thrilled to discover Hollywood (or at least Pendragon Productions) had finally listened to them. For more than fifty years, they had been clammering for an authentic adaptation of *The War of the Worlds*, and now, at last, the great Tripods were ready to stomp onto the silver screen.

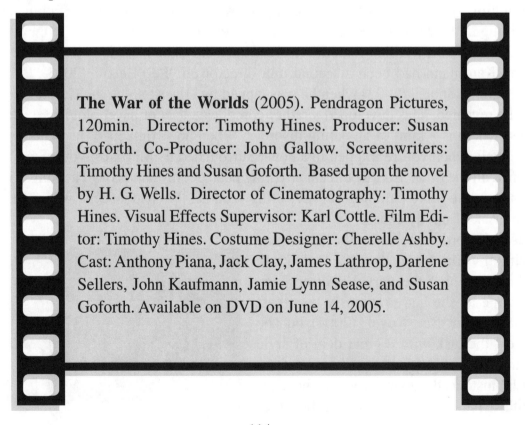

The War of the Worlds (2005). Pendragon Pictures, 120min. Director: Timothy Hines. Producer: Susan Goforth. Co-Producer: John Gallow. Screenwriters: Timothy Hines and Susan Goforth. Based upon the novel by H. G. Wells. Director of Cinematography: Timothy Hines. Visual Effects Supervisor: Karl Cottle. Film Editor: Timothy Hines. Costume Designer: Cherelle Ashby. Cast: Anthony Piana, Jack Clay, James Lathrop, Darlene Sellers, John Kaufmann, Jamie Lynn Sease, and Susan Goforth. Available on DVD on June 14, 2005.

CHAPTER NINE: THE SPIELBERG FILM

I have been thinking about The War of the Worlds most of my adult life. Because number one, I saw the original movie – I think I saw it on television – the George Pal film in 1953. And then, when I was in college, I read the book for the first time, and I thought the book was extraordinary. I always had War of the Worlds in mind. But then a couple of movies came out in the last fifteen years that cherry-picked the best elements of War of the Worlds. And I thought maybe it's just been cherry-picked to death and there's nothing left. Then I read the novel again, and I realized an almost entirely new way of telling the story that no one has ever seen before. I got re-inspired, and I approached Tom [Cruise] and Paula Wagner. We all agreed that it would be a good idea. Any way, it's a movie I have wanted to make most of my career.
—Steven Spielberg, Interview, March 2005

In 2005, Steven Spielberg returned to familiar territory with his big budget remake of "The War of the Worlds," a story that has fueled his imagination for twelve years ever since he bought the radio script of the Orson Welles broadcast. More like "Jaws" (1975) and "Jurassic Park" (1993) than "Close Encounters of the Third Kind" (1977) and perennial favorite "E.T.-The Extraterrestrial" (1982), his latest blockbuster still had the Oscar-winning director looking to the night skies for inspiration. Several other big-budget science fiction films, including "Independence Day" and "Signs," had already "picked the bones" clean of the 1898 classic, and a rival production had moved most of the action to Victorian England. So, when Spielberg looked again at those twinkling lights, he found a new way to tell the familiar story. He planned to focus on a working class family and their reaction to the invasion. Teamed with Tom Cruise, his collaborator on "Minority Report" (2002), and Dakota Fanning, the starchild from "Taken" (2002), Spielberg launched his own assault on the summer cineplexes, and terrified a whole new generation of moviegoers with his invasion from Mars.

"If I could have, I would have begun this movie twelve years ago," Spielberg explained. "I bought at an auction the last surviving War of the Worlds radio script and it was amazing. I guess you could say a distillation of the novel. I thought it would make an amazing movie, but when 'Independence Day' came out, I was convinced they had picked the bones of what I wanted to do, and put me off for a while." But a desire to work again with Tom Cruise brought the project back into mind. He added, "I got interested in it again just in the course of trying to find something to do with Tom."

When Spielberg learned that Pendragon Pictures was readying its own version of the classic alien invasion novel for the summer of 2005, the 58-year-old director put an untitled project about the 1972 Munich Olympics on hold. Then he convinced Cruise to delay the start of principle photography on "Mission Impossible 3" for several months so he could star in "War of the Worlds" first. And finally, following two days of frenzied negotiations with DreamWorks and Paramount Pictures, pre-production was rushed ahead to ensure his adaptation of the H. G. Wells novel would start shooting in November 2004 with a 2005 release date. The first volley in the war of "The War of the Worlds" had been fired.

The Top Secret Plot

The trade ads read: "This summer [2005], the earth goes to war. From Paramount Pictures comes the motion picture even of the year: Steven Spielberg's War of the Worlds, starring international superstar Tom Cruise."

Spielberg's contemporary retelling of the H. G. Wells's seminal classic reveals the extraordinary battle for the future of humankind through the eyes of one American family fighting to survive it. Ray Ferrier (Tom Cruise) is a working class man living in Bayonne, New Jersey. He's estranged from his two children, Robbie (Justin Chatwin) and Rachel (Dakota Fanning), and his ex-wife Mary Ann (Miranda Otto) thinks he is just a lowlife dockworker; his life isn't in order, and he's too caught up with himself and his own problems. But then, the unthinkable and, ultimately, the most unexpected thing happens to him. His small town life is shaken violently by the arrival of destructive invaders from Mars, who have come en masse to destroy Earth. The Martians begin by setting off a pulse weapon that appears to be a simple electrical storm that fries all of the alarm clocks and toasters and cars in town. They then begin to plow through the city and countryside in a wave of mass destruction and violence, ripping up streets, and bridges, and whole towns in their way. Ray recognizes the threat, and comes to the defense of his family. As the world must fend for itself by a new and very advanced enemy not of this world, it's inhabitants must save humanity from a far greater force that threatens to destroy it. He and his friend Ogilvy (Tim Robbins) take arms, escape to the safety of the dense wooded countryside, and fight for their lives and the lives of Robbie and Rachel.

While the actual plot of the film was kept top secret from the press, much of the action was "taken" from several familiar sources. In addition to the H. G. Wells novel, "War of the Worlds" pays homage to several other successful films by borrowing key plot elements and action scenes that had previously worked before. From "Signs" (2002), Spielberg borrowed the family in crisis theme. M. Night Shyamalan's thriller of an alien invasion was told from the point of view of a small family living in rural Bucks County, Pennsylvania. After the death of his wife in a freak car accident, Reverend Graham Hess (Mel Gibson), his two children (Rory Culkin and Abigail Breslin), and brother (Joaquin Phoenix) are still struggling with the loss six months later. The appearance of a gigantic crop circle on his farm signals the beginning of an invasion from space, and Hess must protect his fam-

ily from the onslaught. In "War of the Worlds," Cruise takes on a similar role to Gibson. But instead of playing the grieving father, he is the self-absorbed father who has lost his wife to another man. With his close, socially-inept friend (instead of a socially-inept brother), he finds himself having to protect his two precocious children from the alien onslaught. Not surprisingly, both stories feature rural settings on the East Coast, a stone's throw away from Grover's Mill, New Jersey.

From "Independence Day" and a host of similar films, Spielberg borrowed the larger than life struggle against a superior alien force with grand state-of-the-art special effect set-pieces. But instead of devastating huge metropolitan cities like New York and Los Angeles, he let his aliens rip through the town of Bayonne, New Jersey. The effect of mass panic and fear was the same as the citizens of the town, like Vivica Fox and her son in "Independence Day," raced for safety. The fact that Spielberg's Martians are destroyed by a virus in much the same way that they are killed in the original Wells novel and "Independence Day" was merely providential.

"I think what makes 'War of the Worlds,' at least the version that we're making, really exciting, is you get to really see what's happening to the people in the story," the fifty-eight year-old director explained. "The film is ultra-realistic, as ultra-realistic as I've ever attempted to make a movie, in terms of its documentary style. But at the same time, it's full of the kind of Hollywood production values that the audience is demanding these days. And I think it's the combination, the blend, of these huge events visually and this kind of documentary story, personal story at the center of it, that gives it this very unique—"

Production Notes

The original George Pal version of "War of the Worlds" required nearly three years to make. Spielberg and his team were given less than ten months to do everything, from the rough screenplay through the complex special effects, casting, pre-production, and princi-

pal photography work, and then onto the finished product.

From the beginning, Spielberg was convinced that characterization would be the spine of his film. "We are telling a story about people, not machines," he explained. Yet even before David Koepp had finished the screenplay, Spielberg initiated special effects work that would allow him to use certain special visuals during principal photography. Although an unusual step, it was necessary if the film were to be completed in time for the summer box office season.

"We shot many of the big effect sequences first so ILM (Industrial Light and Magic) could get a jump on their shot list," he said. "New Jersey was all the big effect scenes, and we didn't want snow, because you can't be consistent with snow. You can get a great day and it's beautiful, and it's snowing, and then three days later it's gone. And then it's hundreds of thousands of dollars if not millions of dollars for a combination of digital effects and physical effects to snow in, you know, 50 acres of city streets and farmland. So it was good that we shot it when we did, but we did front load the movie with effect shots so ILM could have a head start and we could make our June 29th release date. There are 400 digital shots in the movie, but I'm not rushing it. This is my longest schedule in about 12 years."

During the coldest November on record, the town of Bayonne, New Jersey (population 68,000) was invaded by Paramount Pictures and Steven Spielberg for filming several key sequences. One local resident told the *Jersey Journal* that he received a knock-on-the-door from Spielberg, who wanted to inspect his home for use in the film. Four hours later, he said, he received another visitor from a location scout who told him that Spielberg wanted to shoot part of the film in his home. Crew members returned to his home to take measurements and to remove his outdoor pool. When city officials were told that the studio wanted to build a structure on a local Little League field and blow it up, they were more than eager to comply with the request. Bayonne Law Director John Coffey II noted that a local ordinance "calls for a payment of $50 a day for a permit to film on city streets, but this (build and destroy plan) is a bit different." At least, while filming the elaborate sequel at the Little League field, the weather cooperated, and it didn't snow.

More important to Spielberg than snow, however, was Koepp's reworking of the hundred-year-old tale. (David Koepp had previously worked to develop Michael Crichton's Jurassic Park into the screenplay Spielberg used to make the hit movie.) The "bare bones" of the Wells novel had already been picked clean by several other, recent blockbusters, including "Independence Day," and the Academy Award-winning director wanted to make certain his film stayed focused on the human element that perhaps had been missing in those previous motion pictures.

Spielberg felt that updating the story to the present day and adding a divorced dad (Cruise) and a couple of kids (Chatwin, Fanning) would make the motion picture more accessible to modern audience members. He was absolutely convinced that the story, not the hardware, was what made *The War of the Worlds* interesting to him when he first read the book. "There are elements of Wells's novel in the movie," the director explained. "We have the tripods. We have the red weed growing all over. But I never thought of doing it as a period piece at the turn of the century. It just wasn't an interesting way to go. I just can't stand the styles of that time."

After he had read and approved the first draft by Koepp, just prior to the start of principal photography, Spielberg set up an unprecedented communications link between the filmmaker's Dreamworks offices, his location sites in New Jersey, and the screenwriter's secluded residence in Los Angeles. The advanced all-digital network enabled Spielberg and Koepp to discuss their story ideas, technical points, and screenplay revisions. From a practical standpoint, Steven Spielberg would leave a file in his computer at the end of his long workday, which Koepp read at his computer. By the time Spielberg returned to his computer the following morning, he would usually find a responding file from Koepp, waiting to be read.

Tom Cruise was also excited by Koepp's adaptation, and didn't mind postponing "Mission Impossible 3" to make the movie. "The minute I read the script, I knew I had to do it" he remarked. "I mean, for me, *War of the Worlds* was always a book that I really enjoyed and I felt that the story could be relevant, that the opportunity for character, all the elements are exciting… Obviously to work with my friend again. I'm playing a father in this. How much of the story am I allowed to give away? (Laughs) All of it! You know, to play a father, the things that are very important to me in my life. It's really a very small, emotional movie."

The last time Steven Spielberg made a very small, emotional movie about aliens, he produced "E.T.-The Extraterrestrial" (1982), which grossed $435 million domestically and landed in the top spot as the highest box office earner in history. So expectations were rather high for his latest "close encounter," particularly with the biggest star in the world sharing screen time with little green men, when the $135 million sci-fi thriller debuted at the local Cineplex in 2005. But Spielberg was the first person to caution moviegoers that "War of the Worlds" was a much darker, scarier film than what his fans were used to seeing. His invaders from Mars were not likely to be satisfied by a handful of Reese's Pieces.

When asked whether the third film in his alien trilogy, which includes "Close Encounters of the Third Kind" and "E.T.," was a reflection of the unsettled times that we live in, Steven Spielberg confessed that he was simply "an equal opportunity director."

"I gave the benevolent aliens a couple of shots, and now I'm going to try my hand at the worst kind," he said with a laugh. "You know, the kind that's just bent on ending civilization as we know it and beginning their own; if you read the original book, you know, they terraform the planet, they reap and sow. So I really have great respect for the book, but not to the extent that I would set the movie back in 1898. I was not going to do a Victorian science fiction movie. There's been others out there very successful and others maybe less successful, but we've seen the sci-fi Victorian period done before, we've all seen the contemporary sci-fi film done before. I feel more at home today, in today's world. And I think, in the shadow of 9/11, there is a little relevance with how we are all so unsettled in our feelings about our collective futures. And that's why I think, when I reconsidered *War of the Worlds*, post 9/11, it began to make more sense to me, that it could be a tremendous emotional story as well as very entertaining one, and have some kind of current relevance."

Fifty-two years have passed since George Pal and Byron Haskin first collaborated with Barre Lyndon on the screenplay that became their hit film. It has been even longer since H. G. Wells wrote the original novel, upon which a radio drama, several motion picture adaptations, and a short-lived television series were based. And in the years that have passed since the first film opened in 1953, men have walked on the moon, sent orbital laboratories and reusable space vehicles into space, and through the use of unmanned probes, photographed, studied and even landed upon some of our neighboring planets, including Mars.

Spielberg assured me that, while his film was totally original, he did not discount the George Pal version. "One of the great things that the Pal film did do was, it did create, before its time, in 1953, a tremendous sense of dread, a tremendous sense of tension and dread. Contemporary dread. And I don't think a science fiction movie had ever done that before or since," he said. "I wanted to capture that sense of dread in my movie. We don't go back to the Pal film, however; we have some obvious homages to the Pal film that I think the audience is going to love, but not many." When I pushed him for details, particularly about whether he was going to have his Martians using tripod machines, he acknowledged with a resounding "yes," but would not reveal anything more. "That's the only secret I'm going to give you, because you know what?" Spielberg quipped. "We have so many surprises in this movie that you're just going to have to see it yourself."

Throughout the production, a strict closed-set policy was enforced by uniformed guards throughout the production. The policy was designed to prevent distractions for the cast and crew as well as to place a veil of secrecy over the film. Pages of the script were color-coded, and each script carried its own code-number. Spielberg and his talented crew were well aware of the rival production that was filming in England and the Pacific Northwest as well as a low-budget quickie, featuring C. Thomas Howell, that was also in production. The last thing the fifty-eight year-old director wanted to discover was scenes (or whole segments) of his carefully guarded production showing up in the dailies of the other two films that were shooting. The pressure to produce a successful motion picture that is enjoyed by audiences wishing to beat the summer's scorching heat as well as satisfy critics of the filmmaker rests squarely on Steven Spielberg's shoulders. The pressure is compounded by a tight production schedule, a huge budget that is shared between Dreamworks and Paramount Pictures, and two rival productions. With barely ten months and a relentless time clock ticking between the start of production in November and the June 29 release of "War of the Worlds" in theatres around the worlds, Spielberg found himself immersed in an incredibly ambitious under-taking all by himself.

"After 'Independence Day' came out, and was successful, I was disappointed that my desire to make 'War of the Worlds' had ended," he commented. "But then I read the book again, and I found a notion that was so wonderful, so startling to me that I felt there was a chance to make a film that was truly moving."

As a filmmaker, Spielberg brings a keen visual sense to his films, a style he endures by talking on the responsibilities of director and producer and sometimes writer. Yet creative insight is something Spielberg grew up with. He was born in Cincinnati, Ohio, in 1946. He started making movies when he was a very young man, often involving many of his local playmates (and even his parents) in the productions. Among his early directing efforts were "Battle Squad" (1961), which combined World War Two footage of an airplane with foot-age he shot of his friends, "Escape to Nowhere" (1961), another World War Two film with his sister Anne, and "The Last Gun" (1959), a western. All of these were short films, but they taught him how to use the camera to tell a story. In 1964, he directed "Firelight," his first film about aliens, and then "Amblin'" in 1968. His artistic training at Long Beach University, which was cut short by his burning desire to learn everything there is to know about film, preceded his early career as a television director at Universal. At the time, Spielberg was assigned to direct an episode of "Columbo" one week or "Fame is the Name of the Game" the next week or "Marcus Welby, M.D." the following week. The regiment was very grueling, and pushed him to the limits of his endurance. All of his work in television was just the beginning of the gathering storm of talent that would become the Spielberg that made the brilliant films he would later become known for internationally.

After filming a segment of "Night Gallery," which featured Joan Crawford, he was assigned a movie-of-the-week titled "Duel" (1971). His creativity and craftsmanship combined with the Richard Matheson story to make one of the most impressive film debuts in the history of the cinema. "Duel," starring Dennis Weaver and a deadly truck from hell, became the highest rated movie-of-the-week in ratings history. In many ways, the tele-film is a precursor to "Jaws," with its relentless chase and its universal theme about man against the forces of nature.

Spielberg realized at that point there was an essential difference between what he was being paid to do as part of his contract at Universal and what he really wanted to do as a feature film director. Shortly after "Duel," he turned to directing feature films, and teamed with Goldie Hawn to make "Sugarland Express" (1974). Even though the motion picture was not a box office success, it was critically well-received, and paved the way for his next outing. "Jaws" (1975), based upon the best seller by Peter Benchley, became a runaway hit at the box office. This classic shark attack tale started the tradition of the summer blockbuster, for no other film in the history of movies had ever earned as much money in such a short period of time. He followed "Jaws" with "Close Encounters of the Third Kind" (1977), "1941" (1979), and "Raiders of the Lost Ark" (1981). "E.T.-The Extraterrestrial" (1982), another one of the biggest blockbusters of all time, not only made him a fortune, but also established him as the top director in Hollywood. He won his first Academy Award as Best Director for "Schindler's List" (1993), as well as an Academy Award for Best Film, and his second for "Saving Private Ryan" (1998). In addition to two other Indiana Jones films (with his pal George Lucas), he has made "The Color Purple" (1985), "Empire of the Sun" (1987), "Always" (1989), "Hook" (1991), "Jurassic Park" (1993) and its first sequel, "The Lost World" (1997), "Amistad" (1997), "Artificial Intelligence" (2001), "Minority Report" (2002), "Catch Me If You Can" (2002), and "The Terminal" (2004), among others.

In addition to his work as a director, Steven Spielberg is also an influential producer and co-creator of Dreamworks Pictures. He produced his first film, the forgettable "I Wanna Hold Your Hand," in 1978, and followed his first effort with "Use Cars" (1980), a critically acclaimed but mostly forgotten Kurt Russell comedy. His stock as a producer continued to rise with "Poltergeist" in 1982, followed by the "Back to the Future" trilogy, "Amazing Stories" (1985), "Twister" (1996), "Men in Black" (1997), and the award-winning "Band of Brothers" (2001).

The filmmaker enjoys a lifestyle away from the traps and trappings of Hollywood. He is happily married to Kate Capshaw, and a proud father.

About the Cast

Moviegoers first met Tom Cruise (Ray Ferrier) in the small role of Billy in "Endless Love" (1981), and from the outset he exhibited an undeniable box office appeal to both male and female audiences. That could explain why he is the biggest star in the world today. But he still remembers humbly his breakout role as Joel Goodsen in "Risky Business" (1983). "Losin' It" (1983) and "All the Right Moves" (1983) were next, along with Ridley Scott's "Legend" (1985). With "Top Gun" (1986), he displayed another side of his persona as the cocky Lt. Maverick Mitchell, and landed him lots of critical acclaim and personal satisfaction.

In his next few films, audiences saw many different sides of Cruise, first opposite Paul Newman in "The Color of Money" (1986), then opposite Dustin Hoffman in "Rain Man" (1988), and finally, as the disabled Vietnam veteran Ron Kovic in Oliver's Stone's "Born on the Fourth of July" (1989). That role landed him a Golden Globe and the first of three Academy Award nominations. His second nomination was for "Jerry Macquire" (1997), and his third came ten years after his first for his role of Frank T. J. Mackey in "Magnolia" (1999)

Born in 1962 in Syracuse, New York, Thomas Cruise Mapother IV, the only son of four children, spent most of his early years eternally on the move with his nomadic parents. By the time he was 14 he had attended 15 different schools in the US and Canada. He finally settled in Glen Ridge, New Jersey, with his mother and her new husband, and contemplated a life as a Franciscan priest. Later, while in high school, he developed an interest in acting and abandoned his plans of becoming a priest, dropped out of school, and at age 18 headed for New York and a possible acting career. The next 15 years of his life are the stuff of legends. He rocketed from an unknown actor in huge cattle calls to one of the top 100 movie stars of all time. His films include "A Few Good Men" (1992), "The Firm" (1993), "Interview With the Vampire" (1994), "Mission Impossible" (1996), "Eyes Wide Shut" (1999), "Vanilla Sky" (2001), "The Last Samurai" (2003), and "Collateral" (2004).

Behind the incredibly cute looks and childlike demeanor lies the distinguished actress of dozen movie performances, and she is only eleven years old. Hannah Dakota Fanning was born February 23, 1994, in Conyers, Georgia, USA. Before her debut into the cinematic world, Dakota would play-act around her house; she would often put a cloth underneath her shirt, and pretend that she was going through labor, using her little sister Elle Fanning as the baby! A local talent scout advised her parents to take Dakota to an agency, which specialized in child actors, in Los Angeles. Her family spent six weeks in California during this process, and now Dakota lives in the LA area. Her first movie role was as a little girl in the park in the movie "Tomcats" (2001), which was soon followed by the role of Clairee in "Father Xmas" (2001). However, her breakout performance as Lucy in the hit film "I Am

Sam" (2001) opposite Sean Penn and Michelle Pfeiffer, won her an award for her outstanding performance - and she was only seven years old at the time! Dakota then went on to star in many more movies, playing Young Melanie in "Sweet Home Alabama" (2002), Sally in "The Cat in the Hat" (2003), Pita Ramos in "Man on Fire" (2004), opposite Denzel Washington, and Emily in "Hide and Seek" (2005). Her first contact with Steven Spielberg came as Allison "Allie" Clarke, the star child, in the Sci-Fi Channel original miniseries "Taken" (2002).

Tim Robbins, who plays Ogilvy in "War of the Worlds," won an Academy Award for his performance as the troubled Dave Boyle in "Mystic River" (2003), but most genre fans remember him as Astronaut Woody Blake who sacrifices himself for his comrades in "Mission to Mars" (2000). Robbins studied drama at UCLA where he graduated with honors in 1981. That same year, he formed the Actors' Gang, an experimental ensemble that expressed radical political observations through the European avant-garde form of theater. He started film work in TV movies in 1983, but hit the big time in 1988 with his portrayal of the dimwitted fastball pitcher "Nuke" Laloosh in "Bull Durham" (1988). Tall and handsome with baby-faced looks, he was perfectly cast as the innocent man in "The Shawshank Redemption" (1994). He has also played his share of slick conmen in films as diverse as "The Player" (1992) and "Bob Roberts" (1992). Miranda Otto, fresh from "The Lord of the Rings" trilogy, David Alan Basche, James DuMont, Justin Chatwin, and Ann Robinson round out the cast with their assorted talents and skills as actors.

Spielberg's Close Encounters With Aliens

For how many years did we gaze into the night sky, wondering, "Are we indeed alone? Is man nothing more than an accident in the universe, an orphan race lost forever in the void of space?" Only Steven Spielberg knows the answer to that question.

When Spielberg was just eighteen, he directed a movie about aliens menacing the citizens of a small town titled "Firelight." For a low-low budget production that was shot with family and friends, the 140-minute film featured all of the familiar stereotypes from a sci-fi thriller, including a mad German scientist. Spielberg premiered the movie at Phoenix Little Theatre (now the Phoenix Theatre) in Phoenix, Arizona, and sold tickets to all of his neighbors. The motion picture was a resounding success. After the closing frame, the entire audience was on its feet cheering. The young filmmaker had reaped his first rewards from a tale about aliens and flying saucers, and that success, in many ways, signaled the direction that his career might take.

In 1977, with a considerably larger budget and the backing of a major studio, Spielberg unveiled "Close Encounters of the Third Kind" to moviegoers, and captured the hearts and minds of his audience once again with a tale about aliens and flying saucers. This classic one-of-a-kind science fiction film told the story of working-class cableman Roy Neary (Richard Dreyfuss) and his "close encounter" with strange visitors from outer space. When

Neary sets out to determine what happened to him, along with several others (including Melinda Dillon), the U.S. Government stages an elaborate cover-up to keep people away from the aliens' landing site. However, Neary and his friends share a vision which draws them to Devil's Tower, Wyoming, and a meeting with the alien visitors. What makes this movie work is not necessarily the extraterrestrials and the special effects that surround them (although they are tremendous) but the stories of the characters who know they've witnessed something extraordinary and are not afraid to pursue their vision without knowing why they're pursuing it. Spielberg does certainly exploit the familiar trappings of flying saucer mythology, with references to the Bermuda Triangle, missing time, alien abduction, and a governmental cover-up to hide the truth. But his wide-eyed, optimistic, childlike vision makes the film one of the most enchanting of all movie-going experiences.

Five years later, Spielberg revisited the mythology with a smaller, more emotional film titled "E.T.-The Extraterrestrial" (1982), which began one of the biggest blockbuster moneymakers of all time. When visiting Earth at night, one of a group of alien botanists is left behind stranded on this planet. Fortunately, the extraterrestrial soon finds a friend and emotional companion in 10-year-old Elliot (Henry Thomas), who discovered him looking for food in his family's garden shed. While E.T. slowly gets acquainted with Elliot's brother Michael (Robert MacNaughton), his sister Gertie (Drew Barrymore) as well as with Earth customs, members of a U.S. Government task force (including Peter Coyote) work day and night to track down the whereabouts of Earth's first visitor from Outer Space. The wish to go home again is strong in E.T., and after being able to communicate with Elliot and the others, E.T. starts building an improvised device to send a message home for his folks to come and pick him up. With the help of Elliot and his friends, E.T. manages to elude the task force, and reach his spaceship safely. Spielberg's film is full of whimsy and charm, and tugs at the heartstrings, particularly in the final scene when Elliot must let E.T. go home. Like "Close Encounters of the Third Kind," the filmmaker brings a sense of awe and wonder to every scene. The fact that the movie was set at Halloween, many years after the famous Orson Welles radio broadcast, suggests that Spielberg was invoking our greatest fears, and saying that there was really nothing to fear at all.

Our greatest fears about an alien invasion were what the U.S. Government hoped to exploit in order to keep the secret about Roswell and alien abductions from the public in Steven Spielberg's "Taken" (2002). Written by Leslie Bohem, from ideas by the award-winning director, the story spans five decades and four generations, centering on three families—the Keys, the Crawfords, and the Clarkes. World War Two veteran Russell Keys (Steve Burton) is plagued by nightmares of his abduction by aliens during the war, and leaves his wife and son shortly after returning home. In 1947, the Roswell incident transforms Owen Crawford (Joel Gretsch) from an ambitious Air Force captain to evil shadow government con-

spirator who will stop at nothing, including the murder of his own wife, to maintain the secret. The unhappily married Sally Clarke (Catherine Dent) is impregnated by an alien visitor (Eric Close), and her offspring triggers several future events. As the decades go by, the heirs of each family are affected by the machinations of the aliens, culminating with the birth of Allie Keys (Dakota Fanning), who is the final product of the aliens' experimentations. She alone holds the key to their future. While the television miniseries, which aired on the Sci-Fi channel, was not without its faults or criticism, the ten-part (877 min.) series returned Spielberg back his early roots. The scope of the project was enormous, and brought the whole flying saucer mythology – from Area 51, Project Blue Book and Roswell to alien abductions, alien autopsies, and missing time – into focus. The earlier episodes are particularly engrossing with the threat and menace of invasion always at hand.

The invasion is real in "War of the Worlds" (2005), and with his latest "close encounter," Steven Spielberg returns full circle to his origins. "The whole thing is very experiential," he concludes. "The point of view is very personal. Everybody, I think, in the world, will be able to relate to the point of view, because it's about a family trying to survive and stay together, and they're surrounded by the most epically horrendous events you could possibly imagine."

War of the Worlds (2005). Dreamworks/Paramount Pictures, 140 min. Director: Steven Spielberg. Producers: Kathleen Kennedy, Paula Wagner, and Colin Wilson. Screenwriter: David Koepp. Based upon the novel by H. G. Wells. Music Composer: John Williams. Cinematographer: Janusz Kaminski. Editor: Michael Kahn. Production Designer: Rick Carter. Visual Effects Supervisor: Brad Alexander. Cast: Tom Cruise, Tim Robbins, Miranda Otto, Dakota Fanning, Justin Chatwin, David Alan Basche, James DuMont, Yul Vazquez, Daniel Franzese, Miguel Ferrer, and Ann Robinson.

CHAPTER TEN: OTHER ALIEN INVASIONS

Good morning. In less than an hour, aircraft from here will join others from around the world. And you will be launching the largest aerial battle in the history of mankind. "Mankind." That word should have new meaning for all of us today. We can't be consumed by our petty differences anymore. We will be united in our common interests. Perhaps it's fate that today is the Fourth of July, and you will once again be fighting for our freedom... Not from tyranny, oppression, or persecution... but from annihilation. We are fighting for our right to live. To exist. And should we win the day, the Fourth of July will no longer be known as an American holiday, but as the day the world declared in one voice: "We will not go quietly into the night! We will not vanish without a fight!" We're going to live on! We're going to survive! Today we celebrate our Independence Day!

—*President Thomas Whitmore, Independence Day (1996)*

H.G. Wells's seminal novel *The War of the Worlds* (1898) has not only inspired several cinematic adaptations, including the most recent one with Tom Cruise, but has also influenced dozens of other films as well. While somewhat of a cliché today, the notion that monstrous invaders from another world would travel vast cosmic distances to conquer Earth was once a completely new one. Back in 1951, when Michael Rennie as Klaatu stepped out of his silver flying saucer with his giant robot Gort and demanded to be taken to our leaders in "The Day the Earth Stood Still," cinema-going audiences had never seen an alien before. Now, slightly more than fifty years later, we've become so accustomed to aliens invading our space, it's really hard to imagine the idea was once fresh. You'll just have to take my word for it. So, what follows is a trip back down memory lane when the word "alien" meant a visitor from space and "invasion" was a cosmic struggle for existence between monstrous invaders and humanity's best and finest.

The Adventures of Buckaroo Banzai Across the 8th Dimension (1984). Twentieth Century-Fox, 103min. Director: W.D. Richter. Producers: Richter and Neil Canton. Writer: Earl MacRauch. Cast: Peter Weller, John Lithgow, Ellen Barkin, Jeff Goldblum, Christopher Lloyd, Lewis Smith, Clancy Brown and Vincent Schiavelli.

What did happen at Grover's Mill in October of 1938? Was Orson Welles part of an invasion plot that involved mass hypnosis? Are there extraterrestrial biological entities living among us? In W. D. Richter's highly imaginative, action-packed, science fiction-romance-adventure comedy, Buckaroo Banzai and his crime-fighting Hong Kong Cavaliers must battle evil creatures from the 8th dimension (all named John) that came to conquer Earth in 1938, and are still hanging around, waiting to get their hands on the oscillation overthruster. Even though the film was dismissed by most critics as "strange" and "unintelligible" and snubbed by the majority of the movie going public for being "too hip," it has since become a cult favorite.

Alien Containment (1981). Cannon Films/Italian Pictures, 85 min. Director and Screenwriter: Lewis Coates. Producer: Claudio Mancini. Cast: Ian McCulloch, Louis Monroe, Sigfried Rauch, Martin Mase, and Lisa Hahn.

In yet another "Alien" rip-off, a cyclopean creature from Mars tricks a former astronaut (Rauch) into helping spread its alien eggs all over the earth. When the ship laden with eggs finally crash-lands in New York City (with every member of its crew dead), the alien threat is discovered. The mission commander (McCulloch) teams with a Brooklyn cop (Mase) and a government agent (Monroe) to track the eggs back to their source. Writer-director Coates guides audiences through a very familiar landscape to a predictable conclusion. Set the snooze alarm on your clock to keep you from dozing off between scenes.

Alien Nation (1988). 20th Century Fox, color, 91 min. Director: Graham Baker. Writer: Rockne S. O'Bannon. Producers: Gale Anne Hurd and Richard Kobritz. Cast: James Caan, Mandy Patinkin, Terence Stamp and Leslie Bevis.

In the near future, an alien civilization comes to earth. These humanoid aliens (with seemingly larger bald heads, different taste buds, and a fear of saltwater), called Newcomers, are slowly brought into humankind's society. Despite facing severe discrimination, a Newcomer police detective Sam Francisco (Patinkin) is teamed with a somewhat redneck fellow detective Detective Sgt. Matthew Sykes (Caan) to investigate a new drug in play in the Newcomer underworld. As a Newcomer crime boss, Terrence Stamp is a scene stealer. The mix of action and comedy is entertaining. Caan's hard-boiled performance was the right note to play off the "humanity" of Patinkin's Francisco. A TV spinoff series followed.

Alien Vs. Predator (2004). (aka AvP). 20th Century Fox, color, 111 min. Director: Paul W. S. Anderson. Writers: Paul W. S. Anderson, Dan O'Bannon, etc. Producers: Gordon Carroll, John Davis, etc. Cast: Sanaa Lathan, Raoul Bova, Lance Henriksen, and Ewen Bremner. When a satellite from the Weyland Corporation discovers an unusual pyramid buried 2000 feet under the Antarctic ice, President Charles Bishop Weyland (Henriksen) and a crack team, led by mountaineer Lex Woods (Lathan), charge off to lay claim. Problem: the pyramid, which has characteristics of Aztec, Egyptian and Cambodian designs, is actually a training ground for young Predators that breeds the most dangerous game every 100 years, Aliens, for their passage into adulthood. As the pyramid changes its room structure every 10 minutes, Lex tries to hold her group together, but not surprisingly, they wander off and get killed off one by one.Only the fierce babe survives (shades of Ripley), and then she has to decide on whose team to play! The battles between the Aliens and the young Predators is well worth the price of admission, even if you are two steps ahead in logic.

Assignment: Terror (aka Dracula Versus Frankenstein) (1971). Italian/International Jaguar, 89min. Director: Tulio Demichelli. Producer: Jami Prades. Writer: Jacinto Molina. Cast: Michael Rennie, Karin Dor, Craig Hall, Paul Naschy, Patty Sherpherd, Angelo del Rozo, Ella Gessler, Peter Damon, and Gene Reyes. Michael Rennie leads the vanguard of alien invaders from a dying world to Earth with one of Ed Wood's leftover plans from "Plan 9 from Outer Space." By reviving the famous monsters of filmland, including Dracula, the Wolfman, the Mummy, the Gill Man, and Frankenstein's monster, they hope to terrorize the world into submission. But sibling rivalries emerge between the various monsters, and soon they are fighting with each other. The advertised confrontation between Dracula and Frankenstein never occurs (leaving this critic to question the alternate English-language title). The script is weak, the direction is poor, and the special effects are far below the credibility level. Rennie, who was never able to shake the typecasting of his Klaatu role from "The Day the Earth Stood Still," is embarrassingly stiff in a part that should have been most familiar to him. With all of their intelligence, you'd think these aliens would come up with a better plan to conquer Earth. Sexy James Bond-girl Karin Dor makes a first viewing palatable.

Battlefield Earth: A Saga of the Year 3000 (2000). Warner Brothers, color, 118 min. Director: Roger Christian. Writers: L. Ron Hubbard (novel) Corey Mandell, etc. Producer: Jonathan Krane, Elie Samaha, etc. Cast: John Travolta, Barry Pepper, Forest Whitaker, and Sabine Karsenti. It's 3000 AD, and the extraterrestrial Psychlos have taken over the planet, and caged humans as animals. Their leader, Terl (Travolta), assisted by Ker (Whitaker), is pirating all the natural resources, while the humans fight with each other over what is left. Jonnie Goodboy Tyler (Pepper) tries to unite the

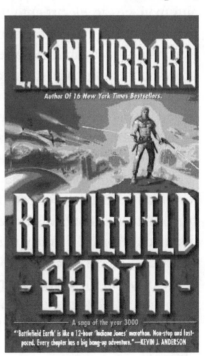

remnants of mankind in a revolt against the Psychlos. The revolution leads to a lot of explosions, and a finale that seems borrowed from "Independence Day" as fighter jets engage alien spaceships in aerial combat. Christian does wonders with the material that he has at hand, but with less than half of the novel to work with, the story seems unfinished. One wonders what a masterpiece this could have been if made into two films or a trilogy, like "The Lord of the Rings." Great score by Maurice Jarre.

Battle in Outer Space (1959). Japanese, Toho Productions, 93 min. Director: Ishiro Honda. Producer: Tomoyuki Tanaka. Writers: Jojiro Okami and Shinichi Sekizawa.

Cast: Ryo Ikebe, Kyoto Anzai, Koreya Senda, , Leonard Stanford, and Harold Conway. When alien invaders arrive from beyond the cosmos and destroy the International Space Station and several Japanese cities, the nations of the Earth unite in a common cause to fight off the space menace. The space battle between rocket jets and flying saucers looked pretty cool when we were kids, but that was many years before the debut of "Star Wars." The rest of the film is pretty much standard fare, with Japanese actors Ryo Ikebe and Kyoko Anzai taking center stage. Its prequel, "The Mysterians" (1957), featured a similar plot with aliens seeking earth females for procreation.

The Creeping Unknown (aka The Quatermass Xperiment) (1955). Hammer Films, b/w, 82 min. Director: Val Guest. Producer: Anthony Hinds. Screenwriters: Guest and Richard Landau. Based on "Quatermass" television series by Nigel Kneale. Cast: Brian Donlevy, Margia Dean, Jack Warner, Richard Wordsworth, David King Wood, and Lionel Jeffries. The sole survivor (Wordsworth) of a doomed space expedition returns to earth with an alien organism growing within his body. Even though he survives the crash of his rocketship, he begins acting strangely as a fungus-like growth creeps over his entire body and ultimately consumes him. Imagine that. Professor Quatermass (Donlevy) is called in to save the day, and manages to electrocute the octopus-blob creature before it can spread over the entire London area. The alien spore, which infects the astronaut's body, and the "creeping unknown," which grows in the human host, anticipate the complex life-cycle of the titular monster in "Alien" (1979). But this idea was certainly not a new one when Guest first began sketching plans for his big screen remake of Nigel Kneale's popular British television series. Pulp science fiction adventures had relied on this familiar formula for years. American Donlevy gives a wooden performance as the British scientist, but Wordsworth's doomed astronaut literally makes your flesh creep.

Dark City (1998). New Line Cinema, color, 100 min. Director: Alex Proyas. Writer: Alex Proyas. Producers: Andrew Mason and Proyas. Cast: Rufus Sewell, William Hurt, Kiefer Sutherland, and Jennifer Connelly.

In a future city, John Murdoch (Sewell) wakes up in a hotel to discover he is wanted for the serial killing of prostitutes, but his memory is almost gone. While the police seek to arrest him for the crimes, Murdoch relies on Dr. Schreber (Sutherland) to help him to escape a deadlier foe-the Strangers, an alien race that wants to dissect Murdoch's brain. The chase is on through the nighttime streets of the city, with Hurt as the police Inspector Bumstead (Hurt) and Connelly as his wife. The film's pace is fast, and "Dark City" ends with a bang. This film's look is a mix of German Expressionism ("The Cabinet of Dr. Caligari" and "Metropolis") and film noir ("The Maltese Falcon" and "Blade Runner"). If you like the original "Matrix" and were disappointed by the sequels, then this is the film you should watch instead. Sexy Jennifer Connelly never looked so good!

The Day the Earth Stood Still (1951). 20th Century Fox Pictures, b/w, 92 min. Director: Robert Wise. Producer: Julian Blaustein Screenwriter: Edmund H. North. Based on the short story "Farewell to the Master" by Harry Bates. Cast: Michael Rennie, Patricia Neal, Hugh Marlowe, Billy Gray, Sam Jaffe, and Lock Martin.

One of the first Hollywood films produced during the science fiction boom of the 1950's, the movie reflected our worst fears about atomic war and our own paranoia, prejudice and bigotry. When an emissary from an alien confederation (not unlike Star Trek's United Federation of Planets) arrives by flying saucer in Washington, D.C., Klaatu (Rennie) warns the peoples of the earth that violence and aggression will no longer be tolerated by the other civilized worlds. But before he can deliver his complete message to a gathering of world leaders, he is gunned down by military forces that view his pacifist ways as an even greater threat to world peace. Subsequently, his eight-foot-tall robot Gort fries a few tanks and soldiers with his cyclopean laser beam, and forces them to reconsider. Klaatu's society has totally eliminated war and hostility by empowering a police force of robots to patrol the planets in flying saucers, and mankind must submit to peace, or else be destroyed. A powerful motion picture way ahead of its time, even if you don't stop long enough to think about its Christ allegory.

Devil Girl From Mars (1954). Danziger Productions, B&W, 77 min. Director: David MacDonald. Writers: John Mather and James Eastwood. Producers: Ed and Harry Danziger. Cast: Patricia Laffan, Hazel Court, Hugh McDermott, Peter Reynolds, and Adrienne Corri. Laffan's Nyah arrives from Mars in a black leather miniskirt, and demands healthy Earthmen to take back to Mars for breeding purposes. But the humans put up a struggle. Are you kidding? Most fan-boys would gladly surrender to this dominatrix from Mars, and willingly climb aboard her spaceship.

Earth Versus the Flying Saucers. (1955). Columbia, B&W, 83 min. Director: Fred F. Stears. Producer: Samuel Katzman. Writer: Curt Siodmak. Based on a book by Donald E. Keyhoe. Cast: Hugh Marlowe, Joan Taylor, Donald Curtis, Morris Ankrum, John Zaremba, Thomas Browne Henry, and Grandon Rhodes.

Warning! Take Cover! Flying Saucers Invade Our Planet! Washington, London, Paris, Moscow Fight Back! Operation Skyhook, under the leadership of Dr. Russell Marvin (Marlowe), has been launching rockets in preparation for future space travel, but the little green men who wear trashcans for spacesuits don't want us going into space. They destroy our rockets, and then start destroying our cities. Marvin and his colleagues built an anti-magnetic beam weapon, and the battle is on! Except for the superior Ray Harryhausen effects, I really don't care who wins. "Earth Versus the Flying Wallendas" (Yes, I know the title!) is a low-rent version of George Pal's superior "The War of the Worlds" (1953) that's better off left at the local Blockbuster Video. "Independence Day" was the superior, big-budget remake.

Fiend Without a Face (1958). Eros, 75 min. Director: Arthur Crabtree. Producer: John Croydon. Screenwriter: Herbert J. Leder. Cast: Kyanston Reeves, Marshall Thompson, Terry Kilburn, Kim Parker, Peter Madden, and Michael Balfour.

The monsters in this low-budget quickie are disembodied brains that wrap themselves around a victim's head (with the help of a spinal cord-like tail) and sucked their victims dry. If only this production had a brain... Unleashed by a mad scientist (Thompson) who has learned to transform thoughts into physical form, these organic parasites scramble around much like the face hugger in "Alien," propelled by the whip of their multi-jointed tails. They depend on human hosts to provide them with greater mobility as they struggle to take control of a remote army base (near the Canadian frontier), and are very difficult to kill. While the idea may be borrowed from Robert Heinlein's *The Puppet Masters* (1951), the climax is clearly inspired by "The Thing (from Another World)" as soldiers of the isolated base fight an all-out war with the parasites. Let's face it: these fiends are pretty laughable, and are with little doubt too embarrassed to show their faces.

The Fifth Element (1997). Columbia Pictures, France/USA, color, 126 min. Director: Luc Besson. Written by: Luc Besson. Produced by: Patrice Ledoux. Cast: Bruce Willis, Gary Oldman, Ian Holm, Milla Jovovich, and Chris Tucker

A few centuries in the future, the planet Earth is threatened by the arrival of the essence of Evil. Only the fifth element (Jovovich in a bikini made of bandages), a gift from a spacefaring race of our distant past with connections to the Egyptian pyramids and an ancient priesthood (Holm), can battle the epitome of Evil. She is helped by an air taxi driver (Willis), who also is a Special Forces commando with a nagging stage mother. The action is non-stop. Gary Oldman is a merchant of death quite willing to kill anything, anywhere, anytime for a price. Chris Tucker is a gender-bending disk jockey good for more than a few laughs. The bad guys are really bad; the good guys are a bit stiff, except for Willis, and Milla Jovovich looks hot in her skimpy Victoria Secret wear. This is as much a comedy as a science fiction-action thriller.

Final Fantasy: The Spirits Within (2001), U.S./Japan, Columbia and Sony, color, 106 min. Directors: Hironobu Sakaguchi and Motonori Sakakibara. Writers: Hironubu Sakaguchi, Al Reinert, etc. Cast: Ming-Na, Alec Baldwin, James Woods and Steve Buscemi.

Based on a popular video game, this animated feature was the first of its kind to attempt an all-digital, computer-generated workspace, and succeeded with a decent storyline. The oppressed humans in 2065 are making an attack on the extraterrestrial phantoms who have invaded Earth. The charming Dr. Aki Ross (Ming-Na), a researcher creating a new type of weapon against the phantoms, joins up with a gung-ho group led by Captain Edwards (Baldwin) with Neal Fleming (Buscemi) and others. They race to succeed before General Hein (Woods) uses the Zeus cannon which may endanger the Earth. The animated characters look close to real people. You will either love it, or hate it, but you will see more of it.

Flash Gordon (1980). MCA/Universal Pictures, UK, color, 111 min. Director: Mike Hodges. Written by: Michael Allin and Alex Raymond (comic strip). Produced by: Dino De Laurentis. Cast: Sam J. Jones, Melody Anderson, Max von Sydow, Topol, Ornella Muti, Timothy Dalton, and Brian Blessed.

No, this is not your father's black and white serial with Buster Crabbe but rather an overblown color spectacular a la De Laurentiis. Flash (Jones), a star football player, blunders aboard the retro rocket ship of Dr. Zarkov (Topol) with the lovely and talented Dale Arden (Anderson). This trio faces the Fu Manchu mustache and evil of Ming (and Dale fends off his advances in the harem) in order to save Earth. The buff Flash attracts the interest of Ming's half-clad daughter (Muti) and escapes. Flash and Prince Barin (Dalton) have a great bullwhip duel on an unsteady platform at the court of Prince Vultan of the Hawkmen (Blessed), a macho guy with a great laugh.

Does the trio save the Earth? Who else? Do we have camp values? We think so. Would we run off with Ornella Muti? Damn straight! If you like Queen, you'll love the music score. The cinematography is gorgeous, a rainbow of color and invention.

Galaxy Quest (1999). Dream Works Distribution, color, 102 min. Director: Dean Parisot. Writer: David Howard. Producers: Mark Johnson and Charles Newirth. Cast: Tim Allen, Sigourneyl Weaver, Alan Rickman and Tony Shalhoub.

Almost 20 years after their Sci-Fi series "Galaxy Quest" (a thinly-disguised "Star Trek") has been cancelled, the cast is still making appearances, signing autographs at media conventions throughout the country. The egotistical captain (Allen) is approached by a race of humanoid aliens who have modeled their lives after the TV show and now need help to fight off a more aggressive race of aliens. Through the magic of show business, the officers including the busty Gwen DeMarco (Weaver), the ham actor-officer (Rickman) and the rest of the cast resume their battle stations and take on the alien menace in outer space. "Galaxy Quest" won a Hugo Award from SF fans who attend conventions. They loved the mix of comedy and melodrama, and Allen's take on William Shatner's Captain Kirk is uproarious.

Horror of the Blood Creatures (aka Vampire Men of the Lost Planet and The Space Vampires) (1971). Fillippino, Independent International Films, 86min. Director, Producer: Al Adamson. Writer: Sue Macnair. Cast: John Carradine, Robert Dix, Vicki Volante, Joey Benson, Jennifer Bishop, and Bruce powers.

Padded with stock footage from "One Million Years B.C." (1940) and "Unknown Island" (1948), this cartoon caricature follows the exploits of Dr. Rynning (Carradine) and his two colleagues (Dix and Volante) as they rocket to a faraway unknown planet (not unlike Flash Gordon's Mongo) to destroy the home base of space-faring vampires. Seeking Spectrum X, the secret power source, they battle bat creatures, cat-men, claw demons, serpent people, and the like. Eventually, they discover the base and emerge victorious. Strictly comic book fare. With the release of "Lifeforce: The Space Vampires" in 1985, this low budgeter was issued on video with the title "The Space Vampires."

Independence Day (1996). 20th Century Fox, color, 145 min. Director: Roland Emmerich. Writers: Dean Devlin and Emmerich. Producer: Devlin. Cast: Bill Pullman, Mary McDonnell, Jeff Goldblum, Margaret Colin and Will Smith.

Atmospheric anomalies on July 2 are matched with giant objects approaching earth, and by July 3, every major city in the world is threatened with destruction by giant spaceships piloted by unfriendly aliens. A scientist (Goldblum), a fighter pilot (Smith), the President of the United States (Pullman), and a cast of just plain folks with a badass attitude decide to get even with the aliens on July 4, Independence Day. The special effects are fun; the characters are borrowed from daily soap operas, and the aliens look like escapees from H. R. Giger's studio. But the film is literally a blast from the past! Rent "Earth Versus the Flying Saucers," and you'll have a great double-bill. Released during the dog-days of the Clinton presidency, audiences literally cheered out load when the White House was destroyed by the aliens. Too bad Bill, Hilary and Monica weren't home that day when the aliens came calling.

Invaders from Mars (1953). Twentieth Century-Fox, B&W, 78 min. Director: William Cameron Menzies. Producer: Edward L. Alperson. Writers: John Tucker Battle and Richard Blake. Cast: Helena Carter, Arthur Franz, Jimmy Hunt, Leif Erickson, Hillary Brooke, and Morris Ankrum.

Little Jimmy Hunt sees a flying saucer land in his backyard, and tries to tell his family and friends about the strange events. Naturally, they don't believe him. When he tells his dad (Erickson), he gets slapped in the mouth for telling a lie. Later, when his dad comes back a zombie, he pleads to the local doctor (Carter) for help. Of course, she believes him, and calls out the Army, Air Force, and Marines to surround the saucer, and duke it out with the Martians. Is it a dream? Is it live or is it Memorex? It seems the studio couldn't make up its mind either, and filmed the ending three different ways. The remake is only marginally better. This film is actually quite a let-down considering that Menzies was responsible for the superior "Things to Come" (1936).

Invaders from Mars (1986). Cannon Films, 100 min. Director: Tobe Hooper. Producers: Golan and Globus. Based on the original film by William Cameron Menzies. Cast: Karen Black, Hunter Carson, Timothy Bottoms, Laraine Newman, James Karen, Louise Fletcher, Bud Cort and Jimmy Hunt.

Like the original, a youngster (Carson) is awakened by the sound of a flying saucer in his backyard. When his parents (Bottoms and Newman) disappear while investigating his claim and then later return as changed people, he seeks out the professional help of a psychologist (Black). Soon, as each of his friends, neighbors and even the police begin to display grossly altered personalities, the boy realizes that he is embroiled in a struggle with evil tentacled Martian creatures that want to take over the world. Hooper makes an honest attempt to recapture the magic of the original 1953 feature, but like Thomas Wolfe opined, there's no going home again. Jimmy Hunt, the original youngster who cried wolf, cameos as a police officer. Stan Winston made the Martian creatures, and Les Dilley, who worked with H.R. Giger on the original "Alien," designed the bio-mechanical look of the production.

Invasion (aka H. G. Wells's War of the Worlds) (2005). Asylum Entertainment, 90 min. Director: David Michael Latt. Producer: David Rimawi. Screenwriters: David Michael Latt

and Carlos De Los Rios. Based upon the novel by H. G. Wells. Cast: C. Thomas Howell, Peter Greene, Andrew Lauer, Rhett Giles, and Jake Busey.

This direct-to-video release was yet another retelling of the H. G. Wells novel. Civilization is laid to ruin when a super race of aliens invades the Earth. In the blink of an eye, massive "walkers" cover the planet, annihilating all in their path. As cities crumble, one man struggles to find the one weapon that will turn the tide for mankind. Produced in 2005, this low-budgeter debuted the day before Steven Spielberg's multimillion dollar spectacular, but caused barely a ripple at the box office.

Invasion of the Body Snatchers (1956). Allied Artists, B&W, 80 min. Director: Don Siegal. Writers: Daniel Mainwaring and Sam Peckinpah. Based upon the novel *The Body Snatchers* by Jack Finney. Cast: Kevin McCarthy, Dana Wynter, Carolyn Jones, Whit Bissel, Larry Gates, and King Donovan.

Residents of the small Southern California community of Santa Mira are systematically being replaced by duplicates grown from strange pods that came to Earth from outer space. Only the local doctor (McCarthy) seems to notice that people are behaving like zombies, but when he pushes his inquiry too far, the "pod people" start chasing after him. A study in terror and paranoia that grew out of the McCarthy hysteria of the 1950's, this was one of the classic movies of the golden age of science fiction films. And while the literate screenplay clearly improves on Finney's novel, the movie still has a few lines of dialogue that are worth rewinding for..."I never really knew terror until I kissed Becky." We recommend this one highly, even if you choose not to kiss Becky.

Invasion of the Body Snatchers (1978). Paramount, Color, 100 min. Director/Writer: Philip Kaufman. Producer: Robert Solo. Based upon *The Body Snatchers* by Jack Finney. Cast: Donald Sutherland, Brooke Adams, Leonard Nimoy, Veronica Cartwright, Kevin McCarthy. Those alien pods are still turning people into zombies, but this time they have progressed as far as the huge metropolis of San Francisco. After a brief introduction, in which we see Kevin McCarthy still running away from "them," the action shifts to Sutherland who works as a health inspector. He starts to notice that people are behaving strangely, and notifies his friend (Nimoy) who turns out to be one of them. The chase is on, and my money is on the "pod people." After seeing this several times, I'm still not sure how much is conspiracy and how much is paranoia and hysteria, but it makes for a very tense two hours in the dark.

It Came From Outer Space (1953). Universal, B&W, 80min. Director: Jack Arnold. Producer: William Alland. Screenwriter: Harry Essex. Based on a story by Ray Bradbury. Cast: Richard Carlson, Barbara Rush, Charles Drake, Alan Dexter, and Russell Johnson. Aliens crashland on Earth when their flying saucer experiences engine trouble, and they take over the minds and bodies of local townspeople to effect repairs. The repair work is slow, and they are forced to employ more and more humans. Eventually the locals decide to take direct action against the stranded aliens, and all hell breaks loose. That's always the trouble with trying to find a good repair shop while on holiday.

It! The Terror from Beyond Space (aka It! The Vampire from Beyond Space) (1958)
United Artists, b/w, 69 min. Director: Edward L Cahn. Producer: Robert E. Kent. Writer: Jerome Bixby. Cast: Marshall Thompson, Shawn Smith, Kim Spalding, Ann Doran, Ray "Crash" Corrigan. Returning from Mars, a space expedition discovers that a blood-drinking monster has hitched a ride to Earth and is relentlessly stalking members of its co-ed crew. Like all low-budget films of this kind, members of the crew behave like numskulls, and make easy prey for the monster by wandering alone into the dark corridors of the rocketship when they should be teaming up to blast it out the airlock. The special effects are laughable, and Ray "Crash" Corrigan as the rubber-suited monster is less than credible, but the film is still fun, particularly when

we know who's going to get it next and no amount of screaming at the screen can save them from going to their doom. Any similarities to the 1979 "Alien" are more than coincidental, even though writers Dan O'Bannon and Ron Shusett would want us to think otherwise.

Kronos (1957). Regal Productions, b/w, 78 min. Director and Producer: Kurt Neumann. Screenwriter: Lawrence Louis Goldman. Cast: Jeff Morrow and Barbara Lawrence.
The menace in Neumann's low budgeter is a 100-foot-tall robot from space that consumes energy and continues to grow stronger and larger. When scientist Jeff Morrow (a regular in sci-fi movies) is unable to retard its march inland from a California beach, the army tries destroying it with a hydrogen bomb. The robot merely absorbs the nuclear energy and grows even larger as result. Anticipating James Cameron's low budget "Terminator" (1984), Neumann mounts an impressive thriller, with superior special effects, on less than $160,000. Like the unstoppable cyborg from the future, Kronos is a robot that can't be reasoned with or bargained with either. And the result is equally compelling. Makes a great double feature with "The Monolith Monsters" (1957).

Lifeforce (aka The Space Vampires) (1985). MGM/United Artists, in association with Cannon Films, 100 min. Director: Tobe Hooper. Producers: Golan and Globus. Screenwriters: Dan O'Bannon and Don Jakoby. Based on the novel The Space Vampires by Colin Wilson. Cast: Steve Railsback, Frank Finlay, Peter Firth, Michael Gothard, Nicholas Ball, Patrick Stewart and Mathilda May.
Space-faring vampires, led by the totally naked Mathilda May, are discovered hiding in the corona of Halley's Comet, and are brought back to Earth by the British-American crew of a

space shuttle. Once on terra firma, the vampires escape their confinement at a London scientific installation and begin to ravage the countryside. Hans Fallada (Finlay), a criminologist known as "the Sherlock Holmes of psychology," enlists the aide of the American shuttle captain (Railsback) to hunt them down, and possibly get a date with May. Patrick Stewart, the future Starfleet captain, warps in for some of the fun and games. Forget trying to figure out how the vampires survive in space without a ready blood supply, and just think

how great the Parisian model looks naked. Director Tobe Hooper, best known for "The Texas Chainsaw Massacre" (1974), has made better films, but none quite so erotic. And if May's performance doesn't get those hormones pumping, consider yourself dead.

Little Shop of Horrors (1960). Santa Clara Films, b/w, 70min. Director, Producer: Roger Corman. Writer: Charles B. Griffith. Cast: Jonathan Haze, Jackie Joseph, Mel Welles, Myrtle Vail, Dick Miller, and Jack Nicholson.

"Feed me!" Nothing is sacred in this zany, crazy horror comedy, and certainly nothing is to be taken seriously. Seymour (Haze), the under-paid, over-worked Jewish fan boy who tends Mushnik's Flower Shop, discovers a blood-thirsty plant from outer space. Naming it Audrey II after the girl he wanted to ask out to the prom (Vail), he puts it on display in the store window. Suddenly, business is blooming at Mushnik's as customers rush in to see the exotic potted plant. However, when it starts crying "Feed Me!," Seymour goes trawling for buxom hookers to feed Audrey. Had he bothered to get laid by one of the hookers, Seymour might just have pulled Audrey up by its roots and had a real life outside his parent's basement. Oh, well! Lesson for all fan boys to learn! Suggested by John Collier's short story "Green Thoughts," this tale of a plant that feeds on blood is irresistible. Jack Nicholson appears in a minor role as a super-masochist who enjoys pain, and refuses to get out of the dentist's chair. A big-budget Broadway musical followed in the 1980's.

Man from Planet X (1951). Independent, B&W, 70 min. Director: Edgar G. Ulmer. Writers: Aubrey Wisberg and Jack Pollexfen. Cast: Robert Clarke, Margaret Field, Raymond Bond, William Shallert, and Roy Engel.

When it appears that a new, rogue planet is heading for a near-miss with Earth, Professor Elliot (Clarke) and his beautiful daughter (Field) and colleague Dr. Mears (Shallert) set up an observatory on a remote island. But when a flying saucer from Planet X deposits the titular character on the island's foggy moors to spearhead the invasion, all manner

of shenanigans begin. Really low production values make this invasion seem rather one-sided, with the little alien outnumbered by solemn-faced scientists. Sleep during this one.

Men in Black (1997). Columbia Pictures, color, 98 min. Director: Barry Sonnenfeld. Writers: Lowell Cunningham (comic) and Ed Solomon. Producers: Laurie MacDonald and Walter F. Parkes. Cast: Tommy Lee Jones, Will Smith, Linda Fiorentino, Vincent D'Onofrio, Rip Torn and Tony Shalhoub.

Those men in the black helicopters are not the UN, but rather a secret organization monitoring the activity of extraterrestrials throughout earth from a hidden headquarters in New York City. A senior Man in Black (Jones) recruits a New York policeman (Smith) to help him collar an ET terrorist (D'Onofrio) who is out to cause trouble for our planet as we know it. It is a fast-moving action film/comedy that never slows down. Jones and Smith are the classic odd couple partners. Linda Fiorentino adds sex appeal to great comic casting. It also contains great parody on popular urban and rural myths about flying saucers and alien abductions.

Men in Black II (2002). Columbia Pictures, color, 88 min. Director: Barry Sonnenfeld. Writers: Lowell Cunningham and Robert Gordon. Producers: Laurie MacDonald and Walter F. Parkes. Cast: Tommy Lee Jones, Will Smith, Rip Torn, Lara Flynn Boyle, Rosario Dawson and Tony Shalhoub.

That secret organization that monitors extraterrestrial activity in "Men in Black" (1997) has a problem that may threaten the balance of the universe and put an end to Victoria's Secret catalogs. An ET threat to peace in the galaxy has landed (Boyle), who looks great in lingerie, and she wants her revenge. Agent J (Smith) learns that Agent K (Jones) has retired with knowledge that must be retrieved. J picks up a witness/girl friend too (Dawson), and the boys are back in town. They serve and protect the universe. If you liked the first film, you will like this one. It is essentially the same film. Most of the fine actors are back, too. The pace is intense; the laughs are frequent. It is, however, a sequel, and for some reason some critics chose not to like it. Their loss, and our gain. Who cares about the plot when we've got Laura Flynn Boyle in various stages of undress!

The Monolith Monsters (1957). Universal Pictures, b/w, 78 min. Director: John Sherman. Producer: Howard Christie. Screenwriters: Jack Arnold, Robert Fresco and Norman Jolley.

Cast: Grant Williams, Lola Albright, Les Treymane, Phil Harvey, and Paul Frees.

Like "Kronos" (1957), the world is threatened by a seemingly unstoppable force from outer space. A strange black meteor crashes near the town of San Angelo, California, and litters the countryside with fragments. When a thunderstorm exposes these meteorite fragments to water, they grow into skyscraper-sized monoliths which then topple and shatter into thousands of pieces that grow into monoliths themselves, and repeat the process. Any humans standing in the way are crushed or turned into human statues. The citizens of San Angelo desperately try to save themselves and the world from the spreading doom. Written by Jack Arnold, the great director behind "It Came from Outer Space" (1953), "The Creature from the Black Lagoon" (1954), "The Incredible Shrinking Man" (1957) and many other films, this is an effective, low-budget chiller. Blink and you will miss teenage heartthrob Troy Donahue as Hank Johnson, the man at the dam.

Night of the Blood Beast (1958). American International Pictures, b/w, 65 min. Director: Bernard Kowalski. Producer: Roger Corman. Writer: Martin Varno. Based on a story by Gene Corman. Cast: Michael Emmet, Angela Greene, and Ed Nelson.

Like "The Creeping Terror," yet another astronaut returns from space with alien embryos growing in his body. Apparently, during his deep space mission, some alien intelligence took control of his rocketship and mind, and implanted fertilized eggs with the astronaut's chest cavity. The astronaut returns to Earth dead, but later revives under the control of his extraterrestrial hosts. A single "blood beast" eventually hatches and turns deadly, with all of the usual death and mayhem that follows. This low-budgeter does not strive for the same epic pretentiousness of its predecessor, but is nonetheless unremarkable. Corman made a career out of making cheap knock-offs of popular films, but he seems to be scraping the bottom of the barrel here.

The Night That Panicked America (1975). Television Movie, 100min. Director and Producer: Joseph Sargent. Writers: Nicholas Meyer, Anthony Wilson, and Howard Koch. Cast: Paul Shenar, Vic Morrow, Cliff De Young, Michael Constantine, Walter McGinn, Will Geer, Tom Bosley, John Ritte, and Eileen Brennan.

The true story of the night that Orson Welles (Shenar) and the players of the Mercury Theater set out to dramatize *The War of the Worlds* by H. G. Wells, and in turn scared an entire nation with their alien invasion. Made for TV and written by a young Nicholas Meyer, who would later to helm several *Star Trek* movies, the tale mixes elements of the broadcast with a number of fictional vignettes charting the terrified reaction of the public. The movie functions at its considerable best when set at the Columbia Broadcast Studio in New York City, with the build up and behind the scenes action really ratcheting up the tension and suspense.

Not of This Earth (1957). Los Altos, b/w, 69min. Director, Producer: Roger Corman. Writers: Charles B. Giffith and Mark Hanna. Cast: Paul Birch, Beverly Garland, Morgan Jones, William Roderick, Jonathan Haze, and Dick Miller.

SOMEWHERE IN THIS WORLD STALKS A THING THAT IS...

NOT OF THIS EARTH

Paul BIRCH · Beverly GARLAND · Morgan JONES

A ROGER CORMAN PRODUCTION · Screenplay by CHARLES B. GRIFFITH and MARK HANNA

Produced and Directed by ROGER CORMAN · An ALLIED ARTISTS PICTURE

When Mr. Johnson (Birch), the alien in the gray flannel suit, comes to Earth looking for isotopically-pure human blood, he stumbles upon the services of a mad doctor (Jones) and his hot-to-trot nurse (Garland). The blood in his veins is drying up, just like that of his people, because of a devastating nuclear war on Davanna. Johnson quickly discovers that a simple transfusion will not do, and starts sending derelicts (and even a vacuum cleaner salesman, played by Dick Miller) through his matter transporter to his home world. Chillingly portrayed, particularly when Johnson removes his dark glasses to reveal pupil-less eyes, this was one of a handful of quickies produced by Roger Corman on a $1.98 budget that paid off. Garland certainly sets the hormones racing in those tight tight sweaters of hers. Talk about putting an eye out! The film was later remade with Traci Lords in the same role. Va-va-voom!

The Parasite Murders (aka They Came from Within) (1974). Cinepix/Canadian Development Corporation, 87 min. Director and Screenwriter: David Cronenberg. Producer: Ivan Reitman. Cast: Paul Hampton, Joe Silver, Lynn Lowry, Barbara Steele, Allan Migicovsky, and Susan Petrie.

A research scientist creates, then implants a parasite that turns people into sexual fiends. Eventually, the vaguely phallic parasites emerge from their human hosts and attach themselves to other victims. A young doctor (Hampton) and his wife (Lowry) fight a losing battle against the creatures in the isolated high-rise apartment building as their friends are taken over one by one. Remarkably similar to Don Siegel's "Invasion of the Body Snatches" (1956), director Cronenberg's analogy of rapidly spreading sexual disease is far more disturbing and real for most of us today. Remember how mom always used to warn us about washing our hands after we used the bathroom...

Plan 9 from Outer Space (aka Grave Robbers from Outer Space) (1956) Reynolds Productions, b/w, 79min. Director, Producer, Screenwriter: Edward D. Wood, Jr. Cast: Bela Lugosi, Vampira, Tor Johnson, Lyle Talbot, Joanne Lee, and Gregory Walcott.

Celebrated as the worst Science Fiction film ever made, Plan 9 relies on one of the most unoriginal plots (and sworn testimony!), wooden acting (thanks to the wooden direction of Ed Wood), cardboard sets (that shake when characters walk), laughable effects (with hubcaps standing in as flying saucers), and Wood's own chiropractor to showcase Lugosi's last role. Having failed with eight earlier plots to conquer Earth, pompous aliens rely on the titular plan of reviving the dead and turning the zombies loose on mankind. Had Kubrick chosen this film to torture Alex in "A Clockwork Orange" (1971), that might have been considered cruel and unusual punishment. Ironically, with the release of Tim Burton's "Ed Wood," this film is very hip today!

Predator (aka Hunter) (1987). Twentieth Century Fox, 107 min. Director: John McTiernan. Producers: Joel Silver, Lawrence Gordon, and

John Davis. Executive Producers: Laurence Pereira and Jim Thomas. Screenwriters: Jim Thomas and John Thomas. Music Composer: Alan Silvestri. Cast: Arnold Schwarzenegger, Carl Weathers, Elpidia Carrillo, Bill Duke, Jesse Ventura, Shane Black, Sonny Landham, Richard Chaves, R.G. Armstrong, and Kevin Peter Hall.

Recruited for a special mission to rescue hostages held by guerilla fighters in the some Central American jungle, Major "Dutch" Schaefer (Schwarzenegger) and his army men embark on a what they believe will be a simple one-day operation. However, as they penetrate the enemy border, the special forces unit becomes the target of an invisible alien predator. One by one, members of the unit are murdered, until it becomes a showdown between the ex-Austrian bodybuilder and the hunter from another world. Packed with state-of-the-art special effects, gut-wrenching combat scenes, a wonderfully realized monster, and a handful of winning performances, McTiernan's first major film was the perfect popcorn extravaganza for summer audiences, and one of the California governors' best roles. Too bad Fox didn't leave better off alone

Predator 2 (1990). Twentieth Century Fox, 108 min. Director: Stephen Hopkins. Producers: Joel Silver, Lawrence Gordon, and John Davis. Screenwriters: Jim Thomas and John Thomas. Music Composer: Alan Silvestri. Cast: Danny Glover, Gary Busey, Ruben Blades, Maria Conchita Alonso, Bill Paxton, Kevin Peter Hall, Robert Davi, Kent McCord, Calvin Lockhart, Adam Baldwin, and Morton Downy Jr.

With Schwarzenegger conspicuously absent, the sequel picks up ten years later in the violence-torn Los Angeles of the future. Police lieutenant Mike Harrigan (Glover minus his "Lethal Weapon" co-star Mel Gibson) discovers the Predator has intervened in a series of gang-land murders between rival drug dealers. As the body count increases, Harrigan allies himself with a couple of Men in Black (Busey and Baldwin) to fight the extraterrestrial hunter. But when he learns they mean to capture the creature, and not kill it, he carries on alone, fighting the Predator to the death. Glover is such a great actor, but compared with Schwarzenegger in a sequel to "Predator," he's a lightweight. The really cool part of the movie occurs when Glover ventures aboard the alien's spaceship, and we glimpse the skull of that now-famous, death-dealing indestructible juggernaut from "Alien" in the Predator's trophy case. Cool stuff! And a nifty set-up for the "Alien Versus Predator" (2004) movie.

Puppet Masters, The (1994). (aka Robert Heinlein's The Puppet Masters). Buena Vista, color, 109 min. Director: Stuart Orme. Writers: Robert Heinlein (novel), Ted Elliott, etc. Producer: Ralph Winter. Cast: Donald Sutherland, Eric Thal, Julie Warner and Will Patton. A flying saucer touches ground in Iowa, and slug-like creatures that look like they're on holiday from Roger Corman's "It Conquered the World" (1956) literally attach themselves to the backs of the Iowans. A father and son team (Sutherland, Thal) from a "secret" government agency come to investigate with an exobiologist (Warner) from NASA. They spot a fraud, but they come to know that the threat real. Sutherland's character is relentless in his pursuit. The action is fast and furious. Unfortunately, though Heinlein's novel was probably the earliest satire of our society's 1950's concerns (in particular, the communist scare and the fear of conformity), similar adaptations or "original" screenplays--such as Don

Siegel's wonderful "The Invasion of the Body Snatchers" (1956)--came to the screen first, and told the story better.

Queen of Blood (aka Planet of Blood) (1966). George Edwards Productions/AIP, 88 min. Director: Curtis Harrington. Producer: George Edwards. Screenwriter: Curtis Harrington. Based on the novel by Charles Nuetzel. Cast: John Saxon, Basil Rathbone, Judi Meredith, Dennis Hopper, Florence Marley, and Forrest J. Ackerman.

In the distant year of 1990, three astronauts (Saxon, Meredith, and Hopper) discover a derelict spacecraft on Mars, and bring its sole survivor, a green-tinted alien (Marley), aboard their rocketship. On the return trip to Earth, members of the crew demonstrate they haven't learned a thing from "It! The Terror from Beyond Space," and make easy prey for Marley's hemophiliac vampire by wandering alone in the spaceship. Ultimately, Meredith learns the titular monster wants to breed with Saxon, and fights Marley to the death because she has designs of her own for the captain. Director Harrington (under the tutelage of Roger Corman) cannibalized the superior Russian film "Niebo Zowiet" (1959) for stock footage, and shot the balance of the motion picture in

eight days with a budget of less than fifty thousand dollars. Regrettably, it looks it. For a bloody awful time, this makes a great double-bill with "Planet of the Vampires." Beware of whiplash when swapping between disks.

Red Planet Mars (1952). Melaby Pictures, b&w, 87 min. Director: Harry Horner. Producer: Anthony Veiller. Writers: Veiller and John L. Balderston. Cast: Peter Graves, Andrea King, Herbert Berghof, Walter Sande.

Graves receives television transmissions from Mars that reveal God lives in residence among the Martians on a utopian world. Don't tell the Baptists. They'll never forgive you for it.

Spaced Invaders (1990). 100 min. Director: Patrick Read Johnson. Producer: Luigi Cingolani. Screenwriters: Scott Lawrence Alexander and Patrick Read Johnson. Cast: Douglas Barr, Royal Dano, Ariana Richards, Wayne Alexander, Fred Applegate, J.J. Anderson, Gregg Berger, Patrika Darbo, Ryan Todd, and Casey Sander.

A crew of dimwitted Martians overhears a rebroadcast of the infamous Orson Welles "War of the Worlds" radio drama, and believing that the Martian fleet is attacking Earth, they land their broken-down flying saucer in a backwater Illinois town. As fate would have it, they arrive on Halloween, and are mistaken for trick-or-treaters. Comedy ensues as the Martians try to get taken seriously. "Buckaroo Banzai" exploited the same material with a much smarter script and more talented cast.

Signs (2002). 106 min. Director: M. Night Shyamalan. Producers: Kathleen Kennedy, Frank Marshall, Sam Mercer, and M. Night Shyamalan. Screenwriter: M. Night Shyamalan.

Cast: Mel Gibson, Joaquin Phoenix, Rory Culkin, Abigail Breslin, Cherry Jones, Patricia Kalember, and M. Night Shyamalan. When members of a family in Bucks County, Pennsylvania, discover a mysterious crop circle in their field, they suspect the work of pranksters. But the five-hundred foot crop circle turns out to be a navigation sign for an invasion force from outer space. The suspense-filled movie focuses on the Hess family and their reactions to world events, and makes what ordinarily would have been yet another "War of the Worlds" rip-off into a very personal, family drama.

Species (1995), MGM, color, 108 min. Director: Roger Donaldson. Writer: Dennis Feldman. Producers: Dennis Feldman and Frank Mancuso, Jr. Cast: Ben Kingsley, Michael Madsen, Alfred Molina, Marg Helgenberger and Natasha Henstridge.

The Search for ET Intelligence Project gets a transmission from beyond the stars on how to structure alien DNA and splice it to human DNA. How could the attractive Dr. Baker (Helgenberger) resist doing that? The result is the beautiful but deadly Sil (Henstridge). Sil hears her mating call, gets naked (often!), and mates with as many guys as she can handle in an R-rated film. The Preying Mantis of Cincinnati would be proud! Earth's only savior Xavier Fitch (Kingsley) recruits a cadre led by Preston Lennox (Madsen), reminiscent of Schwarzenegger's commandos from "Predator," and sets out to stop her before she can score more victims. It's good sexy fun, though a little tough on the guys who inhabit singles' bars. Henstridge is an eyeful of deadly curves and charm, especially when she breaks out of her prison and sheds those prison duds.

Species II (1998), MGM, color, 93 min. Director: Peter Medak. Writers: Dennis Feldman and Chris Brancato. Producer: Frank Mancuso, Jr. Cast: Michael Madsen, Natasha Henstridge, Marg Helgenberger, and Mykelti Williamson.

Two astronauts come back from a manned mission to Mars, and one of them (Justin Lazard) has become half alien. Soon, he's mating like crazy, running off with mutant babies that burst out of women. We all saw Alien, right? With a second "kinder and gentler" Sil, now called Eve (don't ask us why Dr. Baker made a second one?), Lennox (Madsen) leads his crew on a search for the oversexed astronaut. He reproduces amazingly fast. Humankind is challenged. Oh, this is so cheap and dirty. If your prom date stands you up again, give it a try, guys, but don't let her see you watching it a second time. You'll drop in class.

Starship Troopers (1997). TriStar Pictures, USA, color, 129 min. Director: Paul Verhoeven. Written by: Robert A. Heinlein (novel) and Edward Neumeier. Produced by: Jon Davison and Alan Marshall. Cast: Casper Van Dien, Dina Meyer, Denise Richards, Jake Busey, Clancy Brown, and Michael Ironside.

In a futuristic, fascist police state, high school graduates are given the choice to serve in the military and earn the right to vote, or not. Johnny Rico (Van Dien), the scion of a wealthy family, decides to take a chance on the military option, while his beautiful but brainless girl friend (Richards) enrolls as a space cadet. Typecasting? Soon, the buglike extraterrestrials from Klendathu nuke Rico's home town in Brazil, and the war with the bugs is on. But instead of using heavy artillery or rocket launchers against the naturally armored Klendathuites, Verhoeven opted for small caliber assault rifles and nuclear hand grenades (count to three, throw it, and kiss your ass goodbye in real life). Somehow, these humans win. This film bears no resemblance to Heinlein's book, except for the title, but does have a unisex shower scene that will get the hormones racing of most viewers over thirteen.

Star Trek: First Contact (1996). Paramount Pictures, color, 110 min. Director: Jonathan Frakes. Writers: Gene Roddenberry, Rick Berman, etc. Producer: Rick Berman. Cast: Patrick Stewart, Jonathan Frakes, Alfre Woodard, James Cromwell and Alice Krige.

The Enterprise's Pickard (Stewart) and crew save Earth from the space-faring collective known as the Borg, but a Borg ship escapes into the past. The Enterprise must follow the Borg into the middle of the 21st Century. There, the inventor (Cromwell) of the first faster-than-light ship is about to take off, if the Borg don't prevent it from happening. If he doesn't succeed, first contact with the Vulcans won't happen, and, then, neither will the Enterprise. The inventor's helper Lily (Woodard) has some up close and personal discussions with Picard. And the Borg Queen (Krige) has a strange appeal to Data in a sexy, cyberpunk way. Good dialog and three-dimensional characters make this an extraordinary "Star Trek" film, and the best after "Star Trek: The Wrath of Khan."

The Thing (from Another World) (1951). RKO/Winchester Pictures, b/w, 86 min. Director: Christian Nyby (and Howard Hawks). Producer: Howard Hawks. Screenwriter: Charles Lederer based on the novella "Who Goes There?" by John W. Campbell. Cast: Kenneth Tobey, Margaret Sheridan, Robert Cornthwaite, Dewey Martin, Bill Self, Douglas Spencer, and James Arness.

The "thing" was not the metamorphosing creature of its source material and big budget remake, but a blood-drinking carrot, played by none other than Sheriff Matt Dillon from "Gunsmoke," James Arness. It gets worse. Members of an isolated army research station discover a flying saucer embedded in the ice at the Arctic circle, and bring Arness's frozen body back to their post. When one of the soldiers accidentally unthaws the "thing," it begins to run amok, killing and maiming and being generally unpleasant. The station's resident mad doctor

(Cornthwaite) urges the others to capture it alive, while leader Tobey believes that "the only good monster is a dead monster." Ultimately, they trap Arness in the greenhouse and cook him for dinner. Spencer`s final warning to "keep watching the skies" clobbers audiences over the head with their own Cold War paranoia in a heavy-handed way. The movie was the "Alien" of its day, and launched the whole sub-genre of invasions from space, but it's hard to take the "vegoid" monster, played by stalwart Arness, very seriously today.

The Thing (1982). Universal Pictures, 109 min. Director: John Carpenter. Producers: Davis Foster and Lawrence Turman. Screenwriter: Bill Lancaster. Based on the novella "Who Goes There?" by John W. Campbell. Cast: Kurt Russell, A. Wilford Brimley, T.K. Carter, David Clennon, Keith David, Richard Dysart and Charles Hallahan.

The discovery of a flying saucer buried in the ice ignites feelings of suspicion, paranoia, and betrayal among the civilian and military personnel at an Antarctic research station. As in the original, they recover a sole survivor from the wreckage, only this is no blood-thirsty carrot, but rather a carnivorous, shape-changing "thing." Once the creature thaws, it takes on the identity and physical make-up of each person it encounters, killing and draining the very essence of life. The station's resident mad doctor (Dysart) urges the others to capture the "thing" alive, while the rebellious Russell simply wants to destroy it as long as he can figure out which person the monster has replaced. Very few other films scared the shit out of us as much as this one did! Carpenter dispenses with many of the tired, overworked conventions of the original, and plunges his audience into a Gothic horror tale of spine-tingling terror, dismemberment, grue and gore. If you plan to watch this one alone, leave a light on in the hallway. You'll thank me later.

The X Files (1998). 20th Century Fox, color, 121 min. Director: Rob Bowman. Writers: Chris Carter and Frank Spotnitz. Producers: Carter and Daniel Sackheim. Cast: David Duchovny, Gillian Anderson, John Neville and Martin Landau.

When FBI Agents Mulder (Duchovny) and Scully (Anderson) have been pulled off the usual X file search for extraterrestrials, they wind up dealing with a terrorist bomb plot in Dallas, Texas. They learn of yet another conspiracy. A nervous physician (Landau) assists them in a search for a deadly virus or entity which may have originated in outer space. A powerful group of men in London opposes them. The pair travel from Texas to FBI head-quarters, to Antarctica, etc. Is anything resolved here? The atmosphere is wonderful, reminiscent of the perennial search for the real Kennedy assassins in Oliver Stone's "JFK." It is a continuation of "The X-Files" TV series, with the aliens getting closer to launching their "war of the worlds."

Zombies of the Stratosphere (1952). Republic Serial, b&w, 12 chapters. Director: Frank C. O'Brannon. Producer: Franklyn Adreon. Writer: Ronald Davidson. Cast: Judd Holdren, Aline Towne, Lane Bradford, Leonard Nimoy, Wilson Wood, and John Crawford.

Martians plan to blow the Earth up with a hydrogen bomb and then shift Mars into Earth's orbit to take advantage of our superior climate. Really! I'm not making this stuff up! Talk about typecasting: keep your eyes peeled for Leonard Nimoy as one of the alien zombies plotting against Earth.

CHAPTER ELEVEN: THE VISITORS INVADE

In our obsession with antagonisms of the moment, we often forget how much unites all the members of humanity. Perhaps we need some outside, universal threat to make us recognize the common bond that unites all humanity. I occasionally think how quickly our differences worldwide would vanish if we were facing an alien threat from outside this world. We'd forget all the little local differences and find out once and for all that we really are all human beings here on this Earth. And yet I ask you, is not an alien threat already among us? What could be more alien to the universal aspirations of our peoples than war and the threat of war?

—President Ronald Wilson Reagan, Address to the 42nd Session of United Nations General Assembly on September 21, 1987

Inspired by H. G. Wells's *The War of the Worlds*, Kenneth Johnson created a four-hour miniseries, titled simply with the letter "V," for Warner Brothers Television that aired on NBC in May 1983. Johnson's initial idea was that the Martians from the classic 1898 novel would arrive as friendly Visitors from outer space, looking to trade their advanced technology for sea water and other abundant resources, but their intentions for the Earth were far more nefarious. They had already completely depleted the resources on their home world, and were seeking to conquer a new world and enslave humanity. When a journalist reveals their true nature to his television audience, all hell breaks loose, and the "war of the worlds" begins. The show was such a ratings smash that executives at NBC ordered a follow-up sequel. Executives at NBC actually wanted a weekly series for their Fall 1983-84 season, but Warner Brothers could not figure out a way to make a weekly series cost effectively for the network.

A year later, the second miniseries, titled "V: The Final Battle," aired during the May ratings sweep, and swept the competition away with the continuation of humanity's fight with the alien Visitors. Johnson supervised the writing of the script for the sequel, but he left the project shortly thereafter. Daniel Blatt and Robert Singer were hired as co-executive producers. The six-hour series was such a success that NBC pleaded with Warner Brothers for a series, and after some debate among the top executives, the studio agreed to make "V-The Series."

On Friday, October 26, 1984, "V-The Series" picked up right where the second miniseries had left off, and continued for nineteen episodes. At a cost of more than $1 million per episode, the series was the most expensive television show in history. But when the ratings began to drop off, NBC was forced to cancel the show. The final episode aired on March 22, 1985, a cliffhanger never to be resolved, and the show went into re-runs and syndication. While most television viewers living today fondly remember the state-of-the-art make-up and special effects of the ground-breaking show, few recall "V's" metaphor about Nazi Germany or the tough sell it was originally for creator-producer Kenneth Johnson.

In the Beginning...

...it was a classic Hollywood pitch session.

Producer Kenneth Johnson, coming off of the dual success of "The Bionic Woman" (1975) and "The Incredible Hulk" (1978) and looking for a break from the sci-fi genre, had reportedly gone to NBC and Warner Bros. to pitch a series concept concerning the French Maquis, the World War II underground resistance movement that took on the Nazis. Unfortunately, the lack of interest during that meeting quickly became apparent, but Johnson, savvy enough to know what he would need to sell such a concept, added, "The difference is that the Nazis are from outer space."

His day ended with a commitment for a four-hour miniseries. Although seemingly trapped within a genre he desperately wanted a reprieve from, Johnson nonetheless saw the possibility of exploring key sociological issues that television by and large had not been addressing. Most importantly, he had taken note of the fact that in recent years America had become a home base for growing fascist and vigilante movements, all of which dovetailed with his fascination with Sinclair Lewis' 1935 novel, *It Can't Happen Here*.

"That novel concerned a fascist regime taking power in the U.S. and how people reacted to it," says Johnson, whose credits include The Bionic Woman, The Incredible Hulk and the TV version of Alien Nation. "1 tried to find a contemporary framework in which to tell the story and V seemed like the perfect one. It would have been unrealistic, ironically enough, to have the invading force be an Earth-based one. The Chinese and the Soviets were obviously the first thoughts that came to mind, but I thought it would be difficult to believe that they would have the staying power or the presence to be able to commandeer the country."

What Johnson wanted to do was explore what life would be like if America suddenly found itself in a police state, and how Americans themselves would react to an occupying army of fascists. He compares his approach to how the French reacted to the onslaught of the Nazis in the early 1940s.

"I thought there might be a way to parallel the Nazis' falling in Denmark," he says. "They sort of rolled into Denmark and said, 'Hi, we're going to be your friends. We're here to protect you from the imperialistic English, you lucky people.' So I thought about spacecraft being like the Nazis coming into Denmark, and I realized there was a way to do that, that a totalitarian society like the aliens could come in here, showing us one face, if you will, but underneath is another face that's quite different."

"V"- The Second Generation

Since its cancellation, there have been numerous rumors of a possible revival of "V," first by the creative team of the series, then by "Babylon 5" creator J. Michael Straczynski, who actually wrote a four-hour teleplay for syndication. For a short time, Warner Brothers discussed a third final miniseries, but executives ultimately rejected that idea as being too expensive to produce.

In 2003, Kenneth Johnson announced plans for a new miniseries to pick up twenty years after the events of the original miniseries, but that has yet to be made. Now, however, there's been a change of heart, with NBC giving a script order for "V: The Second Generation," which will essentially ignore the events of "The Final Battle" and the weekly series. Instead, it will jump forward 20 years in time (literally the length of time since the airing of the original "V").

As Johnson explains it, his scenario for the follow-up will deal with Resistance leaders Mike Donovan (Marc Singer) and Julie Parish (Faye Grant) who are trying to spark a revolution in a generation that has known nothing but Visitor rule since the moment they were born, so there is a certain apathy when it comes to the notion of revolution. Says Johnson, "NBC wants to move it away from the notion of Europe under occupation to something that has a little more modern feel. But that's tricky. I don't want the heroes of the piece to be considered terrorists, but that's the parallel. If the Visitors are the hyper-power, what does that make the Resistance?"

One key plot element for the new version comes from the final moment of the original four-hour miniseries. In that story, the Resistance discovers that the Visitors have one deadly enemy, leading the humans to jump to the conclusion that, "If it's their enemies, then that makes them our friends." A signal is sent into deep space and it would seem that in "V: The Second Generation" there is finally an answer.

"That's sort of where the story goes," Johnson says, "but part of what I'm dealing with on the network level is, 'Does anybody really care about those old actors?' It's amazing. It's like, 'Let's do the 'Brady Bunch' reunion movie, but not get the Brady Bunch."

The impression is that if the new "V" is a hit, this will leave the door open for a series of TV movie sequels. "Not necessarily," Johnson replies. "I'm looking at this as one piece that ends, basically. But at the same time, the way that I've crafted it, there's an open door. It's a different door than we've been through before triggered by the notion that our world is in a different and better place." He pauses, adding innocently, "Isn't it?"

Now if only he and NBC can settle on the length. The network wants three hours, Johnson is pushing for four. Get set for the "final battle" all over again.

Whatever happens in the future, David Braff has one final thought about the subject: "My feeling about the series," he offers, "is that we were doing two different things in what proved to be unwieldy in an hour form, and that is we were carrying 12 to 14 characters who had soap operatic problems, and yet it was an action-adventure formula. I believe the two were incompatible. If it had been successful, I think we would have spawned a new type of genre. But, unfortunately, it wasn't."

Episode Guide:

"V" (mini-series; four hours)
Airdates: Part 1: 5/1/83; Part 2: 5/2/83
Written and Directed by Kenneth Johnson
Cast: Marc Singer (Mike Donovan), Faye Grant (Juliet Parrish), Richard Herd (John), Jane Badler (Diana), Robert Englund (Willie), Blair Tefkin (Robin Maxwell), David Packer (Daniel), Michael Wright (Elias), Frank Ashmore (Martin)
Plot: One spring day, they arrived. . . tens of thousands of extraterrestrial beings in fifty huge Motherships, and hovered over the major cities of the world: Paris, London, Athens, Moscow, Peking, New York, Los Angeles and other key urban centers. They came from a dying planet, offering their friendship and advanced technology in exchange for small amounts of Earth's mineral resources. But in reality, their purpose was much more sinister: they came to drain the planet of its water and process the Earth's populace, like cattle, as food! At 0100 Greenwich Mean Time, the Visitors made their first contact with the United Nations of the World. Supreme Commander John, the admiral of the small fleet, greeted the assembled political and military leaders with open arms, and revealed that the aliens had traveled 8.7 light years from the fourth planet in the Sirius star system on a mission of mercy. He then invited members of the press, including cameraman Mike Donovan, aboard his ship. The Visitors remained cordial, pleasant-yet something was not quite right. In the weeks that followed, the Visitors were welcomed into every facet of Earth culture. Youngsters played with action figures, teens signed on with the Visitor Youth Corps and social events were planned around the new arrivals. They earned Earth's friendship with unselfish acts of courage, such as William saving Caleb Taylor from a freezing unit; and they gained the love and affection of many. The Visitors became an integral part of Earth culture and the

lives they touched. Skeptical of the Visitors, Mike Donovan infiltrated their rank and discovered their real purpose and identity. The Visitors were really lizards in human disguises, and were not our friends. However, before he could broadcast the information to the world, the Visitors seized control of the media and invoked martial law. Donovan became a fugitive, and the aliens were anxious to kill him before

he could spread the truth. Captured once and interrogated by the evil Diana, he was freed by Martin, and members of a Fifth Column, who didn't believe in what the Leader was doing. Donovan became convinced that the Visitors would have to be stopped at all costs. Soon, others rebelled against the Visitors' stranglehold. Juliet Parrish, a bio-med student, believed Donovan's story and organized a resistance group to fight back. It was composed of an anthropologist, a construction worker, a former cop, a black marketer and others who were disenchanted with the Visitors. They establish an underground base in the city and a mountain hideaway. Juliet composes a plan for the group to strike back-but first they must arm themselves. On the eve of their strike however, Robert Maxwell, the anthropologist, betrays the Resistance's secret mountain base in ex-

change for his daughter Robin's return, and regrets his action when he learns they intend an immediate assault. During the daring, daylight raid on the munitions house, Juliet and the others make off with an impressive supply and hurry to the aid of their comrades in the mountains. United in battle-the Resistance members fight against the Visitors. [Novelization by A. C. (Ann) Crispin, New York: Pinnacle Books, 1984.]

"V: The Final Battle" (mini-series; six hours)
Airdates: Part 1: 5/6/84; Part 2: 5/7/84; Part 3: 5/8/84
Written by Brian Taggert, Diane Frolov, Peggy Goldman and Faustus Buck
Story by Lillian Weezer, Diane Frolov, Peggy Goldman, Faustus Buck and Harry & Renee Longstreet
Directed by Richard T. Heffron
Cast: as above, plus Michael Ironside (Ham Tyler), Mickey Jones (Chris), Sarah Douglas (Pamela)
Plot: Four months later, the world is living under the totalitarian rule of the Visitors. Although more people have joined the Resistance, their hit-and-run tactics have proven only marginally successful. Donovan convinces the group that they need a "bonanza" in order to remain unified, and they decide to crash an upcoming speech and expose the Visitors on network television for what they really are. The plan succeeds and calls attention to the Resistance group. But Juliet Parrish is captured and taken to Diana for conversion. She fights against the conversion and is eventually freed and reunited with the group. In the

interim, the Resistance group is joined by a professional mercenary-Hamilton Tyler. Tyler is known by Donovan as a former CIA operative and a ruthless killer. He advises the group about a master plan that they are working on against "the lizards," and he gives them teflon-coated ammunition which will penetrate the Visitors' protective armor. Meanwhile, aboard the Los Angeles Mothership, Diana not only plots against her, superiors (John and Pamela), but uncovers numerous members of the Fifth Column, including Martin. She insists on total victory against the humans, even if it means using a weapon that will annihilate all life on Earth. In the end, she dispatches all her troops and kills both Pamela and John. Robin Maxwell, who was impregnated by Visitor Brian (under orders from Diana), gives birth to twins-one human and one lizard. The lizard baby dies, but the human one metamorphoses into a star-child of enormous energy and power. Robin begins by fearing the child, but grows to love it as her own, Robin is also able to avenge her honor by killing Brian with an experimental poison-the Red Dust-that chokes of air to the Visitors. Led by William, Martin and other Fifth Columnists, the Resistance launches a two-pronged attack on the Visitors. The Red Dust kills off the ground troops and effectively cripples the command of the Los Angeles mother-ship. Diana arms her doomsday weapon and escapes in a lone shuttlecraft, while the other Visitor ships withdraw from Earth. But thanks to the timely appearance of star-child Elizabeth at the control panel, the weapon is disarmed.

"V" (weekly series):

Cast: Marc Singer, Faye Grant, Jane Badler, Michael Ironside, Blair Tefkin, Robert Englund, Michael Wright, Frank Ashmore (Martin/Philip), June Chadwick (Lydia), Lane Smith (Nathan Bates), Jeff Yagher (Kyle Bates), Jennifer Cooke (Elizabeth), Judson Scott (Lt. James), Aki Aleong (Mr. Chiang), Howard K. Smith (himself)

Episode 1: "Liberation Day"

Airdate: 10/26/84

Written by Paul Monash

Directed by Paul Kransy

Guest Stars: Michael Durrell (Robert Maxwell), Jenny Beck (Elizabeth)

Plot: While piloting the Mothership home, Martin sees Diana steal a shuttlecraft and sends Donovan in pursuit of her. Donavan disables her craft with expert marksmanship and captures her after her shuttle has crashed to Earth. Diana is imprisoned and held for trial as humankind spends a year celebrating its victory over the lizards. During the year, the Resistance fighters attempt to put their lives back together: Donovan, along with his friend Martin, resumes a career in television broadcasting; Juliet Parrish goes to work for Nathan Bates (the man responsible for manufacturing the Red Dust) at Science Frontiers; Robin, her father and her daughter settle down at a quiet ranch; and Elias and Willie open a restaurant-The Club Creole. But Ham Tyler is not content to settle down and is hired by Bates to spring Diana from her prison, so that she can help them unravel the secret of the captured Mothership. The plan, however, goes awry. Diana escapes! She coldbloodedly murders Martin and signals for her troops from a deep-space tracking station. Donovan and Tyler arrive too late to stop her, and the nightmare begins again!

Sub-Plot: While Donovan and Tyler (and others) are pursuing Diana, Elizabeth becomes gravely ill. Her grandfather Robert Maxwell calls Julie for help; but before she can do anything, Elizabeth crawls into a cave and begins a metabolic change. Events are complicated by the fact that Robin has left the ranch for a much-needed rest.

Episode 2: "Dreadnaught"

Airdate: 11/2/84

Written by Steven E. deSouza

Directed by Paul Kransy

Guest Stars: Michael Durrell (Robert Maxwell), Jenny Beck (Elizabeth)

Plot: Once aboard her command ship, Diana orders the fleet (which has been hiding behind the moon) to attack Earth. Lydia, Diana's second in command, informs her that most of the Fifth Columnists have been executed and the Leader has been informed of Diana's poor progress. Diana is infuriated, yet remains cool and reasons that the Red Dust dies in warmer climates. So that is where she will mount her final attack. The Visitor troops strike Los Angeles and demolish all military resistance (clever use of "War of the Worlds" footage here). Diana lands at Science Frontiers and orders Bates to turn over the stolen Mothership. But Bates is too clever for her. He strikes a bargain to make Los Angeles an open city, with himself as head of the provisional government. Diana really has no choice-Bates has armed himself with a failsafe doomsday device that will release Red Dust everywhere if she tries to take the city by force. Diana agrees to his terms, but quickly begins plotting to undermine that agreement. She orders the Leader's Tn-ax particle beam to burn the city to cinders. However, the Resistance, led by Donovan and Tyler, seize the Mothership. Robert Maxwell pilots it into a collision with the Tn-ax while the others escape. The two sides are once again locked in a stalemate.

Sub-Plot: Elizabeth metamorphosizes into a 17-year-old woman. Willie spots the Mark of Zon on her hand and explains that a child of both worlds is prophesied to unite the people in Preta-na-ma, or peace. Elizabeth is the chosen one!

Episode 3: "Breakout"

Airdate: 5/24/85 (shown out of order during initial series run)

Written by David Braff

Directed by Ray Austin

Guest Stars: Xander Berkeley, Christian Jacobs, Pamela Ludwig

Plot: While Donovan and Tyler are on their way to free Sean, they rescue a young boy from the clutches of the Visitors, then are betrayed while hiding in a "safe" house. Together with Robin,

they are sentenced to the Visitors' maximum-security camp, which greatly resembles a Nazi POW stalag. They are determined to escape, but soon discover that the camp is ringed by a sea of sand that is inhabited by crivits-sand sharks. Diana captures Kyle and bargains with Nathan Bates: his son's release in exchange for Elizabeth. Bates turns to Parrish for assistance, but she refuses to reveal Elizabeth's whereabouts. On the eve of their breakout, Donovan and Tyler meet Kyle. At first, their verbal exchanges are not friendly. But they soon earn each other's respect-and break out of the prison camp. Donovan and Tyler steal a Visitor shuttle while Kyle races off on a motorcycle.

Episode 4: "The Deception"

Airdate: 11/9/84

Written by Garner Simmons

Directed by Victor Lobl

Guest Stars: Nick Katt (Sean Donovan)

Plot: Robin, attempting to make her way back home, meets- a young motorcyclist, Kyle Bates, and witnesses the delivery of an important pouch from a downed fighter pilot. Kyle takes her to a place of safety, then takes the pouch to Resistance headquarters. Apparently, the World Liberation Front wants to move Elizabeth to New York, and safety, before the Visitors get her. Once Kyle meets Elizabeth, he becomes involved in the Resistance. Realizing the Resistance plans to move Elizabeth, Diana orders Donovan's capture and creates an elaborate deception in order to get the information she needs. The deception is truly ingenious: by way of holographic generators, Diana poses as Julie and convinces Donovan that the war has been over for a year. Her plan goes awry when she gives Donovan a newspaper featuring a clip of Elizabeth as a child and not the 17-year-old woman. Donovan escapes the Visitor legation and foils the alien's plot moments before they can reach Elizabeth.

Sub-Plot: Donovan's son Sean is given a commission in Diana's Visitor Guard, while Bates and his son Kyle disagree about the elder's collaboration with the enemy.

Note: This was the first episode to feature a broadcast from the Freedom Network, in which real-life Howard K. Smith reports about the international progress of the war.

Episode 5: "The Sanction"

Airdate: 11/16/84

Written by Brian Taggert

Directed by Bruce Seth Green

Guest Stars: Nick Katt (Sean Donovan), Thomas Callaway (Klaus)

Plot: Klaus is a master assassin who has been retained by Diana to pursue and terminate

anyone committing crimes against the Legation. He is also a guru, or zen master, in charge of training the Visitor Youth Corps to kill. His favorite among the group of young trainees is Donovan's son Sean! When Tyler shows Donovan footage of the Youth Corps' training camp, Mike decides that he must stop the indoctrination of his son. He smuggles himself into the Legation and duels with Klaus to the death for Sean's freedom. Diana interferes and Sean remains in the Visitor's control.

Sub-Plot: After mother Robin and daughter Elizabeth are reunited, a struggle for the love and attention of Kyle develops between them. Nathan and Kyle Bates have an argument concerning Elizabeth, and Nathan assigns his personal henchman, Mr. Chiang, to watch his son very closely. Meanwhile, Elizabeth uses her very special powers for the first time!

Episode 6: "Visitor's Choice"
Airdate: 11/23/84
Written by David Braff
Directed by Gilbert Shilton
Guest Stars: Sybil Danning (Mary Kruger), Robert Ellenstein, Jonathan Caliri
Plot: The Resistance intercepts a communication which reveals that all the Visitor Commanders of Processing Units will meet at the Playa Del Mar beachside resort to discuss a new human meat processor-The Encapsulator. Donovan and Julie decide to disrupt the meeting and dispatch Kyle and Tyler to acquire explosives while they contact the local Resistance group in Playa Del Mar. Following a minor (but almost deadly) misunderstanding, Julie, Donovan and the locals organize an attack on the Visitor estate. At the meeting Mary Kruger, a notorious Visitor commander, unveils the new processor, which will triple the speed of food production. The device is indeed a deadly one, and Diana is most pleased with its results. She offers a toast and treats the other commanders to an exquisite dinner. During the Resistance's daring nighttime assault, Julie becomes trapped in a freezing chamber and almost prepared for the food processor. She is rescued by Donovan moments before the estate is blown up. The Encapsulator is destroyed and most of the Visitor guests killed. Diana, unfortunately, escapes.

Sub-Plot: Kyle is captured while stealing explosives and given by his father to Mr. Chiang for discipline. He is later rescued by Elizabeth, using her extraordinary powers.

Episode 7: "The Overlord"
Airdate: 11/30/84
Written by David Abramowitz
Directed by Bruce Seth Green
Guest Stars: Sheryl Lee Ralph (Glenna), Robert Thaler, Michael Champion
Plot: The people of the small town of Rawlinsville, inside the Red Dust contaminated area, are being used as slave labor to mine cobalt for a collaborator named Garrison. Since the Visitors need a large supply of cobalt for their final assault on the Earth, he has struck a deal with Diana-one bar of gold for each ton of cobalt. When a black woman, Glenna, escapes and goes to the Resistance for help, Elias convinces the others that she is sincere. But she betrays them in order to make herself leader of the collaborators, and Donovan, Tyler and

the others must use their best resources to escape and prevent the shipment of the precious mineral.

Sub-Plot: On the Los Angeles Mothership, Diana discovers a Visitor doctor praying to a holographic image of Zon. Zon worship is a forbidden religion amongst the Visitors because it speaks of peace and brotherhood. Its practice is punishable by death. Diana feeds the doctor to a crivit-a sand shark. On Earth, Nathan Bates accuses Julie of being a Resistance fighter and has Mr. Chiang deliver evidence. Julie, however, manages to outwit them both.

Episode 8: "The Dissident"

Airdate: 12/7/84

Written by Paul F. Edwards

Directed by Walter Grauman

Guest Stars: John McLiam (Jacob), Anthony DeLongis

Plot: Moments before Tyler and Kyle rendezvous with a munitions truck, Diana orders the activation of a new force field that obliterates the vehicle. Her plan is to encircle Los Angeles so that the Visitors control everything going in and out, and the Resistance realizes that, if her plan succeeds, it will spell their doom. While Julie attempts to break the security of the transmitting station at Science Frontiers, Donovan and Tyler go hesitant to help either side, but changes his mind when he meets Elizabeth and recognizes her as "The Chosen One." He sacrifices his life to destroy the force field.

Sub-Plot: Angered by Diana's incompetence, Lydia steals a shuttle and attempts to reach the Leader. But she is shot down under Diana's orders.

Episode 9: "A Reflection in Terror"

Airdate: 12/14/84

Written by Chris Manheim

Directed by Kevin Hooks

Guest Stars: Mickey Jones (Chris), Jenny Beck (clone)

Plot: Using Christmas holly, Diana obtains a blood sample of Elizabeth and clones an exact duplicate. The clone, however, escapes and begins terrorizing the city with her unbridled powers. Meanwhile, Donovan and Tyler are using an underground railroad to get children out. They use a church as a hideout and reunite with Ham's old buddy Chris. One of the children reminds Tyler of his little girl, and he finds her presence most difficult. Julie is finally discovered to be a Resistance member, and through an elaborate scheme Bates and his henchmen plot to blow up the Club Creole. Julie is forced to break out of Science Frontiers and hurries to her friends' aid. But she is too late; the Club is destroyed. However, her Resistance friends are all right. In fact, they were the ones who blew the building up.

The clone finally meets the real Elizabeth, and the meeting is a bittersweet one: she sacrifices her life in order to save Elizabeth and Kyle. Reunited in the ashes of the Club Creole, the Resistance offers a Christmas toast to peace and eventual victory. Ham Tyler plays Santa Claus for the fugitive children, and the rebels rejoice in the holiday.

Episode 10: "The Conversion"

Airdate: 1/4/85

Written by Brian Taggert

Directed by Gilbert Shilton

Guest Stars: Duncan Regehr (Charles), Mickey Jones (Chris)

Plot: During a raid on a munitions convoy, Tyler and Kyle are captured by Diana's troops. They become pawns in a very elaborate scheme engineered by Charles, the Leader's special envoy. Charles in charismatic, good-looking and is here to see that the war is won! He demotes Diana back to science officer and makes Lydia (who was not killed when Diana ordered her shuttle blasted in a previous episode) his special assistant. He then begins converting Tyler by brain-washing him into thinking that Donovan raped his wife and stole his child. The Resistance kidnaps Lydia and holds her for a prisoner exchange. Tyler is freed-but only as part of Charles's plan to kill Donovan and destroy the Resistance. A trade-Kyle for Lydia-is arranged, and Charles's scheme is put into motion. At an abandoned stadium, Bates acts as a neutral party in the prisoner exchange. But just as Tyler is about to kill Donovan, Elizabeth intercedes. Bates is critically wounded while Kyle and the others escape. However, the fate of the Open City remains an important, unanswered question.

Episode 11: "The Hero"

Airdate: 1/11/85

Written by Carleton Eastlake

Directed by Kevin Hooks

Guest Stars: Duncan Regehr (Charles), Mickey Jones (Chris), Bruce Davison (Langley)

Plot: A Visitor group, posing as Resistance fighters, strikes Science Frontiers. Word of this heinous attack reaches the city and the real Resistance leaders are put on the spot. Donovan and the others decide to fight back and send Robin to a free newspaper-sympathetic to the Resistance-to print the truth. While there, she and the staff are taken captive by the assassins, who will kill one hostage a day until the Resistance surrenders to the Visitors. Elias and Willie attempt to free Robin and the other hostages, but in the resulting firefight Elias is disintegrated! Willie returns with the news, and the group develops a plan: Donovan will pretend to surrender while the others rescue the hostages. The plan is a sound one, except they don't realize that Diana has planted a spy, John, in the midst of the hostages.

Sub-Plot: Bates lies in the hospital, critically injured from the wounds he suffered at the stadium. Charles and Diana offer Chiang Bates's position of power. A holographic image of Bates is utilized as a puppet to control the city.

Episode 12: "The Betrayal"
Airdate: 1/18/85
Written by Mark Rosner
Directed by Gilbert Shilton
Guest Stars: Duncan Regehr (Charles), Bruce Davison (Langley)
Plot: Willie is injured while attempting to contact the Fifth Column and nearly dies. He is saved by the aid of a Visitor doctor-also a member of the Fifth column-who reveals that Diana is using the hospital to stockpile weapons for the final assault

on Los Angeles. Donovan and Tyler decide to blow the hospital up-but their plans are overheard by Diana's spy (Lt. Langley). Meanwhile, concerned about his father's health, Kyle sneaks into Science Frontiers. He discovers that Chiang has been using his father's power-base, and that Bates has been lying in a near-coma. Kyle attempts to help his father escape, but Chiang shoots Nathan, killing him. Kyle then settles the score by killing Chiang. The Resistance destroys the hospital in a daring daylight raid, and Robin exposes John for what he really is-a Visitor! John is killed by the Fifth Columnist doctor.
Subplot: Diana and Lydia struggle for control and for Charles's attention. By the close of the episode, Robin and Ham are dispatched (permanently?) to Chicago.

Episode 13: "The Rescue"
Airdate: 2/1/85
Written by Garner Simmons
Directed by Kevin Hooks
Guest Stars: Duncan Regehr (Charles), Ian Fried, Darlene Carr
Plot: The Visitors strike and bring Los Angeles to the ground! James and his assault team locate the Resistance headquarters and destroy it-moments after Donovan and company pull out. The totalitarian nightmare rule of the Visitors has returned, and there is no longer any safe place! Charles proposes to Diana, and in an elaborate alien ceremony marries her. Jealous and angry, Lydia poisons Diana's wedding goblet. Charles, however, drinks the deadly potion instead and suffers a horrible death. Diana arrests Lydia for his murder and orders her to stand trial. During the burning annihilation of Los Angeles, Julie helps deliver a baby and becomes trapped by the Visitor assault team. Fortunately, Donovan, Kyle and the others locate her and arrange a rescue.

Subplot: Since the Resistance headquarters were destroyed, Willie and Elizabeth are assigned to find a new base. They move into an abandoned movie studio.

Episode 14: "The Champion"
Airdate: 2/8/85
Written by Paul F. Edwards
Directed by Cliff Bole
Guest Stars: Gordon Ross, Deborah Wakeham, Ross McCubbin
Plot: Lydia is charged with the murder of Charles, found guilty by a Visitor court and sentenced to death. However, while Lydia is being prepared for disintegration, Philip, the Inspector General, arrives and halts the execution. He is a twin brother and look alike of Martin's (having been created by the same zygote mother), and he wishes to further examine the case. While delivering weapons to Tucson, Donovan and Kyle get involved in the problems of a small town. Apparently, the Sheriff has made arrangements with the Visitors to deliver half of the local livestock. Donovan organizes the town's own Resistance and leads them in battle against the Visitors and the local collaborators. On board the Los Angeles Mothership, Philip determines that Lydia's rights were violated and that she was wrongly accused. She is offered "trial by combat" against Diana. The two fight-but just as Lydia is about to finish Diana off, Philip interrupts, explaining he has discovered new evidence. There were additional fingerprints found on the poison vial!

Episode 15: "The Wildcats"
Airdate: 2/15/85
Written by David Braff
Directed by John Florea
Guest Stars: Gela Jacobson (Marta), Rhonda Aldrich
Plot: An epidemic is sweeping through the valley, and even though Juliet Parrish and members of the Resistance are working tirelessly to halt its spread, they realize the only drug that will stop the sickness is under the protection of the Visitors! They reluctantly enlist the aid of a teen group known as the Wildcats and attempt to steal the drug; but they are ambushed and seize a fake drug instead. They quickly come to realize that there is a traitor amongst them. On the Los Angeles Mothership, Diana and Lydia, fearing for their own lives, blame the ship's pharmacist, Marta, for Charles's murder. The duo produces false evidence which is most damning. Philip is fooled by the trumped-up information and sentences Marta to spend eternity with Charles's corpse in its space

coffin.Requesting that Donovan fly the drug in, the Resistance arranges for a landing strip, but its secret location is betrayed to the Visitors by the spy. Julie, Kyle and the others must fight against Lt. James and his hit squad, while Donovan parachutes to safety with the life-saving drugs.

Subplot: After saving Ellen Barker-one of the Wildcats-from the Visitors, Willie becomes the object of her affection. Of course, she doesn't know that he is in reality a Visitor. He tries to tell her the truth, and after much consternation they decide to be friends.

Episode 16: "The Littlest Dragon"
Airdate: 2/22/85
Written by David Abramowitz
Directed by Cliff Bole
Guest Stars: Brett Cullen, Leslie Bevis, Wendy Fulton
Plot: While on a night raid to destroy a new Visitor weapon (the Metamorph), Donovan, Kyle and Willie become involved with two fifth columnists-one of whom is pregnant. They have stolen Berryllium Crystals from the Mothership (which effectively disables its fire-power), and seek a quiet sanctuary in which their child can be born. The Resistance members make them comfortable in an abandoned warehouse. Aboard the Los Angeles Mothership, Philip is angered by both Lydia's and Diana's incompetence in dealing with the traitors and the Resistance. He decides to personally handle the matter, and strikes out-with his private guards-after the man who killed his brother: Mike Donovan. Little does he know that Diana has assigned Angela (a Visitor assassin) to kill him! The Visitors trace the rebels and the fifth columnists to t abandoned warehouse. A fight ensues but, fearing for the safety of the newborn lizard, Donovan agrees to pursue combat with Philip. Donovan wins, then convinces Philip that Martin did not die a traitor's death, but rather that he died a man trying to insure peace. Angela refuses to accept the outcome of the personal combat and attempts to kill Philip Donovan and the others, but her life is ended by someone else.

Subplot: After complaining to Donovan and Kyle that feels like a stranger in a strange land, Willie is asked to the "wantu," or godfather, of the lizard baby. He rejoices the chance to be part of a family.

Episode 17: "War of Illusion"
Airdate: 3/8/85
Written by John Simmons
Directed by Earl Bellamy
Guest Stars: Conrad Janis (Dr. David Atkins), Josh Richman

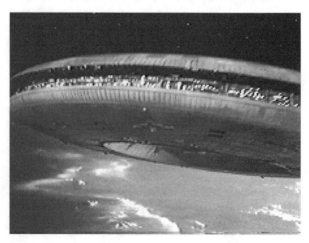

Plot: While Diana and Lt. James plot their next move in Diana's bedchamber, Philip delivers some bad news to Donovan and Kyle. The Leader has ordered the implementation of the Battlesphere-a computerized device that will transmit and execute the Leader's own final battle plans. They realize that it the plan succeeds it will mean an end to the Earth. They immediately undertake a search for a computer wiz (an acquaintance ot Kyle's) who can stop the Battlesphere. Lt. James, meanwhile, traces some guerrilla computer tampering to the home of Dr. David Atkins and his son Henry The Visitors arrest the father, believing him to be the hack who has tapped into the Mothership's central computer. In reality, Henry is the genius. The Resistance finds Henry and convinces him to use som~ stolen data tapes, obtained by Philip, to stop a massive alien attack. Henry neutralizes the attack by re-directing the alien fighters, using the computers at Science Frontiers. He saves the day and is reunited with his father. On board the Mothership, during the celebration of Slutor, Lydia and Diana watch the defeat of the Visitor blitzkrieg.

Episode 18: "The Secret Underground"
Airdate: 3/15/85
Written by David Braff and Colley Cibber
Story by David Abramowitz and Donald R. Boyle
Directed by Cliff Bole
Guest Stars: John Calvin
Plot: This episode takes place almost entirely on board the Mothership. As Lt. James is escorting the latest Resistance captives to their cells, fifth columnists Jonathan and Judith overhear him boast about a list of Resistance leaders and their whereabouts that he possesses. Fearing what such a list could mean, Jonathan steals and hides the metal computer card, on which the list is encoded, under an alien sculpture, a volcano used for part of the Feast of Ramalon ceremony. Philip learns of the list and arranges to have Donovan and Parrish board the Mothership to search for it. Similarly, Diana dispatches Lt. James and his terror troops to find the card. After numerous close calls, Donovan and Parrish enlist the aid of Dr. Maitland, a human who's pretending to help the Visitors develop a plague virus. He is reluctant at first because he and Julie were once lovers, but he eventually helps the rebels find the list and escape the ship.
Subplot: Lydia's brother Nigel is ordered by Diana to serve as a sacrifice for the Feast of Ramalon (the youngest warrior is traditionally sacrificed at the ceremony to insure total victory). Lydia joins forces with Philip, even though she suspects him of being a fifth columnist, and together they prevent Diana from killing Nigel.

Episode 19: "The Return"
Airdate: 3/22/85
Written by David Abramowitz and Donald R. Boyle
Story by David Braff and Colley Cibber
Directed by John Florea
Guest Stars: Marilyn Jones (Thelma), Tawny Schneider
Plot: Moments before members of the Los Angeles Resistance are to be killed by Lt. James and his terror troops, an order is given to cease hostilities. Donovan and company are suspicious of the Visitors' motives, but when Motherships withdraw from cities throughout the world, they begin to accept the fact that the war is over. Apparently, Philip has convinced

the Leader that the Earthlings have fought bravely and would make good allies. The Leader invites Earth's leaders to meet with him for a celebration aboard the L.A. Mothership. He also expresses his wish to mate with Elizabeth, so as to symbolically join the two races. Kyle, naturally, is adamantly opposed to such a proposition, but Elizabeth convinces him that it is the best thing for both worlds. Meanwhile Diana, still obsessed with total victory over the humans, plots the Leader's assassination with Lt. James. When the attempt fails, she threatens to blow up Earth. But her plans are thwarted, and she and James are hand-cuffed and sentenced to death. The Leader's shuttle finally arrives and Elizabeth goes to join him. However, in the final moments of the season, Kyle stows aboard the alien craft. Diana reveals that she has planted a time bomb in the shuttle that will destroy the Leader and all others aboard!

Subplot: Willie meets with his Visitor girlfriend Thelma whom he no longer loves. The two exchange bittersweet memories of their past together.

Episode 20: "The Attack"

Airdate: none (unfilmed)

Written by David Braff and Paul F. Edwards Story by Donald R. Boyle

Plot: Diana regains control of the fleet and launches a devastating attack on Earth; the Resistance attempts to locate Elizabeth and escape the Mothership.

"V" (1983). Warner Brothers/NBC. 2-Miniseries and 19-1 Hour Episodes. Creator: Kenneth Johnson. Writers: Kenneth Johnson, Brian Taggert, Diane Frolov, Peggy Goldman, Faustus Buck, Steven E. deSouza, Paul Monash, David Braff, David Abramowitz, Donald R. Boyle, and others. Producers: Kenneth, Johnson, Daniel Blatt and Robert Singer.

Cast: Marc Singer, Faye Grant, Jane Badler, Michael Ironside, Blair Tefkin, Robert Englund, Michael Wright, Frank Ashmore, June Chadwick, Lane Smith, Jeff Yagher, Jennifer Cooke, Judson Scott, Duncan Regehr, Aki Aleong, Howard K. Smith. Available on DVD.

CHAPTER TWELVE: MARS ATTACKS!

Why are you doing this? Why? Isn't the universe big enough for both of us? Why don't we work together? Think how much we could do! Earth and Mars together! Why there's nothing we couldn't accomplish! Why all this destruction? Why can't we settle our differences and work things out? <u>Why can't we just get along?</u>
—President James Dale, "Mars Attacks!" (1996)

In 1962, following a long, successful tradition of packaging trading cards with bubblegum, Topps Incorporated issued a fifty-five card set that updated H. G. Wells's *The War of the Worlds* to the paranoid Fifties, called "Mars Attacks!" The bubblegum cards told the familiar story of an invasion from Mars and how individual humans responded to the attack. Topps had just released the hugely successful "Civil War Centennial Cards," an unlikely forerunner of the Sci-fi set, earlier that year, and were looking to capitalize on the collaborative genius of Woody Gelman, a former magazine publisher, and Len Brown, an imaginative twenty-one-year-old author. Their follow-up was to make bubblegum card history and turn collectors into fanatics.

"We came up with the idea of doing a modern 'War of the Worlds,' calling the concept 'Attack from Space,'" Len Brown recalled over forty years later. Both he and Gelman had been fans of the pulp science fiction stories of the Thirties and Forties; in fact, Gelman was an avid collector of the pulp magazines, and had a complete run of Hugo Gernsbach's Amazing Stories. "We did the Civil War cards together, and it was during that series that a veteran pulp artist named Norm Saunders was hired to paint some wonderfully detailed" - and very graphic - "pictures that were no bigger than 5in by 7in. The series, gore and all, was pretty successful, and that's when we began discussing science fiction concepts for a card series."

Gelman and Brown worked very briefly with Wally Wood, another pulp artist from the golden era of science fiction pulp magazines like *Amazing Stories* and *Astounding Science Fiction* and E.C. Comics like *Weird Science*, and roughed out some ideas for the card series. They then called back Norm Saunders, and teamed him with Bob Powell, a wonderfully talented and prolific comic book artist. Powell did the pencils, and Saunders painted right over them on the illustration board. The

continuing storyline was developed by Brown and Gelman. The whole process of creating the 55-card set of "Mars Attacks!" cards turned out to be an incredibly creative and wonderfully collaborative venture for all of those involved.

"Woody and I worked together coming up with the scenes," Brown recalled. "The idea was then sent to Bob Powell who would dramatically draw it as if it were a cover of a pulp magazine. When the series was painted [by Saunders], I wrote the descriptions on the back of the cards as well as the front captions; i.e. 'Burning Flesh.' Those were days that I couldn't wait to arrive at work and meet with Woody as we planned the science fiction bubblegum cards. What a way to make a living! I thought I was pretty lucky."

The 55-card set told the story of the titular Martian invasion and how humans responded to the attack. According to the synopsis, Martian leaders take a vote, and decide that Mars will have to invade the Earth. Life on the fourth planet was doomed because atomic pressures had been building up beneath the surface of Mars for many years, and a mammoth atomic explosion was imminent. To protect the survival of their civilization, the Martian officials planned to conquer Earth, and move their population there. With the details of their invasion fully plotted, Mars sends flying saucers through space carrying deadly weapons. The Martians first attack an army base, then blast the Army, Air Force, and Navy. Burning the cities, the Martians destroy much of Earth's population, and devastate much of the planet. The enemy then enlarges insects to over 500 times their normal size and releases them on the remaining humans. The insects destroy railroad trains, high-voltage lines, aircraft, and even the Eiffel Tower, People go into hiding, knowing that death is the consequence if they are discovered by the crea-

tures. Despite its losses, the Earth launches a major counterattack against the Martians on their home planet Mars. They bomb Mars with atomic weapons, smash their cities, and crush the Martians at every stage of their attack. Finally, the atomic pressures in the interior of Mars, having already reached a dangerous level, erupt with terrific force. And as the Earthmen travel home in rockets, they look back and watch as the planet is blown into a million tiny asteroids.

"Mars Attacks!" was really a reflection of the paranoia that gripped Americans in the 1950's. The crash of the flying saucer at Roswell, New Mexico, in July 1947, and the subsequent cover-up by the military, was big news to the generation that had survived the Great Depression and fought World War 2. The story peaked the public's interest in flying saucers. Not long after, a rash of reported sightings of Unidentified Flying Objects (or UFOs) swept throughout the country. Were these flying saucers the vanguard of an invasion from space? People were convinced that they were going to have to fight a new war, an interplanetary war with Martians or little green men. Similarly, the average person was learning more and more each day about the dangerous of the atomic bomb, and many of the movies of the time, including "Them!" (1954), "The Beginning of the End" (1956), "Tarantula" (1956), and "The Deadly Preying Mantis" (1957), exploited their fears by unleashing common insects mutated by nuclear radiation upon the world at large. Add the Soviet menace and the general malaise of the Eisenhower Age, fear and paranoia were plentiful commodities in the 1950's.

And just as Wells's 1898 novel had tapped into something primal in the culture of his Victorian day and age, the "Mars Attacks!" cards were marketed to the eager, young audience of its day that enjoyed comic books and sci-fi movies.

"We did 55 cards in the series and were quite proud of them," Brown continued. "As soon as the product was printed, we placed them in several test stores in Brooklyn. Sales were mixed. A couple of the stores did very well, and sold the cards rapidly. A couple of the stores reported very little interest in the product." Topps Incorporated widened the distribution of the cards to other cities on the East Coast, and planned a marketing strategy for those cities in the Midwest and the rest of the country.

But when parents objected to the gory violence and gruesome depictions, Topps removed the cards from the market-only to make

the infamous card set more valuable on the collector's market. The lurid illustrations by artists Norm Saunders and Bob Powell were apparently too much for the children who spent their hard-earned savings on trading cards and those pinks squares of gum. "It was kind of shocking to top management to get this kind of attention," Len Brown concluded. "After all, our heritage with trading cards had previously been sets depicting 'Flags of the World,' 'Railroad Trains,' and 'U.S. Presidents.' The 'Mars Attacks!' series was never sold elsewhere. No further shipments were made. Only those fortunate to have seen the limited shipments remembered them decades later."

In 1980, Darkstar Marketing produced a limited edition portfolio of reprints of some of the sketches, including pencil drawings by Bob Powell and Wally Wood. "The Mars Attacks Portfolio of Roughs" featured many original drawings, some of the sketches that made it into the final version of the card set and some which did not. Most notable were pencil drawings that depicted the Martians with a third eye sticking out of the middle of their large brain-like foreheads. In 1984, Rosem Enterprises produced a limited set of 13 cards that had been retouched to tone down the gore or sex, the very elements that had caused the cards to be redrawn from the market in 1962. That same year, Renatto Galasso, Inc. produced a reprint series of the original 55 cards plus a 56th card depicting the wrapper. The set was available for collectors who admired Norm Saunders' beautiful artwork, but who couldn't afford the original cards. Renatto also produced a set of 4 premium cards depicting 5" x 7" reprints of 4 original paintings of cards #10, 25, 34 and 35. In 1988, a company called Pocket Comics started to produce a series of tiny (3" x 4.5") comic books based on the 1962 Mars Attacks set. The digest-sized comics elaborated on the original cards, and had a 6" x 4.5" reprint of the card in the middle pages. There was going to be 54 mini-comics in all, one book for each of the original cards. The first books sold well. However, low orders for subsequent books forced Pocket Comics out of business after the first 4 comics.

In 1994, thirty-two years after its first release, the set was re-issued with 45 additional

cards as the "Mars Attacks! Archive Set," and reached a whole new audience with its very graphic portrayal of the titular attack from Mars. Brown worked with Gary Gerani at Topps to produce the new cards, which were drawn and painted by Earl Worem. A series of full-size comics, based on the new cards, followed, and finally, Tim Burton announced plans to make a big budget film.

The film version of "Mars Attacks!" (1996)

was less than stellar despite its all-star cast and high production values. Burton chose to condescend to the material rather than treat it with the respect that it deserved. He indulged his own ego by turning the Martians into irritating little creatures like the Gremlins from the 1984 Joe Dante film, and made the humans into caricatures of real-life people. What could have been a box office blockbuster, like the similarly-themed "Independence Day" which came out a few months earlier, turned into one long, sick joke. U.S. President Dale Ross (Jack Nicholson) learns that the Martians are coming, and alerts the nation in a fireside chat of their imminent arrival. Unfortunately, the aliens do not listen to reason, preferring, instead, to zap large number of Americans. Of course, the Martians get theirs, in the end.

With a wonderful cast that includes Jack Nicholson, Glenn Close, Annette Benning, Pierce Brosnan, and Sarah Jessica Parker, the comedy never really gets off the ground. The jokes are stale, and the only one who seems to be laughing is Tim Burton (not only at his audience but also the material itself). As a parody of 1950's flying saucer flicks, this film never makes it out of the Martian atmosphere. As an adaptation of the 1962 card series, the film is a total travesty.

The "Mars Attacks!" cards are still highly regarded today, despite the film version, and sell on the collector's market for $10 per card or $2000 for a complete set. One can only hope that, at some future time, an innovative filmmaker will be inspired by the cards, and seek to make the serious motion picture adaptation that the fifty-five card set deserves. Even an animated version, perhaps made by a team of Japanese animators! Until then, the cards themselves are worth every penny of their value on the collector's market.

Mars Attacks! (1996). Warner Brothers, color, 106 min. Director: Tim Burton. Producers: Larry Franco and Burton. Writer: Jonathan Gems. Based Upon the Trading Cards by Len Brown, Woody Gelman, Wally Wood, Bob Powell, and Norman Saunders. Cast: Jack Nicholson, Glenn Close, Annette Bening, Pierce Brosnan, Sarah Jessica Parker, Danny DeVito, Martin Short, Michael J. Fox, Rod Steiger, Tom Jones, Jim Brown, Lukas Haas, Natalie Portman, Pam Grier, and Paul Winfield.

Checklist for *Mars Attacks!* Cards

1-The Invasion Begins
2-Martians Approaching
3-Attacking an Army Base
4-Saucers Blast Our Jets
5-Washington in Flames
6-Burning Navy Ships
7-Destroying the Bridge
8-Terror in Times Square
9-The Human Torch
10-The Skyscraper Tumbles
11-Destroy the City
12-Death in the Cockpit
13-Watching from Mars
14-Charred by the Martians
15-Saucers Invade China
16-Panic in Parliament
17-Beast and the Beauty
18-A Soldier Fights Back
19-Burning Flesh
20-Crused to Death
21-Prized Captive
22-Burning Cattle
23-The Frost Ray
24-The Shrinking Ray
25-Capturing a Martian
26-The Tidal Wave
27-The Giant Flies
28-Helpless Victim
29-Death in the Shelter
30-Trapped
31-The Monster Reaches In
32-Robot Terror
33-Removing the Victims
34-Terror in the Railroad
35-The Flame Throwers
36-Destroying a Dog
37-Creeping Menace
38- Victims of the Bug
39-Army of Giant Insects
40-High Voltage Execution
41-Horror in Paris
42-Hairy Fiend
43-Blasting the Bug
44-Battle in the Air
45-Fighting Giant Insects
46-Blast Off for Mars
47-Earth Bombs Mars
48-Earthmen Land on Mars
49-The Earthmen Charge
50-Smashing the Enemy
51-Curshing the Martians
52-Giant Robot
53-Martian City in Ruins
54-Mars Explodes
55-Synopsis/Checklist

Chapter Thirteen: Tripods and Other TV Invaders

The Invaders - Alien beings from a dying planet. Their destination: The Earth. Their purpose: To make it their world. David Vincent has seen them. For him it began one lost night on a lonely country road, looking for a short-cut that he never found. It began with a closed deserted diner .... and a man too long without sleep to continue his journey. It began with the landing of a craft from another galaxy. Now, David Vincent knows that the Invaders are here. That they have taken human form. Somehow he must convince a disbelieving world that the nightmare has already begun.
—William Woodson, Introduction to "The Invaders" (1967)

No book about H. G. Wells's *The War of the Worlds* (and the adaptations it has inspired) would be complete without a mention of the British Broadcasting Company's production of "The Tripods" that aired for two seasons in 1984 and 1985. Based upon a trilogy of children's books by John Christopher (the pseudonym for prolific author Samuel Youd), the series was imagined as an alternate universe to the one in which the Martians had succumbed to the bacteria in Earth's atmosphere. Instead of dying from some unknown virus, the Martians (called here Masters) survived, and enslaved humanity with a mind-control device. Two hundred years after the initial invasion (in 1898), the world has devolved into a new Dark Ages, with the last remaining humans fighting to survive each other and the annual arrival of the Tripods. The show was an ambitious undertaking for British television, featuring nearly 125 speaking parts, lavish costume and set design, ground-breaking model work and video editing, beautifully composed landscape filming, and the painstaking care for detail that is usually only seen in big budget motion pictures.

The first season, which was a collection of thirteen 25-minute episodes, was broadcast between September and December 1984 in the Saturday afternoon timeslot and format of "Doctor Who." The BBC made no secrets of the fact that the series was partly intended as a replacement for their long-running show about the renegade Time Lord and his companions. Based upon Christopher's novel *The White Mountains* (1967), the show was dramatized by Alick Rowe and produced by Richard Bates. The lavish production and sexy cast of young unknowns was hugely popular with the critics and such a ratings smash that the network ordered a follow-up sequel.

A year later, the second season, which was a collection of twelve 25-minute episodes, aired between September and November 1985, once again in the same timeslot that had been reserved for "Doctor Who." Based upon Christopher's *The City of Gold and Lead* (1967), the show was dramatized by Christopher Penfold and produced by Richard Bates. "The Tripods: The City of Gold and Lead" aired during the Fall television series, and swept the competition away with its continuation of the three boy's journey in the world of the Tripods. Bates supervised the writing of the script for the sequel, and while he would have preferred Rowe to continue as the scripter, he was only just satisfied with Penfold's adaptation. The second season was not as successful critically or creatively as the first season, but that did not stop viewers from pleading with the BBC for a third season. After some debate among the top executives, the studio agreed to fund a third and final season.

Pre-production on the third season, which had been planned as a collection of thirteen 25-minute episodes, began in January 1986. Producer Bates hired Alick Rowe to dramatize the new season based upon Christopher's *The Pool of Fire* (1968), and most of the cast was set to return. Then, mid-way through pre-production, the BBC announced that it was canceling the series. The network simply could not justify the enormous cost of the show, especially the expensive model effects and the high production standards that were a cut well above anything that had been seen before. Rowe completed his script, and resolved most of the plotlines that had been set up in the previous two seasons, but no one ever saw the work produced. For a short time, Dreamworks discussed the possibility to producing a big screen adaptation, which would have compressed all three books into one story, but that has yet to be made.

Episode Guide:

"The Tripods: The White Mountains"
(Thirteen 25-minute episodes)
Airdates: September 15-December 8, 1984
Episodes 1-8. Director: Graham Theakston.
Designer: Victor Meredith.
Episodes 9-13. Director: Christopher Barry.
Designer: Martin Collins.
Producer: Richard Bates. Dramatization by:
Alick Rowe. Based on the novel by John
Christopher. Costumes: Phoebe de Gaye.

Music: Ken Freeman. Locations: Andrew Rowley, Gordon Ronald. Make-up: Sally Sutton. Properties: David Morris Vision editing: Sue Thorne, Mike Taylor, Jim Stephens, Angela Beveridge, and Alan Dixon. Video effects: Robin Lobb. Graphic Designers: Charles McGhie, Tom Hartwell and Ewen Maclaine. Visual effects designers: Steven Drewett, Kevin Molloy

Cast: John Shackley (Will Parker), Jim Baker (Henry Parker), Lucinda Curtis (Mrs. Parker), Peter Dolphin (Mr. Parker), Roderick Horn (Ozymandias), Ceri Seel (Beanpole), John Scott Martin (Schoolmaster), Michael Gilmour (Jack), and James Staddon (Nick).

Plot: In the year 2089, survivors of some great catastrophe, two hundred years earlier, struggle for their day-to-day existence. The world has devolved into a new Dark Ages, and life is very harsh. Most people have forgotten that an alien race, presumably the Martians (from *The War of the Worlds*), conquered Earth with their Tripod machines. They don't seem to remember a world that wasn't ruled by the Masters and their Tripods. [The second season suggests that mankind lost dominion over the Earth as a result of a nuclear war, after which the space culture of the Masters felt obliged to move in and take over the planet. This suggestion does not exist in the novels, and is indeed contradicted by Christopher's (later) prequel.] Now, every person who reaches puberty is "capped," and their mind is controlled or at least molded by the Tripods. The Black Guard, which was invented by Rowe for the television series, enforce "capping" laws, and track down youngsters who evade "capping"; in the novel, the Tripods are quite unconcerned with the few who evade, since they never cause serious trouble.

When Will Parker and his cousin Henry are confronted by a Tripod, the reality of their situation becomes very clear; both boys will be "capped" on their next birthday. With the help of a local mystic named Ozymandias (who has primitive maps of England and France), the boys escape from England, and go on an adventure to the "white mountains" (or the Alps) to escape the Tripods altogether. The refuge of free men is located in the Tunnel at the highest peak in Europe-Mont Blanc, the "white" mountain, located at the corner-point between France, Switzerland, and Italy; in reality, this tunnel is located at the Jungfrau, not Mont Blanc. Will and Henry start off down the sandy coast between Rye and Romney, take a boat to Calais, and make they way across France, encountering very interesting people (like Madame Vichot and the Count) along the way. They pick up a third companion, Beanpole, and continue on their journey, all the while narrowly escaping the Tripods and the Black Guard. [In the Tunnel, which becomes a very real place for them, group of runaways and rebels who have never been capped desperately plot to free Earth and its inhabitants. This band of rebels must find a way to defeat the Masters and their Tripods without knowing who they are, what their weaknesses are, or any worthwhile knowledge about them. Worse than that, the rebels have to defeat these space age invaders with technology at roughly 19th century levels.]

"The Tripods: The City of Gold and Lead" (Twelve 25-minute episodes)
Airdates: September 7-November 23, 1985
Episodes 1-4 and 11-12. Director: Christopher Barry. Designer: Martin Collins.
Episodes 5-10. Director: Bob Blagden. Designer: Philip Lindley.
Producer: Richard Bates. Dramatization by: Christopher Penfold. Based upon the novel by John Christopher. Costumes: Phoebe de Gaye. Music: Ken Freeman. Locations: Melanie Howard. Make-up: Helen Barrett. Properties: David Morris and Andrew Clark Vision editing: Alan Dixon, Jim Stephens, John Paroussi, and Susan Brincat. Video effects: Robin Lobb. Graphic Designers: Charles McGhie and Mira Chohan. Visual effects designers: Steve Bowman, Michael Kelt, and Simon Tayler.
Cast: John Shackley (Will Parker), Jim Baker (Henry Parker), Ceri Seel (Beanpole), Jeffrey Perry (Krull), Robin Hayter (Fritz Eger), Alisa Bosschaert (Anne), Peter Forbes-Robertson (Schenker), Karen Seacombe (Brigitte), and Colin Dunn (Kurt).
Plot: The three boys reach the Tunnel, the refuge of free men, at Jungfrau, and Will and Beanpole leave almost immediately on another journey - this time with assumed identities as athletes - to the City of Gold and Lead. Henry remains behind because he is useful to the rebels. When they reach the City, Will is captured, sold into slavery, and bought and befriended by a Master. His Master, while still thinking of him as essentially a badly-trained animal, beats him, but also comes to admire him. Will discovers the most important secret of the City from his Master. Throughout the twelve-part series, Will, Henry and Beanpole seem to discover every important secret, from learning about the City of the Ancients to finding a simple wristwatch. They return to the rebels with the knowledge that the Masters are not Gods, just very advanced creatures (even likeable in some ways), and their Tripods machines are vulnerable. They also reveal that the aliens must be stopped, for their future plans for the Earth do not include humans. In fact, all native life on the planet is doomed!

"The Tripods: The Pool of Fire" (Thirteen 25-minute episodes) Never Filmed. Producer: Richard Bates. Dramatization by: Alick Rowe. Based upon the novel by John Christopher.
Plot: Will and Henry become separated from the free men, and set off on a journey across Europe back to England, recruiting followers as they go. On the way they witness the Hunt of a human by Tripods, apparently for sport. Eventually they return to Wherton (their home village), and on Capping Day, where they are once again rescued by Ozymandias. Meanwhile, the rebels capture a Tripod, with the Master inside, and discover some apparent weaknesses when they subject the alien to experimental tests. The free men then prepare coordinated attacks on all three Cities, joined by an American girl and a Chinese delegation who will be responsible for attacking the second and third Tripod Cities (on the Panama canal and near Peking). In the European City, they succeed in remaining concealed, while preparing the alcohol needed to poison the Masters: they capture the City but find themselves trapped within it. Will, Henry, and Beanpole initiate their own plan of bombing the

City from a hot-air balloon. In the attack, Henry is killed, but they manage to rescue the rebels, and free humanity from the domination of the Tripods and the effects of the Cap. But celebrations are cut short by the news that the American City has withstood the attack.

In 1988, twenty years after the conclusion of his trilogy, John Christopher wrote a prequel of sorts, *When the Tripods Came*, in the aftermath of the BBC series. A century before the action in his trilogy, he creates three young characters, Laurie, Andy, and Rudi, who escape captivity, and form the resistance in the Tunnel in Switzerland. He also settles for all concerned how the Tripods first came and took over. The alien invasion begins with a largely successful attempt to brainwash the population through an animated series called "The Trippy Show." Intended for children but popular with adults, the show takes control of its viewers' minds. So, when the Masters arrive with their Tripods, they are able to conquer the planet without difficulty. Christopher's prequel was not as well received as the books in his trilogy, but his *The White Mountains* (1967), *The City of Gold and Lead* (1967) and *The Pool of Fire* (1968) are still hugely popular among juvenile readers. We can only hope that, when Hollywood gets around to making a big budget film based upon *The Tripod Trilogy*, a director like Chris Columbus makes a worthwhile motion picture.

In addition to "The Tripods," many other television series have borrowed the premise of H. G. Wells's *The War of the Worlds* (1898) to weave spell-binding tales of alien invasion and the small group of humans that resist their interplanetary conquest into the fabric of commercial programming. While the cinema had nearly exhausted the theme (and in fact had made it a cliché), television audiences were eager to sit back in their comfortable homes and watch monstrous invaders from another world travel vast cosmic distances to conquer Earth week after week. Some of the shows were exceeding fresh with their new take on the familiar theme, while others simply updated Wells's seminal novel with a new setting and splashy special effects. With only one notable exception, most of the shows did not last beyond two seasons, and have been largely forgotten or ignored by the passage of time. So, what follows is a flashback to a simpler time when the major networks re-imagined the cosmic struggle for existence between monstrous invaders and humanity's best and finest with appropriate commercial break.

(In Order of Appearance)

"The Outer Limits" (1963-65, ABC/Daystar Productions). Anthology series; forty-eight 1-hour episodes. Created by Leslie Stevens and Joseph Stefano. Producers: Leslie Steven and Joseph Stefano (first season); Ben Brady (second season). Music: Dominic Frontiere (first season); Harry Lubin (second season). Principle Cinematographers: Conrad Hall, John Nickolaus, and Kenneth Peach. Special Effects Supervisors: Jim Danforth, Wah Chang, and Ray Mercer. Airdates: September 16, 1963-January 23, 1965.

"There is nothing wrong with your television set..." Those few chilling words, when first heard on September 16, 1963, introduced what many consider the best anthology series of its kind to American audiences. The three major networks produced few exceptional television shows during the decade of the Sixties, and even fewer ones with a science-fictional premise, yet widespread acclaim for "The Outer Limits" has continued more than forty years after its untimely cancellation. Like its predecessors, including "Tales of Tomorrow," "Science Fiction Theatre" and "The Twilight Zone," "The Outer Limits" offered some bewitching excursions into the realm of science fiction; but it also journeyed beyond the limitless regions of time and space into the human soul. Nearly everyone who remembers the series fondly recalls the monsters that appeared in their living rooms week after week. Each new episode not only brought terrifying aliens into the homes of middle America but also complex themes and ideas about nuclear

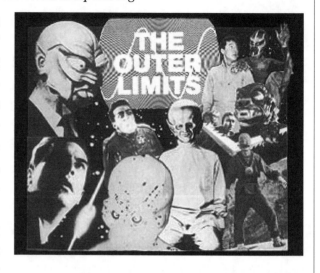

holocaust, racism, political subterfuge, jealousy, obsession, revenge and forbidden love. The show and its social conscience, often represented by the disembodied Control Voice Vic Perrin), were the creation of two brilliant writers, Leslie Stevens and Joseph Stefano. They used the medium of television to introduce us to many alien monsters who were, more often than not, far more civilized than the humans on the show, and were not, in fact, invaders but misunderstood visitors. "The Galaxy Being" (9/16/63), "The Architects of Fear" (9/30/63), "Controlled Experiment (1/13/64), and other tales took the premise of an alien invasion, and gave it a totally new spin. The show that was years ahead of its time!

"The Invaders" (1967-68, ABC/Quin Martin Productions). Forty-two 1-hour episodes. Created by Larry Cohen. Producer: Alan Armer. Executive Producer: Quinn Martin. Music: Dominic Frontiere. Cast: Roy Thinnes and Kent Smith (second season). Airdates: January 1967-May 1968.

From the creative pen of Larry Cohen came yet another take on Wells's *The War of the Worlds*, with some fear and paranoia from "The Invasion of the Body Snatchers" (1956) thrown in for good measure. One fateful night, Architect David Vincent (Thinnes) makes a wrong turn down a lonely country road, and witnesses the landing of a space craft from another world. At first, he can barely believe his eyes; but then, as he gains a bit of perspective, Vincent realizes that he has witnessed an extraordinary event. Reporting it to the authorities, he is considered a "crackpot" when he returns to the landing site with the police and his business partner Alan Landers (James Daly), and finds the craft gone. They dismiss him as just another person who thought he saw a flying saucer. Vincent eventually learns that the "invaders" are from a dying world, and that they have come to conquer Earth by infiltrating all major control centers of human society, including the military. When his partner is killed ruthlessly by the alien invaders, Vincent dedicates his life to convincing the world the threat is real, and ultimately stopping them. The only way that the "invaders" can be

distinguished from humans is by the erect pinkie on each hand or by the way they glow when their human form needs regeneration. During the first season, Cohen's familiar plotline supported a number of suspense-filled episodes (including "The Mutation" and "Panic"); but, by the second year, the writing staff seemed to have run out of ideas. Even the addition of others, including Edgar Scoville (Kent Smith), who believed in Vincent's cause, did not enliven the series, and it was canceled in the Spring of 1968. A four-hour mini-series, featuring Scott Bakula, attempted to bring the television series into the 1990's, but failed to generate much interest on Fox Television.

"U.F.O." (1969, ITC Entertainment). Twenty-four 1-hour episodes. Created by Gerry and Sylvia Anderson. Producer: Reg Hill. Executive Producer: Gerry Anderson. Music: Barry Gray. Special Effects Supervisor: Derek Meddings. Cast: Ed Bishop (Straker), George Sewell (Freeman), Michael Billington (Foster), Norma Ronald (Miss Ealand), Lois Maxwell (Miss Holland), Vladek Sheybal (Dr. Jackson),Anouska Hempel (Operator), Antonia Ellis (Harrington), and Grant Taylor (Henderson). Airdates: September 1969-June 1970. Created by Gerry and Sylvia Anderson, who had produced some of the finest children's programming with "Fireball XL-5," "Captain Scarlet and the Mysterons," and "Thunderbirds," the syndicated British series from ITC Entertainment was yet another re-make of Wells's classic 1898 novel. After investigating reports of Unidentified Flying Objects for more than twenty years, the United States government issued a report in 1968 stating categorically that flying saucers were fantasy. Project Blue Book was closed down, and as far as the average citizen was concerned, no UFOs have ever visited Earth. But according to the show's premise, that was all a lie, a cover-up prompted by the government to hide the fact that the military was engaged in a Cold War with alien invaders from space. Their reasoning was that mass hysteria and panic would result if the common man knew we were being attacked by hostile extraterrestrials bent on world domination. SHADO (Supreme Headquarters, Alien Defense Organization) Command fights a clandestine war, using a fleet of ships and aircraft, and a base on the Moon, against the invaders. Filmed in 1969, the series was very successful in its first season in syndication throughout the world, but despite requests for an additional twenty-four episodes, ITC Entertainment canceled the show. "U.F.O." was revamped and transformed into the highly successful "Space: 1999."

"Project U.F.O." (1978-1979, NBC) Twenty-six 1-hour episodes. Created by: Jack Webb. Producer: William T. Coleman. Writers: Dirk Wayne Summers and Jack Webb. Directors: Lawrence Dobkin, Dennise Donnelly, Richard Greer, Robert Leeds, and Sigmund Neufeld. Visual Effects Supervisor: Tim Donahue. Sound Effects Supervisor: Daniel J. Johnson. Cast: William Jordan (Major Jake Gatlin), Aldine King (Libby Virdon), Caskey Swaim (Staff Sergeant Harry Fitz, and Edward Winter (Captain Ben Ryan). Narrator: Jack Webb. This forerunner of "The X-Files" followed the exploits of two agents of Project Blue Book as they investigated sightings of extraterrestrials and unidentified flying objects. The series, which was inspired by Steven Spielberg's "Close Encounters of the Third Kind" (1977), was way ahead of its time in terms of its special effects, but the "Dragnet"-like style of Jack Webb did not work with contemporary audiences.

"The X-Files" (1993-2001, FOX). 175 1-hour episodes. Created by Chris Carter. Producer: Chris Carter. Music: Mark Snow. Cast: David Duchovny (Mulder), Gillian Anderson (Scully), Mitch Pileggi (Skinner), Nicolas Lea (Krycek), Jerry Hardin (Deep Throat), Tom Braidwood (Frohike), Dean Hagland (Langly), Bruce Harwood (Byers) , Steven Williams (X), and William Davis (Cigarette Smoking Man).Airdates: September 10, 1993-May 2001.

Chris Carter's entertaining and highly original series not only suggested that Earth was being invaded by extraterrestrial beings bent on world domination but also implied that various branches of the United States government were collaborating with the invaders in advance of their alien armada. As agents Fox Mulder and Dana Scully routinely probe cases involving UFOs and alien abduction as part of their duties with the FBI's X-Files Division, they begin to notice a pattern to the cases which suggests that there might be a larger conspiracy at work. Their assignments often put them at odds with other intelligence agencies, notably the National Security Agency (NSA) and a secret agency to which the Smoking Man belongs that is never fully explained. "The Pilot" episode (9/10/93) establishes several important details about the background of the two lead characters, and their assignment with the Federal Bureau of Investigation. Agent Fox Mulder is an Oxford-trained psychologist who earned the nickname "Spooky" from his fellow classmates at the FBI Academy because of his uncanny ability to process information and leap ahead to logical conclusions. During his first three years with the Bureau, while working as a crack analyst in the behavioral sciences department, he stumbled upon a collection of unsolved cases dealing with unexplained phenomena. Agent Dana Scully, a medical doctor with an undergraduate degree in physics from the University of Maryland, is skeptical of anything paranormal, choosing to believe that everything has a logical and scientific explanation. During their nine years of investigation, they uncover the truth that a full-scale invasion is imminent.

"Dark Skies" (NBC/1996-1997) Twenty 1-hour episodes. Creator: Bryce Zabel. Writers: Steve Aspis, David Black, Brent Friedman, Gay Walch, James Parriott. Cast: Eric Close, Megan Ward, J.T. Walsh, Tim Kelleher, Conor O'Farrell, Charley Lang, Jeri Ryan.

The history of the 20th century as we know it is a lie. Aliens have been among us since the 1940's, but a government cover-up has prevented the public from knowing this. John Loengard (Close) and Kim Sayers (Ward) have stumbled upon the truth about an alien invasion, much of it tied to historical events and figures. In addition, the pair must stay one step ahead of a covert government agency, Majestic-12, tasked with fighting the aliens while maintaining the conspiracy of silence.

"The First Wave" (Sci-Fi Channel, 1998). Sixty-six 1-hour Episodes. Creator: Chris Brancato. Writers: Paul Brown, Fergus Cook, Jeff King, Phyllis Murphy, Andrea Stevens, David Wilcox et al. Producers: Matthew Loze and Tara McCann. Cast: Sebastian Spence (Cade Foster), Rob LaBelle (Eddie), Roger Cross (Joshua), Traci Lords (Jordan Radcliffe), Dana Brooks (Col. Grace), and Robert Duncan (Mabus). Airdates: March 1999-May 2001.

Those pesky aliens are at it again, trying to launch the first wave of their invasion of Earth, but reformed thief Cade Foster uses the quatrains of Nostradamus to keep them in check. Clever series with a beguiling cast, including second-season stringer Traci Lords as a gun-toting commando.

CHAPTER FOURTEEN: LITTLE GREEN MEN AND FLYING SAUCERS

The size of the lie is a definite factor in causing it to be believed, for the vast masses of a nation are in the depths of their hearts more easily deceived than they are consciously and intentionally bad. The primitive simplicity of their minds renders them a more easy prey to a big lie than a small one, for they themselves often tell little lies, but would be ashamed to tell big lies.

—Adolf Hitler, Mein Kampf, 1935

If you tell a lie big enough and keep repeating it, people will eventually come to believe it.

— Joseph Goebbels, Nazi Propaganda Minister, 1938

Flying saucers, multi-tentacled alien monsters, and the notion of an invasion from Mars seem so ridiculous to us today that it's really hard to imagine a time when people considered the H. G. Wells novel original and thought-provoking, or were panicked by Orson Welles's "War of the Worlds" radio broadcast, or saw entertainment value in the George Pal film or its numerous remakes and rip-offs. We tend to make jokes about little green men, and ridicule those who claim to have seen them. Films like "Invaders from Mars," "Independence Day," and "Mars Attacks" and television shows like "Taken" and "The X-Files" have so desensitized us to the potential of an alien attack from space that we would probably think the lead story on CNN about an actual invasion was either a hoax or an elaborate publicity stunt to promote the latest summer blockbuster. We'd probably gather on rooftops with hand-painted signs, asking the aliens to expand our consciousness, rather than hide in fall-out shelters. The fact that some unusual kind of spacecraft crashed in the desert outside Roswell, New Mexico, in 1947, or that there have been hundreds of credibly-documented cases of UFO sightings or alien abductions over more than a fifty-year period seems more like the stuff of fantasy than reality. When most of us are reminded of these real invaders from "Mars," we snicker some, and smile, and chalk the reports up to the paranoia of the time. And we happily buy our tickets to the latest cinematic "war of the worlds" and sit comfortably in our summer cineplexes, while some of our government leaders watch the skies with fear and anxiety. Nearly sixty years ago, the top brass understood the threat from alien beings was real, and thanks to a campaign of disinformation and lies, they have kept the secret to themselves. Just how would humanity react if we knew, beyond a reasonable doubt, that the little green men in flying saucers were real?

Roswell and the First Encounters With UFOs

Pilot Kenneth Arnold first cited nine disk-shaped objects, which he called "flying saucers," over Mount Rainer and the Cascade Mountains on June 24, 1947, and launched the modern era of UFO sightings with his detailed report of the encounter. Arnold's descriptions of the craft seemed to match similar sightings over the European and Pacific Theatres of World War II. To the Allied fighter pilots, they were "kraut fireballs" or "foo fighters."

Pilots and their aircrews reported that the unidentified objects flew in formation with their bombers, and actually "played tag" with them on their way to and from bombing missions. The "foo fighters" behaved as if they were under intelligent control, but never displayed aggressive behavior. Reports of these "unexplained transparent, metallic and glowing balls" started turning up in the daily briefings in June, 1944, shortly after the Allied invasion of France. Some thought they were somehow linked to the V-1 and V-2 rockets fired at London and Paris by Nazi Germany, but none of those rumors was ever confirmed. Certainly, no documentary evidence of the "foo fighters" survived the war.

In July 1947, following a rush of UFO sightings in and around the Southwestern United States, an unusual craft crashed in the desert outside Roswell, New Mexico. On the evening of July 2, 1947, Dan Wilmot and his wife saw a shape like "two inverted saucers faced mouth to mouth," come down in the night sky over their farm. The next day, Rancher W.W. "Mac" Brazel found the wreckage near his home in Corona, and reported it to the sheriff's office. Sheriff George Wilcox, in turn, contacted military officials at the 509th Bomb Group Intelligence Office, including Major Jesse Marcel. Ironically, Roswell Army Air Field, 509th Division, was where the nation's stockpile of nuclear bombs (fifteen in all) were stored, including the only planes equipped to fly them and the only pilots and bombers trained to drop them. The base commander assigned Marcel and Sheridan Cavett, a Counter Intelligence Officer, to retrieve the wreckage, which was scattered over a three-quarter mile area, of a flying saucer. Marcel recovered items that were totally foreign to him, and later woke his wife and son to show them what he had found.

On July 8, 1947, the Roswell newspaper published a Front Page Article - taken from the official press release written by Information Officer Lt. Walter Haut of the RAAF 509th acting under orders of Col. William Blanchard - which announced, "RAAF Captures Flying

Saucer on Ranch in Roswell Region." Excitement was high until Brigadier General Roger Ramey, commander of the Eighth Air Force unit, ordered (presumably on orders from Washington) a retraction. Haut recanted the flying saucer press release hours later, claiming in the next day's paper that it was nothing more than a recovered weather balloon. The now-famous photo on the front page showed Marcel crouched over the balloon. While the cover story of a weather balloon was used to obscure the earlier press leak, the actual debris was loaded on a B-29 bomber and flown to Wright Field (now Wright-Patterson AFB) in Dayton, Ohio, for study. In addition to the wreckage, several bodies (four, possibly five) of alien beings were recovered

from the New Mexico desert. At the time, the media and the public "bought" the weather balloon story, but gradually, as the number of credible witnesses came forward recounting their stories - including death threats - of an actual flying saucer and alien bodies, the cover story lost its credibility. The Air Force still maintains this story today, and has actually embellished the story by claiming the alien bodies were "crash-test dummies" in the official report *Roswell: Case Closed* (1997), released just two weeks before the 50th anniversary celebration of the crash.

What happened to the wreckage? The alien bodies?

The Military Cover-Up

On September 24, 1947, President Harry S. Truman formed a special intelligence group, code-named "Operation Majestic-12," to study the remains of the Roswell crash and the bodies that were recovered at the site. The ad hoc group was comprised of a dozen top scientists, researchers and military leaders, and had an intelligence rating higher than those making the hydrogen bomb. Under government auspices, a number of other projects were established to study the question of extraterrestrials. Project Garnet studied the evolution of man on earth, and how that evolution might have been affected or related to aliens. Project Sigma, a forerunner of SETI, dealt with alien communication, while Project Snowbird researched the development and use of alien technology recovered from the crash site. The most secretive of studies, Project Gleem (later renamed Project Aquarius), was devoted to the accumulation of data about alien life forms. One of the earliest government agencies to examine the sightings of UFOs was the United States Air Force, under the code name Project Sign. Project Sign (later renamed Project Saucer) investigated hundreds of reports and gathered tons of physical evidence before giving way to another, far more important project. Project Grudge, attached to the Air Technical Intelligence Center at Wright Field, took a much different approach to the issue of flying saucers. The project was formed to provide disinformation to the public, and to gather intelligence about alien activities.

When President-elect Dwight D. Eisenhower was first briefed on November 18, 1952, by members of the Majestic-12 about the remains of four (possibly five) alien bodies and the wreckage of the flying saucer from Roswell, he was astounded. He insisted upon absolute secrecy, and felt the efforts of Project Grudge were not enough. The crash in New Mexico had been bungled by Army Intelligence, and he was concerned that far too many civilians were asking questions.

By secret Executive Memorandum, NSC 5410 (later amended by NSC 5412/1 in 1954), Eisenhower established a permanent committee (not ad hoc) to be known as Majority Twelve (MJ-12) to oversee and conduct all covert activities related to aliens and UFOs. At the time, those individuals who made up the Majority Twelve were known only to a handful of people, but recent releases of top secret documents through the Freedom of Information Act have revealed that Nelson Rockefeller, the director of the CIA Allen Dulles, the Secretary of State John Foster Dulles, the Secretary of Defense Charles E. Wilson, the Chairman of the Joint Chiefs of Staff Admiral Arthur W. Radford, the Director of the FBI J. Edgar Hoover, and six men from the executive committee of the Council on Foreign Relations (possibly George Bush, Zbigniew Brzezinski, Averell Harriman, and Dean Acheson) were among them. As a result of their recommendations to Eisenhower, a new, low-level effort by the Air Force replaced Project Grudge. Project Blue Book was formed to gather and control information,

and at times mislead the public by explaining away as many reports as possible. MJ-12 and Project Aquarius continued to provide government leaders with the true findings. In subsequent years, the National Security Agency, the Central Intelligence Agency and the Defense Intelligence Agency have assumed control of most investigations under the mantle of national security. Even the Joint Chiefs of Staff, through the Pentagon's National Military Command Center, has its own secret command structure to deal with issues dealing with flying saucers and extraterrestrial visitors.

While it may be a reflection of our tension-filled times, some people today believe that these top secret organizations have been deliberately concealing information about UFOs and alien abduction from the public for decades. This contention is not a new one, and has been raised repeatedly since "flying saucers" first made headlines throughout the world in 1947. Far too many people have actually witnessed or experienced some type of unexplained phenomenon, or know someone who has, to perpetuate this charade. The official denials by the Government of the United States have given rise to the suspicion that not only is the public being told less than the truth, but also a massive cover-up has suppressed the overwhelming evidence that UFOs are real. Not simply paranoia, but mistrust is how most people feel about their government.

The Flying Saucer Conspiracy

Daniel E. Keyhoe's *The Flying Saucer Conspiracy* (Henry Holt & Company, 1955) first exposed key information about the Air Force Project Sign and the Majestic-12 group fifty years ago to an innocent America. Larry Fawcett and Barry Greenwood's *Clear Intent: The Government Cover-up of the UFO Experience* (Prentice-Hall, 1984) and Timothy Good's *Above Top Secret: The Worldwide UFO Cover-up* (Morrow, 1988) both reveal a massive conspiracy on the part of the United States government and other governments to cover-up information about alien landings and abductions. In fact, their use of the more than 10,000 pages of Freedom of Information Act documents about UFOs that are now in the hands of the public detail exactly how the various agencies have conspired to obscure the facts.

Many Americans have witnessed strange craft flying above the Nevada desert, and are convinced that the military is experimenting with alien technology at a top secret site there. Not far from Nellis Air Force Base, Nevada, about eighty miles north-northwest of Las Vegas, extremely advanced and unconventional aircraft routinely traverse the skies over "Area 51" (or "Dreamland"). According to a mysterious Colonel "L," who was stationed there in 1970, and Robert Lazar, a former employee, the facility has at least three captured UFOs, two nearly complete and one dismantled. Designated Project Red Light (or simply "Red Light"), the military supposedly has been researching the development and implementation of gravity-drive systems, flying saucer designs, advanced stealth technology and

alien weaponry. In fact, one of the operational UFOs was said to have exploded in flight with two American test pilots aboard. Whether the facility really studies UFOs or not, two undeniable facts are true. Workers are flown to and from the site aboard a chartered Boeing 737 originating at McCarron Airport every day. And curiosity seekers in the Groom Dry Lake area are routinely searched and turned away by armed security teams.

According to another classified report, the military recovered not one but three alien spacecraft from the Southwestern United States. In addition to the wreckage retrieved near Roswell, New Mexico, officials discovered the wreckage of another alien craft two years later in the same vicinity, and immediately hid the evidence from the public. In 1958, the United States recovered a third alien spacecraft from the Utah desert. The craft was in excellent flying condition, and had been mysteriously abandoned by its occupants. When examined by a group of scientists, the instrumentation was so complex that none of them could fully comprehend its operation. Shortly thereafter, funds were not only appropriated by Project Snowbird to begin a more intensive study but also to contact the aliens who had abandoned their craft.

In addition to wreckage and recovered bodies, the United States Government has also captured a real-life extraterrestrial. In 1977, a top secret document from ORCON (Dissemination and Extraction of Information Controlled by Originator) was made public during the Carter Administration. The document revealed that one alien (called an E.B.E., or Extraterrestrial Biological Entity) survived the second crash in New Mexico (in 1949), and was thoroughly interrogated by military personnel at a secret airbase. The E.B.E. disclosed, before its death of an unexplained illness in 1952, that it had come from a planet in the Zeta Reticula star system, and that its social structure was thousands of years ahead of our own. The alien's body was frozen, like those earlier ones from Roswell, and transported to another facility for study. Project Bando, established in 1949 by the military to collect and evaluate medical information about E.B.E.s, allowed scientists and medical researchers to dissect the alien bodies. Soon after the experiments, contact was established with two other E.B.E.s, and both were invited as guests to live in secret at the base in the Nevada desert.

Project Sign's Report #13 also disclosed that as many as sixteen bodies were found at a separate site in Aztec, New Mexico, in 1948. Dr. Detlev Bronk, a physiologist and biophysicist, was brought in to conduct an autopsy on one of the aliens. The gray figure, which was about four feet in height with large slanted eyes and long pointy ears, confirmed many suspicions scientists had about the origins and evolution of life on earth. Bronk and his colleagues also removed extraterrestrial DNA to see if there was any evidence to confirm genetic manipulation. (Several researchers suspect that aliens may been manipulating our own gene pool to create the best human.) All of the bodies were then frozen by Dr. Paul Scherer, a cryogenics specialist, and transported aboard three trucks covered with tarpaulins marked "explosives." Incredible as that story may seem, the government has been conducting its own genetic tests on these alien visitors for nearly fifty years, and without the knowledge or approval of its citizens.

Alien Abductions

Tales of alien abduction and missing time - often the most shocking and frightening encounters with the unknown - have become as common as UFO sightings in the growing number of reports about extraterrestrial visitors. The most sensational report to date appears to be the night siege experienced by author Whitley Strieber. Strieber writes in *Communion* (William Morrow, 1987) and *Transformation* (William Morrow, 1988) that he and his family were terrorized by an extraterrestrial force at their secluded cabin in the woods of upstate New York.

Of course, "close encounters of the third kind," as coined by Dr. J. Allen Hynek of the Center for UFO Studies to describe encounters with aliens and their spacecraft, are not that unusual. They have been documented, discussed, analyzed, seemingly debunked and re-

examined for over fifty-five years. The most famous case of alien abduction and missing time centers around Betty and Barney Hill, an interracial couple from Portsmouth, New Hampshire. On the night of September 19-20, 1961, the Hills were returning to their home from a vacation in Niagara Falls, New York, when they experienced a bright light above U.S. Route 3. They pulled off the road, and Barney went out onto a field near Indian Head to observe a UFO at close range. Two hours and thirty-five miles later, the Hills were again traveling on the highway with no conscious recollection of what had happened. The couple soon realized that they were missing time from their trip, but it would be over two years later, under intensive hypno-therapy, that Betty and Barney Hill would discover they had been abducted and studied by aliens. Their story has been retold a number of times, most notably in John Fuller's book *The Interrupted Journey* (Dial Press, 1966) and a popular television film with James Earl Jones.

Budd Hopkins, probably the foremost investigator of abductions, wrote the highly-regarded study *Missing Time: A Documented Study of UFO Abductions* (New York: Richard Marek, 1981), in which he interviewed hundreds of people who had experienced the unusual phenomenon of lost time. Similarly, the well-documented abduction of Travis Walton formed the basis of several books (one written by Walton himself in 1978) and the motion picture "Fire In the Sky" (1993). Walton, a twenty-two year-old woodcutter with the U.S. Forest Ser-

vice, was abducted on November 5, 1975, in plain view of his six co-workers (who were subsequently charged with his murder). Five days later, Travis awoke a quarter mile west of Heber, Arizona, and began experiencing nightmares of such unspeakable horror that he sought out a therapist. After months of regressive hypnosis, he remembered being strapped to a table aboard the spacecraft and being tortured by the inhabitants with strange medical instruments. Polygraph and Psychological Stress Evaluator tests have established that he told the truth. He had been abducted by alien visitors.

In 1973, Pat Roach, a divorced woman living alone with her two daughters, was taken aboard a craft standing in the empty field next to her house. Once inside the craft, she was separated from her children, taken to a small medical room and given a gynecological examination by one of the alien creatures. Her daughters, Bonnie and Debbie, were also placed on a machine, and given a full exam. All three were then returned to their home. Another account, taken from 1967, tells of a woman's abduction from her home in South Ashburnham, Massachusetts. Betty Andreasson was abducted from her kitchen, while her seven children, mother and father were placed into suspended animation. During Betty's abduction, her eleven-year-old daughter Becky was revived momentarily as part of the study. Betty was then examined and returned, unharmed, to her home. Both accounts were thoroughly investigated by UFO experts, and deemed credible. Volumes and volumes of voice transcripts, documents, and supplementary materials further substantiate the claims by these and dozens of other individuals that alien abductions are real.

Other UFO Encounters

In addition to the various sightings the United States Government has tried to suppress, or simply explain away, and the eye-witness accounts of alien abductions, many others have had encounters with UFOs. A recent survey, in fact, finds that more Americans believe in the existence of flying saucers and extraterrestrials than do not. That popular belief in UFOs has fueled many of the episodes of "The X-Files" and the recent television miniseries "Taken" as well as dozens of motion pictures, including "Close Encounters of the Third Kind," "E.T.-The Extraterrestrial," "Hangar 18," and "My Science Project."

As depicted in the film "Contact," the giant radio telescope at the Observatory of Arecibo, Puerto Rico, has been transmitting coded messages to the stars for years. Not surprisingly, Puerto Rico has been the main focal point of dozens of UFO sightings dating back to the Fifties. In 1956, local residents reported seeing several disc-shaped craft in the airspace above Laguna Cartagena. In 1964, Quintin Ramirez had a close encounter with a flying saucer outside his home, not far from the location of the other sightings. The wave of sightings in 1980 culminated in a powerful aerial collision between unidentified craft near Cabo Rojo in 1981 that was witnessed by hundreds of spectators. Most recently, ten carloads of witnesses reported seeing five alien beings walking along the road. When one of the cars stopped, the aliens scrambled into the dense tropical rain forest nearby a military complex, long rumored to have played host to visiting E.B.E.s.

Over the years, astronauts and test pilots have logged some of the most convincing reports of UFO sightings. Back in 1962, there were no less than four different accounts. John Glenn, while piloting his Mercury capsule, told Cape Canaveral officials that he saw three objects follow and then overtake him at varying speeds. Similarly, Scott Carpenter reported seeing firefly-like objects, and even managed to photograph one. Test pilots Joe Walton and Robert White detected UFOs during several flights in the X-15, and shot several rolls of film. In 1964, James McDivitt claimed he saw a cylindrical object in the same space as his Gemini IV spacecraft. Both Frank Borman and Jim Lovell reported a bogie on their flight, and photographed twin oval-shaped UFOs with glowing undersides. Even Neil Armstrong and Edwin "Buzz" Aldrin said they saw a UFO chase their craft shortly before their historic moon landing. Recent reports by Shuttle astronauts have added to the sightings, but none of the photographs, possessed by NASA, have ever been released for publication.

Fact may well be stranger than fiction, if not always as easily accessible. Chris Carter, the creator of "The X-Files," reminds us all that the truth is out there, buried in the tens of thousands of reports, voice transcripts, photographs, maps, drawings and other documentation that the United States Government has under lock and key. Maybe one day, if our bureaucracy ever deems us mature enough, we will all know the truth. Until then, we'll keep watching the night skies, and hoping those little green men in flying saucers are just curious visitors and not the prelude to an alien invasion and the beginning of a "war of the worlds."

APPENDIX ONE: A SHORT CHRONOLOGY OF THE SCIENCE FICTION FILM

Together, Jules Verne and H. G. Wells are acknowledged as the progenitors of modern science fiction, but what is truly amazing is how much of their "scientific romances" influenced the science fiction film. What follows is a short, decade-by-decade chronology of the science fiction film:

1901-1910 - Marie-Georges-Jean Melies, an early pioneer in the development of motion pictures, made "A Trip to the Moon" in 1902, the first science fiction film. While the French film owes much to Jules Verne's From the Earth to the Moon (1862) and H.G. Wells's The First Men in the Moon (1901), it was also a whimsical comedy that found the first astronauts who have traveled to the moon in a cannon-shell cavorting with Selenite dancers, who look like they've just stepped out of the Foiles-Bergere. Melies made nearly 800 short films in his career, including two other science fiction films, "An Impossible Voyage" in 1905 and "20,000 Leagues Under the Sea, or a Fisherman's Nightmare" in 1907, relying heavily on trick photography to take us to other worlds and other places. Thomas Edison and his Edison Studios made "A Trip to Mars," a pirated version of Melies's film, and the first of many versions of "Frankenstein," both in 1910. In England, Robert W. Paul tried to create a thrill ride out of H.G. Wells's "time machine," by using cinematic projections as a way to convey the passage of time. When he failed, Paul turned to filmmaking, and produced a handful of science fiction shorts, including "The ? Motorist" in 1905. Other films from the period included "The Dog Factory" (1904), "The Electric Hotel" (1906), "Voyage around a Star" (1906), and "The Aerial Submarine" (1910).

1911-1919 - Filmmakers continued to experiment with trick photography, resulting in more fanciful flights into the unknown. Most of the films of the period, including "One Hundred Years After' (1911), "The Aerial Anarchists" (1911), "The Pirates of 1920" (1911), "Man's Genesis" (1912), "The Black Box" (1915), and "The Master Mystery" (1918), were one-reel wonders that treated science fiction as a kind of joke or novelty. But two motion pictures pointed out the real possibilities of combining trick photography with an interesting story. Germany's "Homunculus the Leader" (1916), yet another retelling of Mary Shelley's Frankenstein, or the Modern Prometheus (1818), anticipated the rise of a master race that would control the world with the birth of an artificial human created by one of the cinema's first mad scientists, and "The End of the World" (1916), a Danish film, was an epic production that featured an all-star cast and the destruction of the world by a rogue comet. Other films from the period included "Conquest of the Pole" (1912), "In the Year 2014" (1914), "A Zepplin Attack on New York" (1917), "20,000 Leagues Under the Sea" (1916), "The Fall of a Nation" (1916), "The Flying Torpedo" (1916), and "The Diamond from the Sky" (1915).

1920-1929 - Following World War I, filmmakers in Germany took center stage with a handful of remarkable motion pictures that characterized the German Expressionist Movement. Films like "The Cabinet of Dr. Caligari" (1919), "Algol" (1920), "Metropolis" (1927), "Alraune" (1928), and "The Girl in the Moon" (1929) featured extravagant sets, elegant costumes, and thought-provoking stories that demonstrated a genuine respect for the genre of science fiction. Fritz Lang (with his wife Thea von Harbou) emerged as a huge talent, and later brought his filmmaking skills to America where he influenced a whole new generation of directors. In the United States, Willis O'Brien made his first stop-motion monsters come to life in Harry Hoyt's "The Lost World" (1925), and the Soviet Union sent its first cosmonauts into space with the first Russian science fiction film "Aelita" in 1924. Other films from the period included "A Message from Mars" (1921), "The Man Who Stole the Moon" (1921), "L'Atlantide" (1922), and "The Last Man on Earth" (1924).

1930-1939 - Universal Pictures produced the first of its monster films based on the classic works of Mary Shelley and H.G. Wells with "Frankenstein" (1931), "The Bride of Franken-stein" (1935), "The Island of Lost Souls" (1932), and "The Invisible Man" (1933), and made cinematic history by turning B-movies into A-list productions, thanks in large part to the superior talent of James Whale. Willis O'Brien continued to bring monsters of his own to life with stop-motion animation in Merian C. Cooper's production of "King Kong" (1933), what some acknowledge as the greatest monster film ever made. After years of disappointments in watching others handle his works, H.G. Wells teamed with Alexander Korda, and produced "Things to Come" (1936), an epic motion picture that follows the fall of man after a decades-long world war and the rise of a new kind of man who takes to the stars. At the time when it was produced, it was the largest, most expensive project of its kind, and while it failed at the box office, "Things to Come" is considered a brilliant milestone in the history of the science fiction film. The decade also saw the rise of Saturday matinee serials, including ones based on the comic book exploits of "Flash Gordon" (1936) and "Buck Rogers" (1939). Other films from the period included "Just Imagine" (1930), "Six Hours to Live" (1932), "Deluge" (1933), "The Transatlantic Tunnel" (1935), "Modern Times" (1936), "The Devil Doll" (1936), "The Son of Frankenstein" (1939), "F.P. 1 Does Not Respond" (1932), "The Phantom Empire" (1935), "The Undersea Kingdom" (1936), "The Walking Dead" (1936), and "The Invisible Man Returns" (1939).

1940-1949 - During the years of World War II, there were few notable science fiction films produced. Most audience members demanded light entertainment, and comedies and musicals were plentiful. With concerns about a master race and its stockpile of super weapons, the more realistic horrors of war supplanted the cinematic thrills and chills of the science fiction film. "Dr. Cyclops" (1940), a throwback to the monster films of the 1930's, was the first science fiction film released in technicolor; regrettably, it featured yet another mad doctor who had invented a device to terrorize his victims; in this case he had created a shrinking ray. Merian C. Cooper gathered his team from "King Kong" together, including newcomer Ray Harryhausen, and produced a somewhat gentler version of the Beauty and the Beast story with "Mighty Joe Young" (1949), while "White Pongo" (1945), the prototype of Bigfoot and the Abominable Snowman in later films, debuted as a white gorilla with superior intelligence. Other films from the period included "One Million B.C." (1940), "The Invisible Woman" (1940), "The Invisible Agent" (1942), "The Invisible Man's Revenge" (1945), "The Lady and the Monster" (1944), and "Unknown Island" (1948).

1950-1959 - The decade of the 1950's produced more science fiction films than any other decade of the Twentieth Century, beginning and just about concluding with the pioneering efforts of one filmmaker, George Pal. Pal produced some of the finest and enormously successful motion pictures of the decade, including "Destination Moon" (1950), "When Worlds Collide" (1951), "War of the Worlds" (1953), "Conquest of Space" (1953), and "The Time Machine" (1960); his success was based, in large part, on the fact that he treated his subject matter with a great deal of respect, and approached each project like it was an A-list production. Almost single-handedly, Pal was responsible for making science fiction films a respectable and entertainment moneymaker. Other studios produced A-list projects, including Twentieth Century-Fox's "The Day the Earth Stood Still" (1951), Universal's "It Came from Outer Space" (1953), Disney's " 20,000 Leagues Under the Sea" (1954), and M-G-M's "Forbidden Planet" (1956). Allegories about the misuse of atomic power and metaphors about the Red scare reflected the fears and anxieties of audiences of the 1950's, and filled the theaters for showings of "The Thing" (1951), "Invaders from Mars" (1953), Ray Harryhausen's "Beast from 20,000 Fathoms" (1953), "Them!" (1954), "Godzilla" (1956), and "Invasion of the Body Snatchers" (1956). The decade concluded on a note of dark pessimism with Stanley Kramer's "On the Beach" (1959). In the motion picture, the remaining survivors of a nuclear war gather together in Australia to await death as the radioactive dust clouds from the final war between the superpowers in the North make their way to the Southern Hemisphere; they know that it is only a matter of weeks before the end, and they try to seize whatever happiness they can; in the final moments of the film, the camera pans through the empty streets, looking for some sign of humanity, but everyone is dead; all that remains is a sign that reads: "There is still time, brother!" The message was clear, and it was trumpeted by a science fiction film. Other films from the period included "Rocketship X-M" (1950), "Flying Disc Men of Mars" (1951), "Five" (1951), "Invasion of the Saucer Men" (1953), "The Creative from the Black Lagoon" (1954), "This Island Earth" (1955), "The Creeping Unknown" (1955), "Earth Versus the Flying Saucers" (1955), "1984" (1956), "The Incredible Shrinking Man" (1957), "20 Million Miles to Earth' (1957), "The Fly" (1958), "The Blob" (1958), and "Journey to the Center of the Earth" (1959).

1960-1969 - Two science fiction films represent the 1960's more than any others produced during the decade, "2001: A Space Odyssey" (1968) and "Planet of the Apes" (1968). Both productions were thoughtful and thought-provoking explorations of what it means to be human in our highly technological and dangerous world, and both relied on topnotch special effects and make-up to tell two vastly different kinds of stories. One used a metaphor to invoke a world in which outside alien forces have been manipulating the destiny of man, and the other created an allegory in which intelligent simians rule over primitive man. Profound images from both films are burned into our collective consciousness: Who can forget that image of primitive man flinging the bone, which he has just used to kill his enemy, into the air and it becoming an orbital platform of nuclear weapons? Or, that image of Charlton Heston riding up to the shattered Statue of Liberty in the sand and realizing that he has been on earth the whole time? But "2001" and "Planet of the Apes" were not the only distinguished films of the decade. The fear of nuclear annihilation provided the subtext for "Village of the Damned" (1960), "La Jetee" (1962), "The Damned" (1963), "Fail Safe" (1963), and "Dr. Strangelove, or, How I Learned to Stop Worrying and Love the Bomb" (1963). Filmmakers trained in the French New Wave school of cinema, including Jean-Luc Goddard, Francois Truffaut, and Roger Vadim, respectively contributed "Alphaville" (1965), "Fahrenheit 451" (1966), and "Barbarella" (1968). Big budget prestige films, like "Robinson Crusoe on Mars" (1964), "Fantastic Voyage" (1966), George Pal's "The Power" (1967), and "Charley" (1968), and low budget quickies, like "Planet of the Vampires" (1965), "Queen of Blood" (1966), and "Night of the Living Dead" (1968) advanced the popularity of science fiction films, each in its own unique way. Of course, the single most defining moment of the decade was not found in science fiction but science fact, the Lunar landing of Apollo 11 on July 20, 1969-the fantasy of so many science fiction films had become front page news on every newspaper in the world. Other films from the period included "The Day the Earth Caught Fire" (1961), "Mothra" (1961), "First Spaceship on Venus" (1963), "Women of the Prehistoric Planet" (1966), "Five Million Years to Earth" (1968), "The Green Slime" (1968), "The Illustrated Man" (1968), "Mission Mars" (1968), "Wild in the Streets" (1968), "Marooned," "Moon Zero Two," and "Journey to the Far Side of the Sun" (all 1969).

1970-1979 - The decade of the 1970's can best be described as schizophrenic; prior to the release of "Star Wars" in 1977, numerous motion pictures, many of them low budget in nature, attempted to continue the thoughtful and sometimes provocative exploration of man and his place in the cosmos that was started with "2001: A Space Odyssey" and "Planet of the Apes"; after the release of "Star Wars," that contemplative style of filmmaking was abandoned in favor of the "wild ride" that the new breakthrough in special effects seemed to offer audience members. George Lucas produced not one, but two science fiction films during this period, one that favored a thoughtful approach and one that debuted the wild ride; of the two, "THX-1138" (1971) was a serious, thought-provoking film that looked at the effects of mind control in a computer-directed, dystopian future, while "Star Wars" was a throwback to the "Flash Gordon" and "Buck Rogers" serials of the 1930's. Other serious films that tried to look at man through the prism of allegory and metaphor were "A Clock-work Orange" (1972), "Slaughterhouse Five" (1972), "Solaris" (1972), "Silent Running" (1973), "Soylent Green" (1973), "The Stepford Wives" (1975), and "Logan's Run" (1976). Comic films, like "Sleeper" (1973) and "Young Frankenstein" (1974), also relied on satire to wring an element of truth about the world in which we lived. Unfortunately, the debut of "Star Wars," followed closely by Steven Spielberg's "Close Encounters of the Third Kind" (1977), changed all of that. The ideas in science fiction film were relegated to the back seat so there was plenty of room up front for the audience looking for its next thrill ride. Not all of the efforts that followed were mindless copies of "Star Wars," but many of them were, including "Starship Invasions" (1977), "Message from Space" (1977), "Battlestar Galactica" (1978), and "The Black Hole" (1979). A few key prestige projects did manage to get made, despite the insistence by many film studios insistence to create yet another rollercoaster ride like "Star Wars," and they were "Superman" (1978), "Star Trek-The Motion Picture" (1979), and "Alien" (1979). Other films from the period included "Colossus: The Forbin Project" (1970), "Beneath the Planet of the Apes" (1970), "The Andromeda Strain" (1971), "The Omega Man" (1971), "The Terminal Man" (1972), "Death Race 2000" (1973), "Westworld" (1973), "A Boy and His Dog" (1975), "Rollerball" (1975), "The Man Who Fell to Earth" (1976), "At the Earth's Core" (1976), "Wizards" (1976), "Demon Seed" (1977), "Invasion of the Body Snatchers" (1978), "The Island of Dr. Moreau" (1978), "The Food of the Gods" (1978), and "Time After Time" (1979).

1980-1989 - The rollercoaster ride that George Lucas first started with "Star Wars" in 1977 continued in its sequels "The Empire Strikes Back" (1980) and "Return of the Jedi" (1983), and in a handful of other lesser efforts that showcased Industrial Light and Magic's superior skills at special effects, including "Dragonslayer" (1981), "Poltergeist" (1983), "Explorers" (1985), and "Willow" (1987). Fellow filmmaker and compatriot Steven Spielberg, who was actually a better director and storyteller than Lucas, made his own prestige pictures, including "Raiders of the Lost Ark" (1981), a throwback to the serials of the 1930's, and "E.T.-The Extraterrestrial" (1982), a reworking of "The Day the Earth Stood Still." Other mavericks like John Carpenter and James Cameron pushed the envelope, and produced a number of noteworthy efforts, including "Escape from New York" (1981), "The Thing" (1982), "Starman" (1985), "Terminator" (1984), "Aliens" (1986), and "The Abyss" (1989), that challenged the studio system mentality with brand new ideas about kinetic, fast-paced film-making. Regrettably, while the technical skills in filmmaking improved, the overall quality of the stories and acting declined. One of the few standouts of the period was Ridley Scott's "Blade Runner," a film that combined effective storytelling skills with superior special effects. Other films from the period included "Altered States" (1980), "Battle Beyond the Stars" (1980), "Somewhere in Time" (1980), "Mad Max" (1980), "Outland" (1981), "Saturn 3" (1981), "The Road Warrior" (1982), "Tron" (1983), "The Adventures of Buckaroo Banzai" (1984), "Back to the Future" (1985), "Cocoon" (1985), "2010: The Year We Make Contact" (1984), "Dune" (1984), "Brazil" (1985), "Mad Max Beyond Thunderdome" (1985), "Weird Science" (1985), "The Fly" (1986), "Robocop" (1987), "Spaceballs" (1987), "Predator" (1987), and "The Running Man" (1987).

1990-1999 - The final decade of the Twentieth Century concluded on a high note as filmmakers began to realize the importance of telling a good story rather than relying solely on special effects. Some of the best efforts of the decade, including "Terminator Two: Judgment Day" (1991), "Jurassic Park" (1993), and "Contact" (1997), did in fact feature some extraordinary advancements in the field of special visual effects, but they also told thought-provoking stories as well. Others, like "Independence Day" (1996), "Mars Attacks" (1996), "Starship Troopers" (1997), "Deep Impact" (1998), and "Armageddon" (1998), became blockbusters by exploiting our old fears of alien invasion, nuclear war, and the end of the world. As computers and technology continued to change the way in which we lived our lives, certain key filmmakers explored the nature of that reality and found deep, black holes into which we had fallen, including "Total Recall" (1990), "The Truman Show" (1997), "Dark City" (1998), "eXistence" (1999), "The Matrix" (1999), "The 13th Floor" (1999), and "Being John Malkovich" (1999). Other films from the period included "Freejack" (1992), "Stargate" (1994), "Twelve Monkeys" (1995), "Escape from L.A." (1996), "Men in Black" (1997), "Gattaca" (1998), "Godzilla" (1998), "The X-Files Movie" (1998), "Galaxy Quest" (1999), and "Star Wars: The Phantom Menace" (1999).

2000-2005 - The new century of science fiction films began with numerous sequels and remakes of classic science fiction films, including not one but two adaptations of H. G. Wells's *The War of the Worlds*. The first half of the decade also saw the conclusion of the "Star Wars" film saga with the releases of "Attack of the Clones" (2002) and "Revenge of the Sith" (2005). Of course, the most interesting trend was a return to adapting famous science fiction and fantasy novels with the big budget releases of two Philip K. Dick stories, "Minority Report" (2002) and "Imposter" (2002), and a trilogy of films from Peter Jackson adapting J. R. R. Tolkien's *The Lord of the Rings*. For the first time ever, a fantasy film with the title "Return of the King" (2003) won the Academy Award for Best Film of the Year!

APPENDIX TWO: TRIVIA

Ever since H. G. Wells first took pen in hand and wrote *The Invisible Man* (1897), *The First Men in the Moon* (1901), and *The War of the Worlds* (1898), science fiction fans, academics, critics and moviegoers have been been examining every aspect of his life and his times and his works. One could argue that H. G. Wells created single-handedly everything that has been written about in the field of science fiction, and the impact of his work has been as great, if not greater, than any other author who has ever written in the field. For example, *The War of the Worlds* is seen as the forerunner of several branches of science fiction literature, including themes related to aliens, alien invasion, first contact, interplanetary war, and the end of the world. His *Island of Dr. Moreau* (1896) gave rise to the notion of genetic engineering; his *The Sleeper Awakes* (1899) introduced audiences to suspended animation and future history, and his *The Time Machine* (1895) created the first device for traveling backwards and forwards in time. But not all of the study related to Wells and the various adaptations of his work has been strictly academic. Trivia buffs have enjoyed collecting and reciting their own kind of arcane information. What follows is an interesting sampling of trivia related to Wells and *The War of the Worlds*.

- Herbert George Wells was nicknamed "Bertie" by his parents.
- H. G. Wells and Amy Catherine Robbins, his second wife, appear as characters in the movie "Time After Time" (1979), which was written and directed by Nicholas Meyer who four years earlier had written "The Night That Panicked America" (1975), a dramatic account of the famous "War of the Worlds" radio broadcast.

- H. G. Wells is the great-grandfather of Simon Wells who directed the 2002 remake of The Time Machine.
- While driving through San Antonio, Texas, H. G. Wells stopped to ask directions to Radio KTSA Studios. The person he happened to ask was none other than Orson Welles who had, only two years earlier, made the famous "War of the Worlds" radio broadcast. After a few tense moments, the two got along very well, and spent the day together. Later, they discussed the broadcast during a radio interview at Radio KTSA.
- As a prophetic writer, H. G. Wells was the first novelist to employ the themes of time travel (in The Time Machine), interplanetary war (The War of the Worlds), genetic manipulation (The Island of Dr. Moreau), a moon landing (First Men in the Moon), and nuclear war (The World Set Free). He predicted the first atomic bomb (a term which he originated) three decades before Los Alamos. He also wrote about a war in the air (well before modern airplanes), tanks, women's liberation, the rise of fascism, and a utopian world where all men were equal.
- No other novelist's work, living or dead, has inspired so many cinematic adaptations as the work of H. G. Wells.
- Prior to making the famous "War of the Worlds" radio broadcast, Orson Welles provided the voice for Lamont Cranston, also know as the Shadow.
- Paramount Pictures first secured the rights for a big budget feature based upon H. G. Wells's The War of the Worlds in 1934. Both Cecil B. DeMille and Alfred Hitchcock were considered for directors. Orson Welles, who rose to prominence with his "War of the Worlds" radio broadcast was pressured by the studio to make the novel into his first feature film, but he turned Paramount down, and made "Citizen Kane" (1942) instead.
- While making his 1953 version of "War of the Worlds," George Pal wanted to make the final third of the movie in 3-D, starting with the sequence in which the atomic bomb is used unsuccessfully against the Martians. But Don Hartman, a Paramount executive, nixed the idea believing that 3-D was nothing more than a passing fancy. He turned out to be right.
- Filming was halted briefly on George Pal's "War of the Worlds," two days into principal photography, when Paramount discovered their filming rights to the novel had expired. But their problems were quickly resolved through the kind permission of H.G. Wells's estate. The estate was so pleased with the final production that they offered Pal his choice of any other Wells property. Pal chose "The Time Machine," which he made in 1960.
- Originally, George Pal wanted the Martian war machines to "walk" on visible electronic beams of light as a kind of tribute to Wells's tripods. This was attempted by having electrical sparks emanate from the three holes at the bottom of the machine, but this was quickly abandoned for fear of starting a fire. The shot of the first war machine emerging from the gully has this effect, but no others. After trying several other techniques, they decided to forego this idea altogether. During filming, how-

ever, the actors were under the impression that they were dealing with the walking tripod machines of the book. Thus, when Gene Barry says, "There's a machine standing right next to us," he believed that one was to have been added later optically.

- The Flying Wing depicted in the movie is the Northrop YB-49. Two were built and both crashed. Stock footage was used in the movie.

- George Pal's 1953 version of "War of the Worlds" had a budget of $2,000,000. Of that sum, $600,000 was spent on the live action scenes, while $1,400,000 was spent on the extensive and elaborate special effects. Those effects won Gordon Jennings an Academy Award, which was awarded posthumously.

- Albert Nozaki based his designs of the Martian war machines on the shape and movements of the swan, even though they look like manta rays.

- During the two-and-a-half minute "grand tour" of the Solar System, images in the prologue of the 1953 film show paintings of all the other planets, except Venus, and it is never mentioned.

- The two Martian machines that crash in Los Angeles are really the same machine from a different angle with the film image reversed.

- When Major General Mann first meets Dr. Clayton Forrester, he refers to an earlier meeting at Oak Ridge. Oak Ridge, Tennessee, was the home to three Manhattan Project plants that enriched and refined uranium in WWII for use in the atomic bombs that ended the war. Two of the three are still in operation today. Ironically, Gene Barry who plays Forrester in the film made the low-budget "Atomic City" (1952), while waiting for production on "War of the Worlds" to begin.

- Byron Haskin, the director of the 1953 version, employed the Martian war machines as alien slave ships that search the surface of Mars for Friday in his "Robinson Crusoe on Mars" in 1964.

- Three of the first season episodes of the "War of the Worlds" television show were credited with pen names: "The Walls of Jericho" by Forrest van Buren; "The Good Samaritan" by Sylvia Clayton, and "Epiphany" by Sylvia van Buren. The names were taken from the two main characters of the 1953 film, Dr. Clayton Forrester and Sylvia Van Buren.

- All the episode titles in the first season of the "War of the Worlds" television series are Biblical references.

- The "War of the Worlds" television series was conceived as a direct sequel to the original 1953 film. In several episodes, the character of Sylvia Van Buren appears, played by Ann Robinson, the original actress who had played the character in the movie. And in one episode, "Time to Recap," several characters travel back through time to the date of the original movie, and everything appears in black and white.

- In the two-hour pilot to the television series, Martians break into a military warehouse where their war machines have been mothballed for thirty-five years. This is the same warehouse where the Ark of the Covenant from "Raiders of the Lost Ark" (1981) is stored.

- In its second season, this series underwent a dramatic format change the show title was changed to "War of the Worlds: The Second Invasion." The present-day setting of the first season was changed to a post-apocalyptic future, several main characters were deleted (presumably killed during the "second invasion", which was never shown), and the plot point that required aliens to "change bodies" every 24 hours was removed.

- In the episode "Dust to Dust," the old Martian war machine that rises at the Indian Reservation is a tripod. This is in reference to the way in which the Martian war machines are described in the H.G. Wells novel.

- Timothy Hines's version of "The War of the Worlds" (2005) is the only film version to be set in Victorian England. The Orson Welles radio broadcast was set in the 1930's; the George Pal version was set in the 1950's; the television series was set in the 1980's, and the Steven Spielberg film was set in 2005. For the record, Jeff Wayne set his rock adaptation in Victorian England as well.

- The Steven Spielberg adaptation is the third incarnation of The War of the Worlds story that Ann Robinson has appeared in, having played Sylvia Van Buren in the original 1953 film The War of the Worlds (1953) and then reprising her role for three episodes in the 1988 television series

- Steven Spielberg owns one of the last copies of the Orson Welles radio script, which he purchased at auction. The director wanted to make the film years ago, but decided against it when "Independence Day" (1996) was released. However, the director wanted to work with 'Tom Cruise ' again after "Minority Report" (2002) and picked "War of the Worlds" (2005) as their next project.

- Initially estimated to have a 2007 release date, this film was abruptly rushed into production in mid-August 2004, for a 2005 release, when director Steven Spielberg and star Tom Cruise learned that a rival production (the Timothy Hines film) was already being shot in Great Britain.

- The Steven Spielberg film was shot under the title "Out of the Night," while the Timothy Hines version used "The Great Boer War" as its alias. Both films used an alias in order to keep unwanted people away from the set, and to keep their rival productions in the dark.

- "War of the Worlds" (2005) marks Steven Spielberg's fifth time working with aliens. His other productions include "Firelight" (1964), "Close Encounters of the Third Kind" (1977), "E.T.-The Extraterrestrial" (1982), and "Taken" (2002).

- While filming in Bayonne, New Jersey, studio Paramount Pictures offered quick cash to residents who lived on First Street and Pointview Terrace to move their cars off the block, between a Tuesday and Friday. This was in order for the film crew to resume shooting.

- The voice-over dialogue from the first trailer for the film paraphrases and updates the first paragraph from H.G. Wells's novel. For example 19th century is changed to 21st century.

SELECTED BIBLIOGRAPHY

Ackerman, Forrest J., editor. *Famous Monsters of Filmland* Magazine. Philadelphia: Warren Publishing, 1958.

_____. *Monsterland Magazine*, nos. 1-6. Los Angeles, California: New Media Publishing, 1986.

Aldiss, Brian W. *Billion Year Spree: The True History of Science Fiction.* New York: Schocken Books, 1973.

Andrews, Nigel. *Horror Films.* New York: Gallery Books, 1985.

Aylesworth, Thomas G. *Monsters from the Movies.* New York: Bantam Skylark Books, 1972.

Baxter, John. *Science Fiction in the Cinema.* New York: Paperback Library, 1970.

Cantrill, Hadley. *Invasion from Mars: A Study in the Psychology of Panic.* New Jersey: Princeton University Press, 1940.

Christopher, John. *The White Mountains.* London: Simon Pulse, 2003.

_____. *The City of Gold and Lead.* London: Simon Pulse, 2003.

_____. *Pool of Fire.* London: Simon Pulse, 2003.

Clute, John and Peter Nicholls. *The Encyclopedia of Science Fiction.* New York: St. Martin's Press, 1993.

Cohen, Daniel. *Horror in the Movies*. New York: Houghton Mifflin Company, Inc., 1982.

Edelson, Edward. *Great Monsters of the Movies*. New York: Doubleday and Company, 1973.

Fawcett, Larry, and Barry Greenwood. *Clear Intent: The Government Cover-up of the UFO Experience*. New York: Prentice-Hall, 1984.

Flynn, John L. *Cinematic Vampires: The Living Dead on Film and Television*. North Carolina: McFarland Books, 1991.
_____. *Dissecting Aliens*. New York: Image Publishing, 1994 and London: Boxtree Ltd., 1995.
_____. "Afterward" to *The Island of Dr. Moreau* by H.G. Wells. New York: Signet Classic Books, 2005.
_____. "V-The Series Episode Guide." *SFTV* June-September, 1985.

Fuller, John. *The Interrupted Journey*. New York: Dial Press, 1966.

Good, Timothy. *Above Top Secret: The Worldwide UFO Cover-up*. New York: Morrow, 1988.

Halliwell, Leslie. *Halliwell's Film Guide*. New York: Scribner's, 1984.

Holmsten, Brian and Alex Lubertozzi, eds. *The Complete War of the Worlds*. New York: Sourcebooks, 2001.

Hopkins, Budd. *Missing Time: A Documented Study of UFO Abductions*. New York: Richard Marek, 1981.

Huss, Roy Gerard. *Focus on the Horror Film*. New York: Prentice-Hall, 1972.

Keyhoe, Daniel E. *The Flying Saucer Conspiracy*. New York: Henry Holt & Company, 1955.

Koch, Howard. *The Panic Broadcast*. New York: Avon Books, 1970.

Lowry, Brian. *The Truth Is Out There: The Official Guide to the X-Files*. New York: HarperPrism, 1995.

Maltin, Leonard. *Leonard Maltin's Movie and Video Guide*. New York: Signet Publishers, 1994.

Mackenzie, Norman Ian. *H.G. Wells: A Biography*. New York: Simon and Schuster, 1973.

Official "The Tipods" Website, The. *http://www.gnelson.demon.co.uk/Tripods.html*, 2005.

Official "War of the Worlds" Website, The. *http://www.pendragonpictures.com,* 2005.

Pohl, Frederick. *Science Fiction Studies in Film.* New York: Ace Books, 1981.

Stanley, John. *The Creature Features Movie Guide.* New York: Warner Books, 1981.

Strieber, Whitley. *Communion.* New York: William Morrow, 1987.
_____. *Transformation.* New York: William Morrow, 1988.

Vera, Hernán and Andrew M. Gordon. *Screen Saviors: Hollywood Fictions of Whiteness.* Lanham, MD: Rowman & Littlefield, 2003.

Von Gunden, Kenneth and Stuart H. Stock. *Twenty All-Time Great Science Fiction Films.* New York: Arlington House, 1982.

Wagner, Chuck. "Martian Inspiration: The Bubblegum Cards." *Cinefantastique,* January 1996, 16.

Walton, Travis. *Fire in the Sky: The Walton Experience.* New York: Marlowe & Co, 1997.

Wells, H. G. *The War of the Worlds.* 1898.

INDEX OF TITLES

ABOUT THE AUTHOR

Dr. John L. Flynn is a three-time Hugo-nominated author and long-time science fiction fan and critic who has written six books, countless short stories, articles, reviews, and one screenplay. He is a professor at Towson University in Towson, Maryland, and teaches both graduate and undergraduate writing courses. His most popular course is one that teaches budding authors how to write science fiction. Born in Chicago, Illinois, on September 6, 1954, he has a Bachelor's and Master's Degree from the University of South Florida and a Ph.D. from Southern California University. He is a member of the Science Fiction Writers of America, and has been a regular contributor and columnist to dozens of science fiction magazines, including "Starlog," "Not of This Earth," "Sci-Fi Universe," "Cinescape," "Retrovision," "Media History Digest," "SF Movieland," "SFTV," "Monsterland," "Enterprise," "Nexxus," "The Annapolis Review," and "Collector's Corner." In 1977, he received the M. Carolyn Parker award for outstanding journalism for his freelance work on several Florida daily newspapers, and in 1987, he was listed in *Who's Who Men of Achievement*. He sold his first book, *Future Threads*, in 1985. He has subsequently published four other books related to film, including *Cinematic Vampires*, *Phan-*

toms of the Opera, *The Films of Arnold Schwarzenegger*, and *Dissecting Aliens*. Brickhouse Books published *Visions in Light and Shadow* (2001), a collection of his literary short stories. For the past three years, John has been nominated for the prestigious Hugo Award, which is the Science Fiction Achievement Award, for his science fiction writing, which includes film reviews and cinematic retrospectives. He has appeared on television (including the Sci-Fi Channel), spoken on the radio, and been a guest at national conferences because of his advocacy work in bringing the science fiction film into the mainstream. With Dr. Robert Blackwood, Flynn formed "the Film Doctors," a team of credentiated academics which studied science fiction films and rendered a scholastic view of the genre. Their first project was *The Top Ten Science Fiction Films of the Twentieth Century*. In 1997, John switched gears to study Psychology, and earned a degree as a Clinical Psychologist. His study, "The Etiology of Sexual Addiction: Childhood Trauma as a Primary Determinant," has broken new ground in the diagnosis and treatment of sexual addiction. For the last several years, he has also worked tirelessly with Bridge Publications, Galaxy Press, and Author Services on behalf of the Writers of the Future contest, in an effort to promote the work of new and emerging science fiction writers.